Palgrave Studies in the Enlightenment, Romanticism and Cultures of Print
General Editors: **Professor Anne K. Mellor** and **Professor Clifford Siskin**

Editorial Board: **Isobel Armstrong**, Birkbeck; **John Bender**, Stanford; **Alan Bewell**, Toronto; **Peter de Bolla**, Cambridge; **Robert Miles**, Stirling; **Claudia L. Johnson**, Princeton; **Saree Makdisi**, UCLA; **Felicity Nussbaum**, UCLA; **Mary Poovey**, NYU; **Janet Todd**, Glasgow

Palgrave Studies in the Enlightenment, Romanticism and Cultures of Print will feature work that does not fit comfortably within established boundaries—whether between periods or between disciplines. Uniquely, it will combine efforts to engage the power and materiality of print with explorations of gender, race, and class. By attending as well to intersections of literature with the visual arts, medicine, law, and science, the series will enable a large-scale rethinking of the origins of modernity.

Titles include:

Scott Black
OF ESSAYS AND READING IN EARLY MODERN BRITAIN

Claire Brock
THE FEMINIZATION OF FAME, 1750–1830

Brycchan Carey
BRITISH ABOLITIONISM AND THE RHETORIC OF SENSIBILITY
Writing, sentiment, and slavery, 1760–1807

E. J. Clery
THE FEMINIZATION DEBATE IN 18TH-CENTURY ENGLAND
Literature, Commerce and Luxury

Adriana Craciun
BRITISH WOMEN WRITERS AND THE FRENCH REVOLUTION
Citizens of the World

Peter de Bolla, Nigel Leask and David Simpson (*editors*)
LAND, NATION AND CULTURE, 1740–1840
Thinking the Republic of Taste

Anthony S. Jarrells
BRITAIN'S BLOODLESS REVOLUTIONS
1688 and the Romantic Reform of Literature

Mary Waters
BRITISH WOMEN WRITERS AND THE PROFESSION OF LITERARY CRITICISM, 1789–1832

Forthcoming titles in the series:

Ian Haywood
BLOODY ROMANTICISM

Palgrave Studies in the Enlightenment, Romanticism and Cultures of Print
Series Standing Order ISBN 1–4039–3408–8 (hardback) 1–4039–3409–6 (paperback)
(outside North America only)

You can receive future titles in this series as they are published by placing a standing order. Please contact your bookseller or, in case of difficulty, write to us at the address below with your name and address, the title of the series and the ISBN quoted above.

Customer Services Department, Macmillan Distribution Ltd, Houndmills, Basingstoke, Hampshire RG21 6XS, England

Of Essays and Reading in Early Modern Britain

Scott Black

© Scott Black 2006

All rights reserved. No reproduction, copy or transmission of this publication may be made without written permission.

No paragraph of this publication may be reproduced, copied or transmitted save with written permission or in accordance with the provisions of the Copyright, Designs and Patents Act 1988, or under the terms of any licence permitting limited copying issued by the Copyright Licensing Agency, 90 Tottenham Court Road, London W1T 4LP.

Any person who does any unauthorized act in relation to this publication may be liable to criminal prosecution and civil claims for damages.

The author has asserted his right to be identified as the author of this work in accordance with the Copyright, Designs and Patents Act 1988.

First published 2006 by
PALGRAVE MACMILLAN
Houndmills, Basingstoke, Hampshire RG21 6XS and
175 Fifth Avenue, New York, N.Y. 10010
Companies and representatives throughout the world

PALGRAVE MACMILLAN is the global academic imprint of the Palgrave Macmillan division of St. Martin's Press, LLC and of Palgrave Macmillan Ltd. Macmillan® is a registered trademark in the United States, United Kingdom and other countries. Palgrave is a registered trademark in the European Union and other countries.

ISBN 13: 978–1–4039–9905–4   hardback
ISBN 10: 1–4039–9905–8   hardback

This book is printed on paper suitable for recycling and made from fully managed and sustained forest sources.

A catalogue record for this book is available from the British Library.

Library of Congress Cataloging-in-Publication Data

Black, Scott, 1964–
   Of essays and reading in early modern Britain / Scott Black.
     p. cm. – (Palgrave studies in the Enlightenment, romanticism and the cultures of print)
   Includes bibliographical references and index.
   ISBN 1–4039–9905–8
   1. English essays–Early modern, 1500–1700–History and criticism.
2. English essays–18th century–History and criticism. 3. Reading–Great Britain–History–17th century. 4. Reading–Great Britain–History–18th century. 5. Authors and readers–Great Britain–History–17th century. 6. Authors and readers–Great Britain–History–18th century. I. Title. II. Series: Palgrave studies in the Enlightenment, romanticism and cultures of print.

PR924.B55 2006
824.009–dc22
                                                    2006045379

10 9 8 7 6 5 4 3 2 1
15 14 13 12 11 10 09 08 07 06

Printed and bound in Great Britain by
Antony Rowe Ltd, Chippenham and Eastbourne

for Rona

Contents

Acknowledgements	ix
Introduction	1
Part 1: Of Essays	
1. Draughts of Reading	15
2. By Way of Essays	36
Part 2: Essay Exapted	
3. Boyle's Essay	67
4. Social and Literary Form in the *Spectator*	86
5. Fleeting Habitations in *Tom Jones*	107
Appendix A. Whitlock, from 'The Author to the Reader'	127
Appendix B. Cornwallis, opening of 'Of Essaies and Bookes' (1601)	128
Appendix C. Cornwallis on Moral Philosophy and Reading	129
Appendix D. Culpepper, 'Of Essayes'	132
Notes	133
Bibliography	178
Index	190

Acknowledgements

This book continues my part of conversations with two friends who died much too soon, Michael Current and Pablo Cepeda. Both would have written better books than this one, but I hope I've been able to get into it some of what they taught me.

Many people have helped me with this project, both in the particulars and in the general moves, readings, and formulations it tries out. I'm very happy to thank the following teachers, friends, and colleagues. At the Johns Hopkins University: Ronald Paulson, Jerome Christensen, Mary Poovey, Oren Izenberg, Daniel Denecke, Ruth Mack, David Glimp, Jane Thrailkill. At Villanova University: Vince Sherry, Evan Radcliffe, Jean Lutes, Heather Hicks, Seth Koven, Erin Connelly. At the Huntington and Clark Libraries: Roy Ritchie, Ben Schmidt, Tom McLean, Mark Canuel, Kirstie McClure. In Philadelphia (WIP): Kathy Rowe, Julian Yates, Kristen Poole, Jane Hedley, Nora Johnson, Steve Newman, Laura McGrane. In Salt Lake City: Barry Weller. Two friends have helped me think through the materials of this book, and much more, far beyond the call of friendship: Lauren Shohet and Andy Franta.

For not caring about the details of this project, but unstintingly encouraging its progress, I am grateful to my family. In Boston: my parents, Sandy and Paul, who've been constantly supportive and always believed this would get done one day; Marc; Jeff, Laurie, and Zoe. In Philadelphia: Doris and Joe; Lisa, Ed, Amy, and Erin; Donna, Ivy, Lea, and Micah.

There aren't words to properly thank Rona, my Rose of Sharon, but happily she reads well between the lines. What's best in this is hers too.

Support for the research and writing of parts of this book came from fellowships from the Ransom, Clark, and Huntington Libraries, and a Villanova University Summer Research Fellowship. An earlier version of Chapter 4 appeared as 'Social and Literary Form in the *Spectator*,' *Eighteenth-Century Studies* 33:1 (1999), 21–42. © American Society for Eighteenth-Century Studies. Reprinted with permission of The Johns Hopkins University Press.

Introduction

Essays were a common feature of the printscape of early modern Britain. Throughout the seventeenth and eighteenth centuries writers wrote 'by way of essay.' By the time Cowley produced what would become for generations of schoolchildren one of the standard templates of the form, his 'Discourses, by Way of Essays' (1668), the genre was as well-worn as his title phrase. John Florio had used the phrase in his translation of Montaigne's 'Of Friendship' (1603) and so had Henry Peacham in his *The Truth of our Times: Revealed out of One's Man's Experience, by Way of Essay* (1638).[1] Montaigne's *Essais* were translated again later in the century by Charles Cotton (1685), but this interest in the French essayist only begins to suggest the breadth of the English habit of essay-writing. From the *Essayes* of William Cornwallis, Montaigne's first English imitator (1600), through Mary Chudleigh's *Essays upon Several Subjects* (1710), 'essay' names a bewildering array of compositions and spans a wide range of practices.[2] There were philosophical essays and poetic essays, essays by ancients and essays by moderns, essays of moral philosophy and essays of natural philosophy.[3] Essays could be lists of single-line observations, often culled – imitated, stolen – from a student's reading. They could be slightly more mortared prose that threads a way through the borrowed quotations to narrate the thought lit by those sparks. And they could be masterful voices that seem less to hold the citations together than flow through them.

In exploring the evolution of the essay in English from Cornwallis in the early seventeenth century to Fielding in the mid-eighteenth century, I offer an account of the genre in its early development and in doing so recover an important but neglected aspect of Britain's emerging print culture. Scholars of literary history and the history of the book have recently begun to turn their attention from writing to reading, shifting from questions of how texts are constructed to how they are received.[4] This study participates in that shift but suggests it could go further. Work on *reading* often focuses on *readers*, on issues of self-fashioning, authority, and authenticity – on the exigencies of writing. Reading is taken as latent writing, becomes writerly.[5] But reading has its own dynamics, what Certeau characterizes as renting and poaching, making a home in a house you don't own, passing through another's field.[6] Early modern essays registered this kind of adaptive reading. Writing in the shape of reading, offering first thoughts instead of final words, these works follow the twists of interest and the by-ways of imagination rather than the rigors of system or scholarship. The genre enabled different moves than writing construed in terms of systems of production, maps of identity, or dynamics of power.[7]

For Cornwallis, 'writing is the draught of reading,' and this dynamic organizes both his own *Essayes* and the early modern genre more generally: it is 'no triall to haue handsome dapper conceites runne inuisibly in a braine but to put them out and then looke vpon them.'[8] The key moment here is not 'to put them out' but 'then look upon them.' Essays facilitated what was classically, and neo-classically, called the 'digestion' of books.[9] Remnants of response, not engines of production, such works disclaim authority and even authorship. In a typical stance, one seventeenth-century essayist maintains he's a 'digestor,' not an 'author,' and the genre enabled this digestive mode of reading throughout the early modern period.[10] Such texts foreground their own work in interweaving and assimilating other texts, and they invite the same of their readers. In this way, essays register and enable the kind of feedback loops that drive print culture as readers read and respond to other readers. Print culture, indeed, is the name we give to the traces of these activities. From the perspective of the essay – a perspective this study adopts – those traces are less occasions to locate such texts in their original contexts than to undertake again that activity and practice again that kind of reading.

Ann Moss and Ann Blair have discussed such 'digestive methods' of reading in relation to commonplace books.[11] The essay was an offshoot and extension of these humanist tools of reading and indeed some works titled 'essay' seem to be little more than published commonplace books. If commonplace books enable the collection of the textual gleanings that furnish an educated mind, essays enable the work of digestion that integrates those findings into one's thinking. The literacy named by 'essay' thus involves the skill of working through gathered texts, registering on the page the commentary – one's own processing of the texts – that comprises the fundamental lesson and activity of humanist education.[12] Early modern essays extended these humanist practices into the print marketplace, disseminating them through its anonymous, far-flung, and decentralized mechanisms. They offered a space in print where such assimilative and adaptive reading could be practiced, modeled, and enabled.

Early modern readers used essays to develop a skill of reading that was distinct from writing, a way of cycling through texts and using their resources in a complex interplay of adoption and adaptation. Instead of the stark, sublime choice between self and system (in which the only options are refusal or capitulation), the essay facilitates a different mode of response, one denser and richer than allowed by many recent critical models. Indeed even this genre, by definition tentative, unfinished, and exploratory, has been presented as foundational, a site of resistance, a locus of authenticity, a place where one can recognize one's true nature off the grid in an excess that can't be contained by any system.[13] Such accounts go too far. Essays don't work in the register of 'as such' – finding sources or origins or new worlds or true voices.[14] Rather, they are registers of 'such as' – the work of recognizing connections, hearing echoes, moving through networks; neither outside, nor against, but a way through. Less appropriative than participatory, essays register a practice of digestive, assimilative reading that isn't fully explicable in terms of the categories of authenticity and self-fashioning. And as the genre offered early modern readers a tool that trained the readerly skills required in an evolving print culture, so they provide us with another approach to early modern literary history, one that's less concerned with locating texts within contexts or subjects within texts than with recognizing the interactive, mediated, and mediating activities of reading.

The residue of reading

John Uffley articulates several of the recurrent features of the essay and provides a first sketch of its generic repertoire in his *Wits Fancies: or, Choice Observations and Essayes, Collected out of Divine, Political, Philosophical, Military, and Historical Authors*. Calling his work a 'small Treatise,' 'the Maiden flowers of my young age,' Uffley stresses both the size and scale of the genre, little, young, and tentative.[15]

> When you have surveyed each Page of this little Treatise, you (I hope) will be able to render an account of it, how you like the Fabrick, and if

it be well rear'd, the thought of falling is not to be feared, though he that did erect it, did not serve many years to the Profession, nor deserved the attribute of an *Architect*, yet he hath used his best endeavours to write truly those things that (by his own Experiences) he knows, and thought it meet (without the least offence) to Entitle it, *Wits Fancies, or choice Observations, &c.* being the marrow of all that ever he read in any History, either sacred or Prophane.[16]

Uffley emphasizes the provisionality of his form. He's a builder but not really an architect, and he rests his case on his sincerity, not any kind of trained professional ability. Essays are amateur, immature, even premature; so much we expect. But the sudden explication of 'his own Experiences' as 'the marrow of all that ever he read' is a surprise and suggests the space between this early example of the essay and our more familiar points of reference. Experience here is in books, and Uffley's book of *Essayes* doesn't go the way of an Emersonian essay, say, an occasion to trace, develop, or follow out original thoughts on the page. Instead, Uffley gives us the occasions of thought, passages from his reading that have struck him as worth writing down, textual moments that have caught his attention and he suggests might be worth ours. The work of thought seems to be registered in the attention implied by selection, not by any further mark. And his selection also begs our attention in turn. We're invited 'to render an account' of his work, rerendering what he has rendered, perhaps copying out what he has copied, or at least reading what he has read. In this way, essays are textual bridges that register the effects of one's reading and enable further reading in turn.

One of my purposes in this study is to explore this process of participatory reading at the size and scale of the essay, to 'experience' (as Uffley would have it) its model of textuality. Toward that end here are a somewhat randomly selected couple of pages that give a feel of the texture of Uffley's work and offer a chance to read along with him. They offer less a map of a mind than a record of reading, and, while they could be fruitfully explicated in terms of their particular references, Uffley's own focus on the 'Fabrick' suggests less a report on his world than a mechanism by which he seeks to participate in it.

> Something it is to have a fame go of a man; yet words are as fame, soon blown over, when *Libera scripta manet*; Books out live men.
> Boldness or Valour is not terrified with mans own danger, but to fear in behalf of others, is humanity.

> Boldness and fear are commonly misplaced in the best hearts, when we should tremble we are confident, and when we should be assured we tremble.
> A cold and moist brain is an inseparable companion of folly.
> Brevity although it breed difficulty, yet it carrieth great gravity.
> Brevity when it is neither obscure nor defective, is very pleasing even to the choycest judgements.
> Brevity makes counsell more portable for memory, and easier for use.
> The Brownists say, they did not make a new Church, but mended an old.
> The Brownists separate, for these four causes or points, A hateful Prelacie, a devised ministry, a confused communion, and an intermixture of errors.
> The Brownists charge Episcopacie with four heresies, first their Canons, secondly sin uncensured, thirdly their Hyrarchy, fourthly their Service book.
> The agreement of brothers is rare, by how much nature hath more endeared them, by so much are their quarrels more frequent and dangerous.
> *Butidius* a man well qualified, and if he had taken a right course, a man likely to have come to honourable preferment, over much haste pricked forwards, and at the first went about to out-go his equalls, then his Superiors, and at last of al to fly above his own hopes, which hath been the overthrow of good men, who contemning that, which by a little patience is had with security; hasten to that which is gotten before his time, breedeth their ruine and destruction.
> Buying and selling of men and women, which was used in *England* until the third year of *Henry* the first was then prohibited.[17]

This is strange. As a reader's notebook, it might make some sense. But it's not immediately clear why someone would publish this, or want it published. After spending some time with it, though, I find it fascinating, as much for what it lacks (or leaves out) as for what it includes. These notes seem to be the stimulants of thinking, or perhaps the ashes of it. There's even perhaps a suggestion of trust or discretion in Uffley's willingness to leave us, further readers, to our own responses. We're guided by his selections, but left to do our own readings of them.

Organized alphabetically and otherwise undigested, Uffley's work is thoroughly unoriginal, a collection of quotations from his reading, a commonplace book. That it calls itself an 'essay' suggests that the early modern genre evolved out of this practice of commonplace reading. It also offers one kind of answer to questions being posed by historians of the book and reading. As I was researching this book at several libraries, I met numerous scholars looking for evidence of readers and their readings in the margins of books. The fruits of such work have been both exhilarating and disappointing. For every book copiously annotated by an Alberti there seem to be hundreds of empty margins, or simply nominal registration of the fact of reading. (This was true of the copy of Uffley I read at the Huntington, signed 'Elizabeth Cox' at the end of the text with no other markings.) It may be that we're looking for readers' responses to books in the wrong places. Works like Uffley's redirect our search from the margins to the text, but with a renewed attention to title and genre. Uffley's *Observations and Essayes* register a reader's response to his texts, and the title he uses announces as much, indicating the genre within which readers did that kind of work.

Uffley's book was published in 1659. The quoted passage shows the kind of notation of various commonplaces that can be found in 'Essays' throughout the century.[18] Uffley notes topical debates like those concerning the Brownists that belong to his moment alongside universal topoi like *Libera scripta manet* that recur in many essays.[19] In this sense, essays change because things change. But this practice of writing – writing as a register of reading that invites further reading – doesn't change. Literary historians seem less interested now in such questions of continuity, but the persistence of this kind of writing by a wide variety of writers with a wide array of projects across the politically, religiously, and socially diverse worlds stretching from 1600 to 1750 asks us to find a space for a literary form that doesn't develop in lockstep with cultural changes, and perhaps doesn't develop that much at all.

Passages from one book in another, essays tend to be less works than workings out. Passages from one book to another, they leave little but the accidental remnants of response. They don't so much announce an author as invite, in turn, our response in kind. Turnings and returnings, halfway points between one reading and another, essays register exercises in reading that don't necessarily pay off in writing, in authorship or authenticity. The essay, that is, puts pressure on our professional predilections to use texts as historical windows and on historicist ways of reading. Uffley wouldn't have brought together this particular grouping of readings and references (with Butidius butting up against the Brownists) ten years before or after. Yet there are plenty of examples of texts like this that call themselves essays and do what Uffley does with their own local material. To locate such texts in their precise contexts may tell us about the moments that produce them, but won't fully address the works' own projects. Essays direct readers to take account of their 'own experiences' with contents rooted in many locales. Such a mode of reading is necessarily anachronistic, stringing readers between their own moment and the moment of the text, which itself registers the writer's own moment engaging with other texts, which are versions of the same practice, and so on.

All texts interweave the residue of many times, and to lock them to any one time is to limit both what they've achieved (a bridging of various times) and what they allow (a participation in that historical process, that process of being in time or, necessarily, in the middle of time, *in medias res* and in media). Starting from the perspective of the mediate and mediating mode of reading enabled by this genre, we end up with a different kind of literary history. No essays without print, perhaps, but the same practice of essay-writing under the Stuarts and the Hanovers – in Grub Street, Oxford, and Edinburgh – in the City and, of course, the country – in ale-houses, in coffeehouses, and at tea-tables. My account of the essay, then, starts with an assumption that its ubiquitous and widespread practice of writing has a generic profile that is interesting precisely because of its continuity and because of the continuities it enables.

Tools and skills of reading

In organizing this study, I've tried to take seriously the exigencies of essays, to practice the kind of literacy I describe evolving through them – a way of reading that's secondary, that comes late, that responds to what it finds and makes no claims to be originary or even original. Because these practices were tentative and shared, rather than exhaustive and authoritative, I am less concerned with locating a normative model of the genre than with exploring the range of variations that went under the name 'essay' in the first century of its development. For instance, Lady Gethin's *Remains*, her personal notebooks published in 1699 as a memorial at her death, were presented as 'Written by Her for the most part, by way of Essay' shortly after Locke used the term for the title of his *Essay concerning Human Understanding* (1690).[20] Gethin's work was 'written for the most part in hast … her first Conceptions, and overflowing of her Luxuriant Fancy, noted with her Pencil at spare

Hours, or as she was Dressing ... and set down just as they came into her Mind, as never designed for any others view but her own.'[21] Locke may have chosen to title his philosophical work an 'essay' to make a similar gesture of modesty, but he does take pains at the outset to describe the work more broadly in terms drawn from the essay's generic repertoire. In the 'Epistle to the Reader' he describes the *Essay* as 'the diversion of some of my idle and heavy Hours,' focused on the pleasures of process ('sport' and 'pursuit') not product, and presented as occasion for readers to think along with him: 'This, Reader, is the Entertainment of those who let loose their own thoughts, and follow them in writing; which thou oughtest not to envy them, since they afford thee an Opportunity of the like Diversion, if thou wilt make use of thy own Thoughts in reading. 'Tis to them, if they are thy own, that I referr my self.'[22] If Locke's *Essay* stretches the limits of the genre, it nevertheless uses it and, indeed, makes the participatory reading sponsored by the essay integral to its epistemology more generally.[23]

A generation after Locke presented his experiment in a mode of participatory thinking 'fitted to Men of my own Size,' Chudleigh offered her *Essays* as a record of her own first steps toward thinking, a way to assimilate her reading and test out her understanding (and show that women can be of Locke's size too).[24] In doing so, Chudleigh echoes Cornwallis's rationale for his *Essayes* a hundred years earlier. On the one hand a wide range of contemporary practices are named 'essays' and on the other the genre exists as a recognizable practice across a long and in many ways discontinuous period. Early modern essays remind us that print culture is a complex, layered phenomenon, at once more continuous than histories of a ruptural modernity would have it and less continuous than the synchronic focus of cultural studies suggests. An account of the essay must negotiate these two problems, addressing the continuity of a discursive practice across the epochal divides that tend to organize literary histories as well as the variety of particular applications within a single genre at a specific time.

In order to grasp this complex generic history my study presents the evolution of the early modern essay as three intertwined strands. I offer an account of a practice (a skill that emerges out of humanist commonplace reading), an account of some of the ways this skill comes to be modeled on the page (beyond enabling a certain kind of work off the page), and an account of various adaptations of this tool that reapply the skill it sponsors to new projects. In this way, I braid a history of three threads, each of which runs concurrently with the others. Each of these co-existing strands can be found in a slice from any part of my period, as with Gethin and Locke, and all of them stretch throughout the whole of it. Chudleigh is in one sense contemporary with Cornwallis – they both use essays as occasions to practice a mode of commonplace reading – even as she shares a bookseller's stall with the *Spectator* and its innovative use of the genre for a different kind of project.

The two chapters of Part 1, 'Of Essays,' explore the co-evolution of this tool of reading and the skill it sponsors. The first chapter, 'Draughts of Reading,' centers on a Senecan figure for reading and discusses the essay as an aid to the 'digestion' of texts. I reconstruct the early modern generic repertoire through a range of self-conscious accounts of the form – prefaces, dedicatory epistles, occasional comments, and two essays, 'Of Essays' – by several of its early practitioners, Cornwallis, Tuvill, Felltham, Culpeper, and others who disseminated this humanist exercise of readerly writing through print. The second chapter, 'By Way of Essays,' takes up another classical figure of reading, traveling, and charts another way through the evolution of the genre. From early essays 'Of Travel' by Palmer and Peacham to Cowley's *Essays*, I show how this tool of reading evolved into a model of reading, coming to register on the page the kind of responses it had enabled off the page. This suggests an a-modern alternative to various modern and post-modern theories of the essay, which I review at the end of the chapter in light of the genre's early history.

Part 2, 'Essay Exapted,' looks at the ways the essay and its mode of reading are made central to three other kinds of projects, natural science, a sociable public sphere, and the novel. I borrow Stephen Jay Gould and Elizabeth Vrba's neologism 'exaptation' to suggest that genres, like other forms, do not evolve to fit functions but rather the reverse; functions develop once the forms are available to be used, reused, or even misused – adapted or exapted.[25] Chapter 3, 'Boyle's Essay,' locates Robert Boyle's 'Proemial Essay' (1661), a key methodological statement of his reformed natural philosophy, in its generic context. Boyle adopts the essay as a formal tool of his natural philosophy not because, as recent historians of science have argued, it serves to isolate facts but rather because it enables a kind of reflection that was as important to his project as the reporting and witnessing of experiments. Boyle makes the essay's skill of participatory reading the motor of his epistemological reform. By following the evolution of the essay through Boyle's adoption of it, I explore one specific mechanism by which humanism evolved into natural science.

In the 1710s, Addison and Steele turned the printing technology of commercial and political news-sheets to other uses, creating a literary form, the periodical essay, that both structured and mediated the emerging commercial metropolis. In Chapter 4, 'Social and Literary Form in the *Spectator*,' I discuss how both the press and the modern public sphere were shaped by this adaptation of the essay. Distinct from neo-classical and republican uses of print like Shaftesbury's, on the one hand, and personal and confessional uses like Puritan diaries, on the other, Addison and Steele's periodicals both model and enable a social and sociable public. Developed at the intersection of the city and the press, the *Spectator* used the resources of the essay to offer an indigenous literature to a public organized by commerce, conversation, and association.

Tom Jones is punctuated by essays and Fielding declares them essentially necessary to his work. Chapter 5, 'Fleeting Habitations in *Tom Jones*,' explores the 'reflection' and 'learning' that are associated with these intrusions. I show that the critically suspect essayistic voice is indeed integral to the novel – not only as a way to reflect self-consciously on the themes of the plot but also in order to reflect on the construction of a work self-consciously engaged in dialogue with the range of texts of a complex print culture. *Tom Jones* offers readers an opportunity to practice, in a text densely layered with a wide range of adapted texts and parodied conventions, the skills required to negotiate a world densely layered with works of all kinds, all ages, and all pedigrees. Fielding orchestrates various forms, styles, and voices into a novel that models and trains the skills needed to participate in a culture mediated by print, a further exaptation of the essay in, or indeed as, a genre of the novel organized by its digestive and dynamic mode of reading.

Print culture

In tracing the spread of the essay's mode of literacy into these various fields, I hope to suggest a different way of approaching early modern print culture. Directing readers to a particular scale of engagement and enabling a skill of reading – a way of cycling through texts without either simply claiming or disdaining them – the genre suggests a model of print culture that looks less like a system than an ecosystem. Essays enable a practice of engagement through which, on the one hand, readers participate in their cultures, and, on the other, cultures evolve through such myriad and unpredictable uses of the genre. They offer little models of the practice of mixing that defines both how we read and how that enables us to participate in a world mediated by print – a world in which genres and practices co-evolve in response to the mutually defining engagements of readers, books, and further readings. In essays, writes Culpeper ('Of Essayes,' 1671), 'a man may read an Epitomy of himself, and the world together.'[26] Essays record the blends that readers work out, not in the interest of better knowledge but in the interest of local use. And they are the tools with which readers negotiate a print culture composed of numerous other negotiations and negotiators. 'Essay' names the work of recognizing such agents and their works, and participating with them in a cycle of reading organized by such contingent uses – mediating and adapting texts by other agents doing the same.

Putting such skills, and the tools that enable them, at the center of our work as scholars of literature would reorient us to a study of genres that have their own rhythms of development. Genres name historical literacies. They are tools that enable certain skills – skills which, in turn, adapt those tools for new projects, which develop new skills, which lead to reformed tools, and so on. Rather than being organized by watershed moments or the epochal divides proposed by stories of modernity, a literary history based on the essay's mode of reading would be shaped like an ecosystem of co-evolving tools and skills of literacy. The condition of understanding such a model is a willingness to participate in it.

Tentative and exploratory, 'imperfect offers' in the early modern phrase, essays are exercises in reading.[27] In the mildness of this claim is the thrust of my intervention: an argument for focusing on a skill or practice that makes no claim to change the world, or even to understand it comprehensively, but rather offers one way to participate in it, the ordinary work of attention, interaction, and response. In thinking about reading in the essay's terms, a literary history based on 'usage' may take shape: 'it is harder to give usage back its value as a constraint, to awaken in ordinary language the order that has been effaced from it, to adhere to habit as to the summons of reflection itself. To give a purer meaning to the words of the tribe can be to give words a new meaning, but it is also to give words their old meaning, to grant them the meaning they have, by reviving them as they have not ceased to be.'[28] The discipline of English can be understood as the study of reading as well as writing, a way of modeling and enabling practices of literacy. We shouldn't lose sight of these skills, this art, in our rush to make sociology or self-fashioning the default position of literary scholarship. Essays remind us that any historical account of reading is contingent on our ability to do it ourselves, to engage those texts and grasp that history as our own. The essay offers us a name for the practices of reflection and recitation, and response and adaptation, that define what we do when we read.

Finally, the disclaimers entailed by my topic. Essays don't do everything, they don't see everything ('Je ne voy le tout de rien'), and they offer only a particular tool that facilitates a specific skill (other genres are tools for other jobs).[29] Organized by reading, essays allow you to do things other than build new houses. Every reader, perhaps, like a young student who can't wait to be a scholar and live in a big house, wants to be a writer and make if not a book at least a creative life for herself. When you do that, you use a different tool. Essays don't help you grow up in that way, and they offer a resource for a different kind of activity.[30]

I've found myself involved in a genre that sponsors a kind of reading that doesn't lend itself to many of the moves, or rhetoric, of our critical moment. Nothing happens in essays. Modernity is not initiated; no selves are fashioned or politics undertaken by other means; no regimes of publicity, ideology, or subjectivity are instituted or resisted. Essays don't lay foundations, but make connections and enable the negotiation of borrowed spaces. They don't dream new beginnings but reread old texts.[31] They come late, don't claim to be everywhere, or do everything, or know anything as such. But then, too, they remind us that any writing that does make such claims can be read otherwise too.[32]

This is a book 'of essays,' at once an exploration of the early evolution of the essay in English and an experiment in practicing what I understand of the mode of reading and writing it enables. Registering passages and forgoing the grails of authority, authenticity, and origins, essays are effects of contingent engagements with texts and they invite the same in turn. A practice of writing in the service of reading, the genre invites others, further readers, to connect the dots for themselves – not to finish but to continue. I've tried to perform what I mean by this loose, light way of reading, leaving you, unknown reader, to make what patterns you need out of the ones I've assembled from the texts I've found.

Part 1
Of Essays

1
Draughts of Reading

Salted greens

Essays are like salt, says Bacon, 'that will rather give you an appitite, then offend you with satiety.' '[B]riefe notes,' 'dispersed Meditacions,' such works are aids to the digestion of commonplaces. 'And althoughe they handle those things wherein both Mens lives, and theire pens are most conversant, yet (What I have attained, I knowe not) but I have endeavoured to make them not vulgar; but of a nature, Whereof a Man shall find much in experience, litle in bookes; so as they are neither repetitions, nor fansies.'[1] Essays stimulate, they are obvious, and they register a particular kind of engagement. Salt for ordinary eating, offering readers occasions to engage the common without being either bound by it (simply repeating) or liberated from it (fancifully), essays occupy a middle ground between copying and creating, mediating text and mind, and enabling the work of each on the other. The genre names a place where one's wheels hit the road and that traction conveys you; they are neither about the road, nor about the wheels. The essay, that is, offers a vehicle for a kind of reading that falls between the gaps of our historicist terrors and our post-structuralist desires, neither blindly following nor freely fleeing, but thinking through the ordinary.

Recent accounts of the essay construe it as a romantic genre organized by the dynamics of excess and resistance, or voice and expression.[2] None of these categories adequately accounts for the genre's profile in the seventeenth century. Early modern essays are first and foremost part of a practice of moral philosophy, tools that help one engage, not resist, the commonplace. 'For curious method, expect none,' says Fuller (1642), 'Essays for the most part not being placed as at a Feast, but placing themselves as at an Ordinary.'[3] Goddard describes his *Miscellanea; or, Serious, Useful Considerations, Moral, Historical, Theological ... An Essay* (1661) as 'a poor dinner of green herbs.'[4] Less metaphorically, Ralph Johnson's *Scholars Guide* (1665) defines an essay as 'a short discourse about any vertue, vice, or other commonplace.'[5] The essay is an 'ordinary' serving of commonplaces, and a tool with which to undertake the work of thinking through the ordinary: thinking it through (riding the train to its terminus) and thinking through it (riding that particular train of thought).

Registering readers' engagements with texts, the genre enables a practice of response through which, on the one hand, readers participate in their cultures and, on the other, those cultures evolve. From one perspective, essays are how cultures propagate and spread in a world of print. From another perspective, they are how readers make homes in their cultures, furnishing rooms with the available materials. In the essay the two perspectives are inseparable. The genre names at once a hybrid work (something more than simple repetition and something less than pure fancy) and a tool for that kind of mixing – enabling readers to adopt and adapt commonplaces for their own use and enabling commonplaces to live and evolve, and so too allowing these dynamics to be seen as necessarily entwined and entailed by each other.

Commonplace reading

In *Reading Revolutions*, Kevin Sharpe offers a detailed account of an early seventeenth-century reader. He carefully reconstructs William Drake's commonplace books, his reading notes over the course of his life, and does so in the service of a compelling argument to include readers in our accounts of early modern politics and add the experience of authority to our studies of its exercise.[6] Sharpe's case study is a thick description of the early modern commonplace method of reading and highlights how different it is from our assumptions about reading. Instead of moving through a book in the order it establishes, 'the commonplace method places the reader in a more dominant position and forces the text into categories he has conceived – albeit as a consequence of earlier readings, as well as experience.'[7] In this kind of reading, one detaches texts from their original contexts and appropriates them for one's own uses.[8] (Drake cites Seneca on this process of digestion, a commonplace that directs one how to use commonplaces.)[9] In pursuing one's own use, one could of course go beyond the text's letter. Reading opens a hermeneutic freedom that potentially compromises authority, and such 'radical rereading' could leave one at odds with dominant values.[10] In this way 'an ambiguity at the heart of commonplacing' expresses a central tension of the period between individual and communal authority: 'Though what the compiler copied was extracted from a common storehouse of wisdom, the manner in which extracts were copied, arranged, juxtaposed, cross-referenced or indexed was personal and individual.'[11] Commonplace reading enacts a political problem. Is a reader limited by the authority of commonplace wisdom or does she claim it for herself?

Sharpe's is a big and generous study, and in that spirit I hope I can digest what he writes to ends that, like the kind of history he practices, may have unintended consequences. Sharpe's focus is on readers who read for 'action in the public realm,' or the moments in their reading when they read for this, moments in which they 'were able to construct meanings for themselves, and constitute themselves as political agents.'[12] This was one effect of humanism, which 'enabled a self-education and permitted an independence of judgment that began to constitute a subjectivity that was anything but passive or uncritical.'[13] My question is whether such independence of judgment could lead one to constitute oneself as an *a-political* agent as well, and not just a revolutionary political agent. Sharpe's conclusions are entailed in the way he frames his topic. He notes that his subjects, Drake and here Clarendon, copied into their commonplace books 'passages about beauty, love and marriage, as well as lessons of statecraft.'[14] One doesn't ask everything of everyone, but it's not hard to imagine working through these same materials and telling a very different story. Sharpe's topic, reading, and his own fine skills as a reader allow one to make this critique of his book an extension of it. If the commonplace method depends on, and trains, active readers, I wonder how completely the genie can be put back into the bottle. Readers who could read themselves into revolutionary political positions could also read themselves out of politics altogether, or at least have extra-political moments as well.

I'm not saying that we should read against the politics we find in texts (and return to that false separation of aesthetics and ideology), but rather that we should recognize that non-political moments have their own cultural spaces; not every tool does everything. Another virtue of Sharpe's study is his attention to genre and form.[15] So when I want him to go further, I want him to fulfill his own terms. Genres name the way cultures organize differences, and fuller attention to generic categories will flesh out some of Sharpe's implications. He uses Montaigne and Bacon to exemplify the possibilities that inhere in reading: 'Writers like Bacon and Montaigne could not but be aware of the potential freedom of the reader, given their own often audaciously independent rereading of the classical texts they revered.'[16] Yet while he discusses these writers as examples of the reader's freedom, and notes the importance of genre, he never puts the two together to note that this readerly freedom has a particular generic profile in the period.

It's within the genre of the essay that the reader's freedom is most audaciously worked out. In the commonplace method the reader 'performs a very individual reading and interpretation, and an act of power "over" the text, an act which makes what he writes and thinks his own ... All of Drake's notebooks evidence the permeability of the author/reader boundary.'[17] But if the boundaries are blurred, don't we need an account that starts from that fact, and doesn't introduce the either/or logic that such blurring disrupts? Though reading is said to be free of authority, we seem automatically to go for those categories of authority when we explain reading: Montaigne is said to have 'plundered the established "auctores" of his day,' 'claimed the work as his own,' and 'appropriate[d] authority from the source to the author.'[18] In contrast, I want to suggest that the genre of the essay is the site where that 'freedom' starts to offer an alternative to politics as well as an alternative politics. The form registers a kind of reading that can't fully be defined by those political categories – power, authority – or be collapsed back into the terms they blur. In essays, readers develop a competence in a mode of reading enabled by the commonplace method and its freedom of use, and this skill of reading is not fully explicable in terms of a politics of reading.

In bringing the reader into the story, the story also changes. In their introduction to *A History of Reading in the West*, Cavallo and Chartier also describe Montaigne as 'a singular reader who rejects the rules and postures of studious reading.'[19] Isn't that, though, just what readers do? Every time they study particular cases, historians seem to find exceptions to rules they formulate when they look at global patterns. Chartier's Montaigne, or Ginzburg's Menocchio, or Sharpe's Drake is presented as an exception that proves rules, but in claiming a readerly freedom these examples could suggest, not that such readers are atypical, but that that's how reading works.[20] The history of the book, though, remains framed by questions of 'authenticity and authorship,' and the turn to reading – which has mainly been a turn to readers as actors in stories about social history, cultural identity, and politics –

could go further.[21] Such studies haven't let their new concerns affect their old categories. They're still concerned with the efficacy of writing and 'absolute positions' but reading doesn't necessarily operate in those terms.[22] Stories of reading need not be organized by the same exigencies as stories of writing.

Practicing in public

The expectation of a kind of writing obscures the fact that in their early evolution essays register reading. The genre doesn't facilitate originality or authority but digestion, enabling a kind of work off the page instead of a new work on the page. This creates problems for literary historians as well as social historians. Daniel Tuvill's editor, John L. Lievsay, for instance, has done such a good job of editing Tuvill's essays that the text has all but unraveled. In establishing the sources of Tuvill's two volumes, *Essays Politic and Moral* (1608) and *Essays Moral and Theological* (1609), Lievsay has established how little else there is but those sources. Tuvill is thoroughly commonplace and unoriginal, full of quotations, and those often 'pillaged' from other secondary sources: 'he no doubt justified his somewhat shady practice by pretending to himself that such pillaging was the function of the art which in those days bore the label of "imitation."'[23] Lievsay describes Tuvill's method in apt if negative terms, noting a 'general looseness of structure and imprecision of thought which characterize the whole collection' which he calls 'unmortared' and lacking 'form and centrality.'[24] I agree with Lievsay; the more closely you look at Tuvill (and a close look is possible because of Lievsay's excellent edition), the more the text disintegrates into its separate components. But at the same time, I find Lievsay's expectations foreign and imported into a text that operates with different ones.

Tuvill's text is an assemblage of commonplaces, a tour through his reading, 'unfashioned,' as Tuvill himself says, and indeed unmortared.[25] It looks to me like a published commonplace book, the effects of which are not registered by the writer but rather performed by the reader. Near the beginning of 'Of Civil Carriage and Conversation' Tuvill writes, 'There is no man but will willingly delight in him that is affected with those passions where unto himself is subject and inclined. Experience teacheth and reason proveth it.' A few pages later he cites Solomon: 'For, as the Wise Man saith, all flesh will resort to their like, and every man will keep company with such as he is himself.'[26] It seems as if Tuvill has spoken Solomon's point as his own and then returned to it as a quotation. Perhaps, but it is a commonplace (available from experience, reason, and books) and the work of commonplaces is to allow people to inhabit a discourse without attribution. What's important is not that Solomon says it, but that Tuvill gets it, uses it, makes it his own. Essays offer a space where the thinking of a thought is more important than the origin of it, a space where one redeems the cliché by using it – or by, necessarily, re-using it. A secondary form, made up of quotations and even unacknowledged borrowings, the essay marks a space of participation and continuation.

Lievsay has good reason to be appalled by Tuvill's 'writing,' but he refashions the *Essays* into the shape of his expectations. 'Nowhere does Tuvill's scissors-and-paste, commonplace-book method of composition more clearly reveal his essential unoriginality; for he has digested nothing.'[27] I want to reverse Lievsay's point, not to say that his negatives should be positive (it's really not okay to plagiarize, nor to let someone else do your thinking for you), but rather to suggest that his assumptions get in his way at a much more fundamental point. The commonplace method isn't really a tool of composition, and Lievsay's analysis points out what his expectations deny. He expects Tuvill's *Essays* to operate as a kind of writing when they seem more legible, and less offensive, as a kind of reading. The copious copying of the *Essays* suggests a genre that makes no claim to originality (which Lievsay indeed recognizes), but rather offers a chance to mingle insight with what's given, a mechanism of learning, reading, and rereading the given.

Thomas Greene situates the Renaissance practice of *imitatio* against a backdrop of this kind of commonplace reading:

> Where one is indubitably dealing with a topos, the etiological itinerary is far more jagged and less than fully knowable. It is also to some degree dehistoricized: if the topos has been everywhere, then it derives specifically from nowhere. The reader is not expected to know its history but to recognize its conventionality, to know it as a product of history. Reading an eclectic texture of topoi is a sharply different activity from reading heuristic or dialectical imitations.[28]

Early modern essays are closer to this kind of tissue of *topoi* than to humanist poetry. If 'the humanist text reaches across a cultural gap and takes the risk of anachronism,' essays dwell less anxiously in the anachronistic spaces of reading where another, everyone, or even no one speaks, and precisely in one's own voice.[29] Greene's account of this process of commonplace reading performs what it presents, repeating without citing the everywhere/nowhere cliché from (or at least also in) Seneca – a buried pleasure that Greene certainly includes for our delight and to involve us in the dynamics he describes. Greene notes that Seneca's account of imitation 'arguably consists of a theory of reading as much as of writing'; in epistle 84, 'Seneca's dominant analogies, mellification and digestion, stress a process of transformation. There is a shift from the penetration of a containing outer world to the absorption of the outer world within the self ... Seneca is not concerned with the flow or passage onward of a heritage; he is concerned with what a single individual can do with it.'[30] This focus on reading instead of writing, intake and use instead of output and dissemination, reorients attention to a different side of the complex practice of literacy, and suggests a different kind of historical project than that of much historicism: not a process of grounding, of reading through texts to origins or locking uses to sources, but a way of being historical, existing in time. It's not so much that the present is tied to a past but that a past provides the necessary organizing materials for any activity in the present. (History, of course, is not something you can just step outside of, and, for all the pious invocations of historicism, there couldn't be ahistoricist reading; historicism serves as the commendably conventional kitsch of that recognition.)

'Essay' was the name for a tool of reading that enabled a certain competency and skill – a kind of commonplace book where the work of selection and collection that is key to humanist reading is practiced and undertaken.[31] Sometime in the 1620s, Jonson excoriated essayists in these just terms.

> Some that turn over all books, and are equally searching in all papers, that write out of what they presently find or meet, without choice: by which means it happens that what they have discredited and impugned in one work, they have before or after extolled the same in another. Such are all the essayists, even their master Montaigne. These, in all they write, confess still what books they have read last, and therein their own folly so much, that they bring it to the stake raw and undigested; not that the place did need it neither, but that they thought themselves furnished, and would vent it.[32]

Jonson's complaint anticipates Lievsay's. Both find essayists too raw, mere copyists, and not good digesters. The accusation of essayists doing their dirty work, their reading, in public is repeated by Shaftesbury a century later (1711), and shows that 'essay' named this practice throughout this period.

> 'Tis observable, that the Writers of Memoirs and Essays are chiefly subject to this frothy Distemper. Nor can it be doubted this is the true Reason why these Gentlemen entertain the World so lavishly with what relates to *themselves*. For having had no opportunity of privately conversing with themselves, or exercising their own *Genius*, so as to make Acquaintance with it, or prove its Strength; they immediately fall to work in a wrong place, and exhibit on the Stage of the World that *Practice*, which they shou'd have kept to themselves; if they design that either they or the World, shou'd be the better for their Moralitys. Who indeed can endure to hear *an Empirick* talk of his own Constitution, how he governes and manages it, what Diet agrees best with it, and what his Practice is with himself? The proverb, no doubt, is very just, *Physician cure thyself*. Yet methinks one shou'd have but an ill time, to be present at these bodily Operations. Nor is the reader in truth any better entertain'd, when he is oblig'd to assist at the experimental Discussions of his practising Author, who all the while is in reality doing no better, than taking his Physick in publick.[33]

Essays are private matters, exercises that relate to one's own 'Moralitys,' and so best kept to oneself.[34] Shaftesbury isn't complaining about the practice but about the sharing of it, the way essays oblige a reader 'to assist at the experimental Discussions of his practising Author.' For purposes of sketching out the terrain of the genre, such complaints are invaluable. Foregrounding the core features of the generic repertoire – a practice of writing geared to the absorption of what one reads as part of a practice of moral philosophy – these accounts show that the essay named a particular practice that existed over the course of a century (one that crosses other kinds of social, political, and cultural periodizations). Shaftesbury's England certainly wasn't Jonson's, but the essay named a set of practices, a relatively stable generic repertoire, that was available to both.

Both Jonson and Shaftesbury chastise the practice of publishing the 'raw and undigested' stuff one writes for one's own use because to involve others in one's digestion is unseemly and gross. Their complaints at one level are well taken (if there are relatively few worth reading who write carefully polished books, there are even fewer worth reading who write carefully unpolished books). But at another level, their remarks indicate a commitment to different models of authorship, ones that are not shared and participatory, and that don't ask the reader's assistance, but rather are more regal, the kind of 'absolutist' authorship on display in Jonson's commanding folio *Works* or Shaftesbury's exquisitely produced *Characteristics*.[35] Essays require a different practice of reading, not one geared to observing an author on display, but to learning a skill. Jonson and Shaftesbury take the models of reading on which their own texts depend and apply it to texts organized differently. They only see public display where essays offer examples of something else. (Again, their points are not completely off-base. It's not only ungenerous readers who make essays look vain, but ungenerous writers who use the form to show instead of share.) Their screeds concern the public sharing of a necessary private practice. Shaftesbury himself kept a commonplace book as part of his practical stoicism, but only in the bourgeois public sphere, the emergence of which he observed with clarity and scorn, does the vain publishing of such work become something to applaud.[36] Jonson kept one too, and indeed Lievsay's problem with Tuvill's *Essays* echoes Castelain's with Jonson's *Discoveries*.[37] Both were taken at first to be collections of essays but, through careful research into sources, were discovered to be collections of notes and quotations, registers of reading. Both Jonson's *Discoveries* and Tuvill's *Essays* are better read as effects of reading instead of writing, tools that enabled readers to engage their books.

Only matter well digested

T. C. introduces his *Morall Discourses and Essayes, Upon Severall Select Subjects* (1655) by describing the kind of work essays do:

> They are thought to have a very hard, but have indeed, perhaps, an easie Taske, that are to treat of Subjects, wherein many Excellent Pens having gone before, may seem to have anticipated all that can be pertinently spoken: It is, I confess, in some measure true of those which will handle Arts and Sciences, from whom some new discovery is justly expected; Neither will their Modern Termes absolve them from the Censure of affecting to write somewhat, though to no purpose, if they deliver nothing new in substance. [But] From an Essay or Morall Discourse, we are to require nothing, that was never harped on by any Orpheus; For the Theory of Morality is a path so trodden with throngs of Authours, that perhaps Solomon himself, if

he were now alive, would find it hard to say something in this kind, which might be as new to us, as Gunpowder and the Load-stone once were.

From it therefore we are to expect only matter well digested, with such a trimming and furbishing of the Argument, that the Reader may be tempted, like some Gentlemen, as it were to buy that Horse in Smithfield, which himself lately sold in a Country Fair. Such an Art of new compounding the same notions in variety of Expression, that the Herbalist shall have much adoe to discern his own Simples.

The Consideration hereof hath encouraged me to publish these Essayes, most of them written upon Themes very popular, Whereby, though I may well despair to purchase the name of an Authour, Yet I may seem to be a digestor of what I have read in this kind, and without assuming to inform any mans Iudgement, may serve in some sort to clear his Notions, or at least entertain his Passe-times; which, as it is not a work of much moment, so I am confident, it is as useful as many larger Volumes, which have been published in our Age so fertile of abortive Births.[38]

Essays here are synonymous with moral philosophy, and are organized by different exigencies than knowledge (arts and sciences). They are less concerned with novelty and innovation than with new compounding the same old stuff, a point made by signposting the work of the essay with references to Orpheus and Solomon. T. C. makes a double distinction, between old texts and new things (gunpowder and magnets), and between digesters and authors. Essays deal in books but not in authors. They are tools of reading that do not claim to be original or originary. T. C. figures the essay as a trick and a medicine, or perhaps a trick to get you to take your medicine. (I wish for a moment that Bacon had said sugar instead of salt, for the chance to say, a spoonful of sugar helps the medicine go down.) But of course this is not a practice of sugarcoating, disguise or trickery, but of flavoring. Salt brings out flavor, it doesn't change the taste, and T. C.'s point is that if you buy the old horse back, the proof is in the riding of it. The gentlemen are foolish not because they buy horses they don't recognize, but because they sell horses they don't know.

Essays don't claim to teach anything new or offer any news, but rather clear up your notions. Or at least they'll entertain you. But T. C. says more. Essays are 'as useful' as the larger volumes which fall, abortive, from the press. It's one thing to say they may be old, small, inconsequential, *but* they're entertaining. T. C., however, says his essays work better than larger volumes *because* they're 'not a work of much moment.' What does that mean? What is the efficacy of essays?

The figure of birth is common enough in prefaces.[39] Tuvill describes his *Essays* as a 'young and tender Infant': 'His capacitie is not of the weakest: and therefore, howsoeuer he may now seeme altogether vnfashion'd, I make no doubt, but by conversing with your Ladiship ... his ruder ignorance may be reduced to a better forme. Essaies are the things hee uttereth. His yeeres deny him that length of breath, which should enable him to hold out in a continued, and long discourse.'[40] Essays are explicitly 'unfashioned,' their formal shortness an aspect of their function – immature trials, at best showing promise if taken under a good wing.[41] Here Lady Harrington is asked to oversee the raising of the child, offering a figure for a reader who, by 'conversing' with the *Essays*, will fashion them in her own image. I don't want to milk too much the formulae of dedicatory epistles, but in them, as here, can often be heard moments of generic self-consciousness where the expectations of writers and readers are pronounced, delineated, and assigned. In the abjectly groveling terms of the fawning client, Tuvill articulates an important aspect of the essay's generic repertoire. Entrusting the reader with the work of 'raising' the *Essays*, Tuvill places the burden of conversation on her. The burden of essays falls on the reader, not the writer. Essays ask to be fashioned in the image of their interlocutors, offering a mechanism of response at the heart, and as the heart, of their discourse. They are texts that explicitly assume their final shape in the reader's response, in the form of that response.

Essays are recursively structured by response. The shape of the essayists' converse with commonplaces, Tuvill's or T. C.'s response to them, constitutes their invitation to the reader to do the same.[42] (This is the hopscotch movement, or relay, or feedback mechanism by which cultures reconstitute themselves via the energy of reading.) Essays facilitate a particular kind of reading, one not driven by expectations of originality, novelty, or knowledge, but by a smaller scale, a slower speed. Size matters, and too big a book will bore a reader. Whitlock (1654) describes his project in these terms, by citing Montaigne's 'Of Books' (see Appendix A for the full passage). 'I make no doubt (saith he) but I handle many Themes that are farre better handled in the scattered works of able Writers: But my intent was not to beat my Brains in the Acquisition even of Knowledge it selfe that was too difficult; Nor have I[:] what came easily among Authors or Observations to my understanding; what conduceth to living or dying well, that I communicate.'[43] It's not about acquiring knowledge but using it, and to that end what comes easily is valued more than what's difficult. Ease facilitates use. Whitlock quotes Montaigne contrasting books that are 'variously useful' with books of 'proper Method'; the latter are useful but lack, Whitlock continues,

> the Dulce, Pleasure of variety, and convenience of more contracted brevity: the paines of reading them is seldome bestowed on them, especially if they swell into Tomes of that bignesse, that he that can have no leisure, dareth not look on them, and he that will have none, careth not. I know not, how but as Montaigne saith of himselfe, Tracts of a continued Thread are tedious to most Fancies, which of it selfe indeed is of that desultory nature, that it is pleased with Writings like Irish Bogs, that it might leap from one variety to another, than tread any beaten Path.[44]

Big books are too daunting and boring, and so don't get used – as Montaigne's do here. The *Essais* give warrant for using them, and, by repeating the point, Whitlock proves their point. The efficacy they describe is exhibited in his very use of them. The passage combines an appeal to 'use' (what conduces to living and dying well, moral philosophy) and ease, the latter geared to the fancy and the pleasures it takes in movement and variety, in this case the surprise of finding oneself bounding through Irish bogs. (These are the pleasures of the imagination that Addison will categorize as 'novelty' in the *Spectator*, though by then Steele will have left Ireland far behind and the movement translated into a practice of walking in cities.)[45] Such movement makes pleasure and *dulce* into a motor of use and *utile*. Essays are organized by the desultory movement of 'fancy,' at once responding to and enabling such fanciful reading.[46]

Essays ask readers to read them as they read, and Whitlock's account of his manner of writing records the results of his reading:

> would you know (saith he [Lipsius]) my manner of writing? it is a kind of voluntary Tiding of, not Pumping for; Notions flowing, not forced; like Poets unconstrained Heats and Raptures; such is mine, rather a running Discourse than a Grave-paced Exactnes; having in them this Formality of Essayes (as Sir W. Cornwallyes saith of his) that they are Tryals of bringing my hand and Fancy acquainted in this using my Paper, as the Painters Boy a Board he blurs with Tryals. I may say in my defence as another before me ... As in Hunting he is the best Huntsman that catcheth most, and not bad

because he catcheth not all: To comprehend all, or most can be said on any of these Themes, I professe not.[47]

The quotation from Lipsius allows Whitlock to say his is a 'running discourse.'[48] Movement and trial are the terms of such discourse, and they orient one to the chase itself, to one's own observations, one's own scale and reach. All of this points to a discernable generic profile, a 'Formality of Essayes,' that is more concerned with assembly and application than with originality or coverage. Such work is dense with quotations, using others, self-consciously, to say what one means.[49] The concern is not with owning ideas but with using them well, so it's only appropriate that Whitlock uses Cornwallis to make his point.

> To all gaping Expectaltees (that look for more than here they are like to finde) my Book replyeth with this its *motto*; not queint, but useful; or, not rare but honest, at least in the Authors Iudgment and Intention; and I will use the words of an Ingenuous Author of our own, being so apt to my purpose: [']I like much better to doe well, then to talke well, chusing to be beloued rather than admired, aspiring to no more height then the comfort of a good conscience, and doing good to some, harme to none. If my Essayes speak thus, they speake as I would haue them.['] Thus far he, as fit as if he spoke for me of any thing amongst them.[50]

But for every honest reference, there's a hidden theft, perhaps not of a rare phrase, but worth noting, if only to make a point about the irrelevance of such scholarly reading to this kind of writing. Felltham explained his original *Resolves* (1623) 'To the Pervser' in these terms: 'Rare, I know it is not: Honest, I am sure it is: Though thou findest not to admire, thou maist to like.'[51] Whitlock borrows this statement about scaling down expectations, trading admiration for liking, in order to announce the mode of reading endorsed by the genre he uses, a mode of reading that foregrounds use instead of originality. This is a key feature of Cornwallis's *Essayes*, as well, and especially the one Whitlock cites here ('Of Essaies'), but I think the best way to get there is to flow through the bogs of borrowings that make up the stuff of essays in the seventeenth century.

Felltham lurks, unannounced, between Whitlock's quotations of Lipsius and Cornwallis. In 'To the Readers,' the new preface to the second edition of the *Resolves* (1628),[52] Felltham offers his own book as an example of what he calls a 'running Discourse':

> I am to answer two Obiections, One, that I haue made vse of Story, yet not quoted my Authorities; and this I haue purposely done. It had beene all one Labour, inserting the matter, to giue them, both the Author, and place. But while I am not Controuersiall, I should onely haue troubled the Text, or spotted a Margent [margin], which I alwaies wish to leave free, for the Comments of the man that reades. Besides, I doe not professe my selfe a Scholer: and for a Gentleman, I hold it a little pedanticall. He should use them rather, as brought in by Memory, raptim, and occasionall; than by Study, search, or strict collection: especially in Essay, which of all writing, is the neerest to a running Discourse.[53]

Gentlemen don't steal but borrow, and likewise we don't accuse others of stealing. But, at the risk of being pedantically scholarly, I'll spot Felltham's margin with a note about his borrowing from Tuvill, who writes, 'I coulde adde more; but the humour of *Essaies* is rather to glaunce at all things with a running conceit; then to insist on any with a slowe discourse.'[54] Within the capacious category of 'use,' the line between stealing and borrowing is a fluid one. Essays that register one's use of books work within a mazy cluster of things we all know and use in passing. Tuvill's 'essay' is a running conceit, not a slow discourse (in 1609), which becomes Felltham's running discourse (in 1628), which becomes Whitlock's running discourse, not a grave-paced exactness (in 1654). Felltham's margins, for just this reason, are left free for the reader's own running discourse, the reader's own reading notes. Felltham's free use models the reader's own, and the empty margin serves as a figure for such reading even as it provides a space in which, and on which, to exercise it. Free margins are at once a metonym of and a tool for this kind of reading.

Such writing is part of a practice of moral philosophy, writing for the sake of curbing passions – the effects of which, that is, are registered off the page, not on the page.[55]

> All the externall pleasures that mortality is capable of, can never enkindle a flame, that shall so brauely warme the soule, as the loue of vertue, and the certaine knowledge of the rule wee haue ouer our owne wilde passions. That I might curbe those, I haue writ these: and if in them, thou find'st a line may mend thee: I shall thinke I haue diuulg'd it to purpose. Reade all, and vse thy mindes liberty; how thy suffrage falls, I weigh not: For it was not so much to please others, as to profit my selfe.[56]

Felltham writes for his own use, and invites the reader to do the same, to use his writing for one's own. His margins are left 'free' to enable the reader's 'mindes liberty.' Such free reading passes through texts, not to study but to use them, and the mode of non-studious and 'running' writing that follows this practice of reading is called 'essay.' Essays shift from 'strict collection' – what scholars do – to gentlemanly 'use,' from stocking up to taking profit and fully absorbing such classroom practice into praxis.

While Whitlock makes his points through Montaigne and Cornwallis, Osborn gets to Montaigne through Cornwallis:

> For, though the Generality of Readers, are scandalized at all [that] is not mouldy through Age, or guilded with Novelty; yet, I remember, to have heard from Sir William Cornewallis, (esteemed none of the meanest Witts in his Time) That Mountaign's Essay's, was the likelyest Book, to advance Wisdom: because, The Authours own Experiences, is the Chiefest Argument in it. For as St. Augustine saith, of Short and Holy Ejaculations; That they pierce Heaven as soon, if not quicker, then more Tedious Prayers: So, I have reaped greater Benefit, from concise and Casuall Meditations, on severall Topicks, then long and voluminous Treatises, relating meerly to one and the same thing.[57]

Montaigne's *Essays* at once model and enable a kind of 'experience' – experiment, trial, essay – a mode of 'vigilant and erect attention' (as Hooker glosses Augustine) that flows through books, through Cornwallis's recommendation of Montaigne, and Hooker's recommendation of Augustine, and Osborn's use of all of these to show what he does and so what we should too.[58] The generic repertoire of the essay, its cluster of concerns, is organized around such experience and attention. Essays do not discover new things but compound old stuff. They enable digesters instead of authors, putting the burden on the reader and enabling her own use of such material by organizing a 'running,' 'tiding,' flowing discourse of short, occasional, and various pieces ('concise and Casuall Meditations, on severall Topicks') that appeal to the 'desultory nature' of the fancy. Facilitating this kind of use instead of knowledge, enabling 'profits' and 'benefits' instead of stockpiles, the genre of the essay offers a way of reading through others, or borrowing, that is less concerned with the possession of those objects of thought than with the kind of attention they enable. Montaigne's way of 'advancing wisdom' steers a path between old books and facile novelty, which I take to echo Bacon's remark that essays are neither repetitions nor fancies. They re-engage those books, and register that reading, allowing readers to do the same; a way of passing down a mode of attention in – and as – the experience of reading.

Draughts of reading

In the essay Whitlock quotes from, 'Of Essaies and Bookes' (1601), Cornwallis, Montaigne's follower, opens by dismissing Montaigne's *Essais* as essays, and claims that name for his own work (see Appendix B). 'I Holde neither *Plutarche's* nor none of those auncient short manner of writings nor *Montaigne's* nor such of this latter time to bee rightly tearmed Essayes; for though they be short, yet they are strong and able to endure the sharpest tryall.'[59] At first glance this makes one snort: And so the English essay was conceived, a form of writing that brags about its own feebleness, proudly dissociated from any claim to being smart. But on a second pass, a further and more interesting points lurks here, one that fills out another aspect of the genre, an intriguing suggestion that successful trials aren't real trials. Can an essay be successful? Can it realize its points, hit its mark, and still be an essay? Isn't it then a <whatever else it becomes>? Isn't it then absorbed into its product? If it succeeds, it is no longer preparation but product, no longer the apprenticeship but the profession, the race that's run, the provision that's bought (to use Cornwallis's figures). It's done. And like Plutarch's or Montaigne's, it has too much knowledge to bear inquisition – too many answers to allow questioning. Cornwallis announces his own *Essayes* are properly essays because they are registers not of successful thought but of a process of thinking.

> But mine are Essayes, who am but newly bound Prentise to the inquisition of knowledge and vse these papers as a Painter's boy a board, that is trying to bring his hand and his fancie acquainted. It is a maner of writing wel befitting vndigested motions, or a head not knowing his strength like a circumspect runner trying for a starte, or prouidence that tastes before she buyes. For it is easier to thinke well then to do well, and no triall to haue handsome dapper conceites runne inuisibly in a braine but to put them out and then looke vpon them.[60]

Here thinking happens via the page, but isn't recorded on the page. Writing that benefits undigested thoughts is not an expression of knowledge, what's already been digested, but a way to convert or transform those ideas or those books into use, to make them one's own. Writing is a mechanism of this, but Cornwallis is clear that it isn't the product of it. The stress falls on 'then looke vpon them,' not 'to put them out.' Essay writing is a practice of reading – or rereading, a way to aid the uptake, the absorption, of what one reads. It's a kind of notetaking that enables better comprehension, a testing of one's ideas by running them through the page.

As Cornwallis's paragraph develops, it stages two dramas, one about promise and disappointment, and another that addresses that problem by shifting the terms from books (writing) to persons (reading). Essay is a mode of writing that honors promises, as the triple repetition of 'promise' stresses.

> If they prooue nothing but wordes, yet they breake not promise with the world, for they say, 'But an Essay,' like a Scriuenour trying his Pen before he ingrosseth his worke. Nor, to speake plainely, are they more to blame then many other that promise more; for the most that I haue yet touched haue millions of wordes to the bringing forth one reason; and when a reason is gotten, there is such borrowing it one of another that in a multitude of Bookes, still that conceit, or some issued out of that, appeares so belaboured and worne, as in the ende it is good for nothing but for a Prouerbe. When I thinke of the abilities of man, I promise my selfe much out of my reading, but it prooues not so. Time goeth, and I turne leaues; yet still finde my selfe in the state of ignorance; wherefore, I haue thought better of honesty then of knowledge.[61]

Cornwallis's essays won't break their promise, unlike those books that promise more, and won't mislead youngsters who (it turns out) promise themselves too much, mistakenly, by taking those books' promises at face value. It's finally, of course, not the books' problem that a reader expects so much, a point that Cornwallis recognizes when he shifts from general commentary about books to the first person, 'I promise my selfe much out of my reading, but it prooues not so.' The rhetoric in the accounts of books that promise a lot but don't deliver is curiously impersonal; books seem to borrow conceits from other books, belabor them, empty them. And the actor himself only appears after the props have done their work, or when they are shown to fail at it. The point is that he has to do the work, but first he has to accept responsibility for it. 'Time goeth, and I turne leaves; yet still finde my selfe in the state of ignorance; wherefore, I haue thought better of honesty then of knowledge.' The failure of books causes Cornwallis to reconceive the terms of his project, shifting from books of knowledge to honest reading, reading for use, even in a state of ignorance – a shift of expectations from what books have to what you can use them for. Essay names a practice of writing pegged to this switching of gears from reading for knowledge to reading for use. 'What I may know, I will conuert to that of vse; and what I write, I meane so, for I will chuse rather to be an honest man then a good Logitian.' Such writing foregrounds its utility, a tool or mechanism that teaches you how to use it – that is, how to read it – and offers this skill instead of knowledge.

Essays transform knowledge to use, and the passage winds up with a statement that, in a way familiar from Montaigne and Whitlock, stresses freedom of movement, a kind of free reading that essays are written to facilitate.

> There was neuer Art yet that laid so fast hold on me that she might iustly call me her seruant. I neuer knew them but superficially, nor indeed, wil not though I might, for they swallow their subiect and make him as Ouid saide of himselfe.
>
> *Quicquid conabar dicere versus erat.*
>
> I would earne none of these so dearly as to ty vp the minde to thinke onely of one thing; her best power by this meanes is taken from her, for so her circuit is limited to a distance, which should walke vniuersally. Moreouer, there growes pride and a selfe opinion out of this, which deuours wisedome.[62]

Logicians and those who use 'art' turn out to be those who are used by art – which swallows its subject and makes it speak, zombie-like, or poet-like: Cornwallis uses Ovid to make poetry look like a visitation, making you speak like it.[63] Essay is the energy of claiming such agency for oneself. This is figured in the expected contemporary way, as a distinction between servant and master. It may be that when Cornwallis, Felltham, and others call this a gentlemanly practice of reading, it's not simply to attach the practice to the status but to use the status to describe the practice. Not that only gentlemen can read this way but that this reading asks the reader to use the same freedom gentlemen have.

Does this confuse the earlier figure of apprenticeship? Essay describes a different kind of service, one that is apprenticed to knowledge for the sake of use, not for the sake of knowledge. What's learned by 'using these papers as a Printer's boy' is a skill not a craft. It turns out that all you get from that apprenticeship is the opportunity to continue using knowledge, but never the knowledge itself. The practice leads to praxis, as essays participate in the classical reorientation of philosophy from knowledge to morality that wears Socrates' name and Montaigne's imprimatur.[64] Such writing for use, a practice of moral philosophy, enacts all the familiar neo-stoic and humanist claims about philosophy as a tool with which to master oneself and one's passions as well as the vagaries of the world and its movements. Reading gives you surrogate problems that serve as exercise machines to help you train your strength.[65] (See Appendix C for the proof texts for these claims.) One reads in order to get material to work with, but one must digest what one reads, making it one's own. One writes in order to aid this process of digestion; reading is a mechanism of moral philosophy, digestion a mechanism of reading, writing a mechanism of digestion. Cornwallis says, 'Writing is the draught of reading, and by this I haue disburthened my head and taken account of my profiting.'[66] As 'Of Essaies' makes clear (it is 'no triall to haue handsome dapper conceites runne inuisibly in a braine but to put them out and then looke vpon them'), the name for this kind of writing is 'essay,' part of a cycle that moves from reading through writing to better reading.

Cornwallis's modern editor, Allen, remarks that his 'habit of quoting from adjacent pages of the same book gives the impression that he was reading as he wrote.'[67] But by Cornwallis's own account he was writing as he read; his essays are tools of reading. The misunderstanding is instructive – we expect something more than reading notes in essays. We expect them to exhibit not only what's being worked on but the work itself, and not just to be tools of reading but models of reading. This evolution from tool to model can be seen at the level of individual careers as essays come to register, for instance, Montaigne's – or Bacon's or Felltham's – responses to their reading as well as their notes, and so offer readers models of response as well as texts to respond to.[68] Felltham's final edition of his *Resolves* (1661) substantially revised his original short century, cutting many pieces, adding some, and substantially revising others. The net effect, according to Pebworth, was to transform the work into essays, featuring a 'more relaxed, informal manner' that 'ceases to be dependent on bookish models and moves towards a more confident reliance on his own experience and judgment.' For these reasons, Pebworth suggests that the 'revised short century' influenced the development of essay in England.[69] In a sense, though, the history of Felltham's *Resolves* is the whole history of the genre, offering an example of the essay's evolution at the level of a particular career that recapitulates the development of the genre itself. Like Montaigne and Bacon, Felltham offers an example of essays first being used to enable the uptake of what he reads and then developing into registers of that process. When that happens the essay comes to serve as a re-uptake inhibitor, interrupting the process of reading, in a sense, so it can be more closely examined and more self-consciously undertaken.

Culpeper's 'Of Essayes' echoes Cornwallis's 'Of Essaies,' repeating its point that in essays the mind is able to 'walke vniuersally.' (See Appendix D for the essay.) Essays, says Culpeper, offer 'a generality of knowledge' that uses any and all sciences but isn't bound to particular ones, a point figured by expanding an image borrowed from another Cornwallis essay.[70] Like a building with many builders, none of whom completes the whole, 'so in *Essayes* there is required instructions from Philosophy, History, and what else can be usefully expressed for other observations, and moralities of life, that in them a man may read an Epitomy of himself, and the world together.' Essays 'come nearer ourselves,' offering a mode of reflection that is not limited to particular fields but is rather geared to use ('application and benefit'), the familiar ('men and manners'), and the way this is related to texts ('histories'), 'giving us besides an useful acquaintance both of the dead and the living together.' The repetition of the connective, 'together,' stresses Culpeper's account of the genre as a model of engagement, between oneself and the world and between the present and the past. Not a mechanism of disarticulation from the world, or a choice of experience over texts (or texts over history), essays provide exemplary little models, epitomes, of the way these work together. They are a way of engaging one's world, a place where particular knowledges are used, where the familiar is registered, and use privileged over building.

Towards the end of his essay, after making claims about essays' using the language arts, poetry and oratory, in ways analogous to their use of the arts and sciences – limited by none but again bringing them 'nearer ourselves' – Culpeper catches himself talking about what everyone knows. Everyone, he says, knows what essays are ('it needed not to have been instanced to the judicious Reader, who cannot be unknowing thereof'), and he's probably creating undue expectations. Backing off from his grandiose claims, he enacts the move he describes essays making. Essays 'come nearer ourselves' and this one winds down into a private key: 'it was but the result of private thoughts, by which I endeavoured to take some prospect of the opinions, business, and manners of the world (being indeed the chief accomplishments of humane life) though not without hopes, that if these papers at any time were to be made bold, as to be seen by the world in Print, it would not be altogether without that profit, which I have reapt from them my self.' Feeding back into the world at which his essay looks, the passage suggests a shift from Cornwallis's claim about essays being an occasion for 'tak[ing] account of [his] profiting' to essays being an occasion for the world to profit too. Here the essay is said to be at once a tool by which to engage the world and a part of that world as well. And if Culpeper's direction (from private thoughts to the world) is reversed, one can see the essay as epitomizing not just the way we take the world but the way the world offers us instructions about how to take it. The world consists of such reflections (the world is full of essays), and these reflections train one in a way of reflecting on the world, giving you a particular skill with which, and scale on which, to engage it.

In the move from Cornwallis's to Culpeper's 'Of Essays' I think can be seen a shift from tool to model. The genre becomes a tool on which are inscribed not just instructions for use but also examples of use. These models, epitomes of particular engagements, can't finally map use (the whole point of essays is that you have to do it yourself), but rather offer a register of one trail, one trial, through the world they engage. In his shift to a personal key, Culpeper offers occasion to note both the scale and skill enabled by the genre. As the essay trails off into its personal note, it enacts the hesitancy with which it opened, 'The word *Essay*, we have From the French, in which Tongue it signifies a tryal or probation.' In its move from the obvious through discussion that arrives back, again, at where you started, reaffirming what you already knew, but now reclaiming it as your own by thinking it through, this essay enacts the dynamic the essay as a genre exists to enable – a way to claim such truths as one's own by using them and thinking through them. Culpeper offers us his private thoughts, and in wishing that the reader reap the same profit in reading that he did in writing, he invites us to do as he did, 'take some prospect of the opinions, business, and manners of the world,' which now includes his own work. The point may be to recognize that the works that make up the world of print are made up of such exercises. A chance for us to recognize that 'Print' offers occasion for use, and the work of private thoughts, as well as the claims of knowledge and mastery – and perhaps to recognize even these latter kinds of texts as potentially legible in the other way as well.

2
By Way of Essays

Of travel

In his shift to questions of use, Culpeper epitomizes the scale and skill enabled by essays. His hesitant claims don't offer knowledge but a draught of reading and ask to be read in turn at that scale, in that way. It's difficult to address these skills of reading through categories of writing, authority, or authenticity. Instead of asking what work *writing* does – formation or foundation, whether social or psychological – essays direct us to questions of reading and response. In this chapter, I've set out to explore such questions by casting two lines into the archives. One uses the hook of Cowley's intriguing phrase, 'Discourses, by Way of Essays,' and the other uses another Senecan figure for reading, traveling. What do you do with texts that leave only an incidental residue? That make no claim to found or ground? That are effects of reading, tools of learning, and not tools of teaching and works of writing? I want to try to read along.

When you find that someone named Palmer wrote an essay on travel, you're having a good day. (Was he fated 'to seken straunge strondes'?) In Thomas Palmer's preface 'To the Reader' of *An Essay of the Meanes how to make our Trauviles, into forraine Countries, the more profitable and honourable* (1606), I've found what may be the first native English use of the phrase (though Florio used it first to translate Montaigne's 'manière d'essay' in 'Of Friendship' [1603]): 'I have been encouraged (worthy Reader) upon the vertue of the yonger sort of such noble gentlemen as intend so recomendable a course [foreign travel], to prepare and address the same, by way of Essay.'[1] Palmer claims his work is 'by way of essay' because it is a rough draft, a first attempt to explain to outwardly mobile Englishmen the rudiments of foreign travel: 'It seemeth unto mee (vertuous Reader) a faire dutie (where other worthie men have beene so long silent, in giving a perfect rule of Trauailing, as it is in use at this day) to begin the hewing out of one, that by some master workman, it may hereafter be better planed, formed, and tried.' Despite such protestations, Palmer's work is quite finished and very regular, an orderly breakdown of the topic into heads and subheads.[2]

Cornwallis had figured reading as travel: 'I thought last of Fame [this is the last essay in the first edition], and my thoughts haue ridden (as I thinke) ouer her whole circuite. What I haue seene in my trauaile, I will trust this peece of paper with and so ridde my braine of that carriage.'[3] This kind of writing as an aid to thinking-as-travel (a figure that crosses the two senses of the polyvalent early modern 'travail' – travel and labor) is recommended by Felltham for one's literal travels too:

> That a man may better himselfe by Trauaile, hee ought to obserue, and comment: noting as well the bad, to auoyd it, as taking the good, into vse. And without Registring these things by Pen, they will slide away vnprofitably. A man would not thinke, how much the Charactering of a thought in Paper, fastens it. *Littera scripta manet*, has a large sence. He that does this, may, when he pleaseth, reiourney ouer all his voyage, in his Closet.[4]

Palmer's 'Essay' is not such a register of his travels (or his thoughts) but rather an organizing map for the departing English gentleman (and 'in speciall cases' English gentlewoman), a first draft of a guidebook, not the travel log we might expect.

One can trace the movement of the phrase, 'by way of essay,' towards our expectations by following it through three examples 'Of Travel,' moving from Palmer's essay to Henry Peacham's pair of them. Peacham's first 'Of Travel' was a chapter in his courtesy book, *The Complete Gentleman* (1622).[5] It is similar to Palmer's, offering advice to young gentlemen in the form of the kind of 'catalogue' Cornwallis had contrasted with 'an essay.'[6] Peacham starts off by giving a commonplace book-like series of classical statements about the value of traveling: 'And Xenophon, to intimate unto us the benefit and excellent use of travel, saith that Cambyses by his travel learned many excellent things which he taught Cyrus, his son' and so on.[7] He then provides, in the rest of the chapter, a kind of *Let's Go* for France and Spain, safety tips, information about food, and customs, and language, as well as sight-seeing suggestions and capsule histories of famous places that tell the reader what to look for and look at: 'Blois is an ancient castle situate from the river of Loire upon an hill. Here the old kings of France were wont to reside. Especially Louis the Twelfth took delight in this place, who was called *Pater Patriae*.'[8]

Peacham wrote another 'Of Travel' as part of *The Truth of our Times: Revealed out of One's Man's Experience, by Way of Essay* (1638), and in this essay the genre begins to take its familiar shape. In place of the humanist authorities of *Gentleman*, it offers, as promised, a story of his own experience.

> The true taste of our lives' sweetness [he begins] is in travel upon the way, at home, or abroad in other countries. For not only it affordeth change of air, which is very availful to health, but variety of objects and remarkable occasions to entertain our thoughts, besides choice of acquaintance with able and excellent men in all faculties and of all nations, and perhaps some such as you would ever after think your labor and expense of money well bestowed if you had but only passed the sea for their acquaintance. Such an one I met withal traveling in a very rainy evening through a muddy part of Westphalia where I had lost my way.[9]

After this story, which I'll get back to in a moment, the essay launches into the kind of advice of the earlier essays ('Let your observations be of such things whereby you may profit yourself and your country'), though often filtered through his own experience ('I have observed as I have gone along those countries many excellent points of good husbandry in fields and gardens which we here in England have not been acquainted withal').[10]

In this essay there are also residual traces of the method of commonplacing, though here such sources are offered as illustrative stories, less authorities than another form of experience that illustrates the point:

> It is a great want of discretion, besides very dangerous, to tell or show your money openly in strange places where you are unknown, or to travel upon the way extraordinary rich in your clothes. Hereby many have been betrayed and lost their lives, as a gentleman and acquaintance of mine, Master W. T., was pistoled by his guide in the forest of Ardennes because, riding in a suit laid thick with gold lace, he was supposed to have had store of crowns.
>
> Erasmus, I remember, in his Epistles tells us how narrowly he escaped his throat-cutting one night in an inn where he drew store

of money out of his velvet pouch, which commonly he wore at his girdle.[11]

Too much display indicates a dangerous lack of discretion, and Peacham recommends a mode of travel that doesn't attract too much attention. He uses Erasmus to support his point about Master W. T. while at the same time echoing Erasmus in his own example. I take this flow between the two kinds of stories to constitute writing 'by way of essay.' Peacham writes his book in the way he uses Erasmus, not as an exemplar (though he is that too) but as an example, a figure legible at a certain scale, familiar because he is informed by his contingencies in the same way we are informed by ours. Peacham offers 'one man's experience' as an effect of reading at this particular scale, in this particular way, an evolution from 'raw and undigested' commonplace reading to a digest of one's work with such materials.

Essays register one's travails, one's way of working through the materials one finds in a world that must be negotiated with discretion. Peacham writes 'To the Reader':

> It fareth with me now, honest reader, as with a traveler in winter, who, having foolishly ventured over some dangerous river or passage quite frozen with ice, stands on the other side pointing with his finger and showing his following friends where it cracked. In the same manner I have ventured before, tried the coldness of these frozen and hard times, together with the slippery ways of this deceitful and trustless world. Standing, I hope, now at the last safe on this other side, I show those that are to follow me where the danger is.[12]

Ice flows, its cracks shift, its dangers remain unpredictable. Peacham embeds a recognition of contingency in his figure of his book's rationale. It's not, obviously, about these particular cracks but the way ice cracks. That is, you don't read Peacham's book as a map but as a register of his experience, 'by way of essay,' not as a guide but as a trace of one way across. Peacham doesn't offer himself as an authority in the way the ancients were taken as authorities, but rather offers himself as an example in the way Montaigne's *Essais* read those classical authorities as examples.[13]

The space between Peacham's two essays 'Of Travel' is the space between two kinds of writing practices, one that directs and one that models. The kind of writing enabled by the latter doesn't replace the other but offers a discursive space – a genre – in which to foreground on the page the work done off the page with the other. As Peacham begins to include his own experiences on the page, he offers a text adequate to a mode of reading that takes texts as registers of particular engagements with local contingencies, to be negotiated in those terms. 'By way of essay' foregrounds the scope and scale of texts that are effects of such reading and so enable it, providing occasions to read in the terms of 'one man's experience' (as Peacham puts is) and 'my private thoughts' (in Culpeper's terms).

> [W]e ought to remember [says Culpeper] that as other men thought before they writ, so should we use the like Freedome to instruct our selves, since Learning at first, could be no more, then the best way of thinking ... we can [take] little advantage by reading of books, if we do not first come to their perusing with a genius equal to what we read, as he that finds a Diamond must be able to distinguish it from a pebble, so that in conversing with books, we are but made more acquainted with our selves by the assistance of others.[14]

The idea that you would read texts, even classics, as if you were operating a machine, or being operated like a machine, blindly following their moves, is one of those myths that makes one modern (a dream of purity and autonomy, whether realized as power or pleasure).[15] But books are not occasions to sleep but occasions to think. They can't *enforce* thinking – that's the whole point – but only provide materials to work with, and perhaps a model of such work. Culpeper's thoughts direct us to think, and think in a certain way. 'A cursory Knowledge, though it be not exact enough for the Schools, is more pleasant, and perhaps more useful then to over burthen the Brain with Books, which may be called a Gentleman-like Learning, or one who is in *Omnibus aliquid*, I mean so disposed, that he knows how to make the best use of his acquired and natural parts together, which well joyned cannot but render an accomplished person.'[16] The distinction between gentlemen and scholars keeps recurring in these texts, and while it has a clear sociological significance, I'm more curious about it right now as a procedural distinction, less a way to map identity than to define a mode of reading that leads to other kinds of connections. 'Gentleman-like Learning' here signifies something of everything (*omnibus aliquid*), a 'freedom' claimed less to distinguish oneself than declare dependence on 'the assistance of others.' If the learning of 'schools' is construed as mastery, the learning of essays is construed as dependence on others, 'joining,' and use.

Cornwallis remarks, 'Rethoricke's Cookery is the vomit of a Pedant.'[17] Conversely, essay's cookery is the vomit of a gentleman, a way of spitting up, cow-like, in order to digest better. ('Writing is the draught of reading, and by this I haue disburthened my head and taken account of my profiting'; it is 'no triall to haue handsome dapper conceites runne inuisibly in a braine but to put them out and then looke vpon them.') At once, in Cornwallis's terms, a manner of writing well befitting undigested motions, and a way to process those thoughts, essays enable the digestion that is at the heart of the conception of reading articulated by Seneca.[18] When Cornwallis refers to this passage, though, he selects another figure from it, another way to describe 'lingering among': 'I am of Senecae's minde concerning this variety of Bookes, who compares an vnsettled reader to a traueller that has many Hostes and few friendes.'[19]

Essays are a mechanism of digestion, a way of reading that turns hosts into friends. Returning to Peacham's story:

> Such a one I met withal traveling in a very rainy evening through a muddy part of Westphalia where I had lost my way, and it grew near night and, in Latin demanding of him the way toward Oldenburg and how I had lost my way, using the word deviavi hic [I've gone astray here], he answered humanum est errare [it's human to wander]. To be short, he would not suffer me to pass any further, but carried me home to his own house, which was almost half a mile off, where I never found better entertainment or had more friendlier respect in all my life.[20]

As good travelers do, Peacham records a souvenir of his travels, and in doing so offers an example that registers a route through those cold and trustless times. In Peacham's story he's lost and meets a stranger. The stranger, wittily, recognizes his own question in the one asked by Peacham; the universalizing humanum elevates Peacham into a general condition, enclosing him in a category that the stranger too shares, making them similar in their wanderings. Yet at the same time, with a smile, this elevated language answers the earnest question with a joke. The slippage of the phrase isn't really an answer (and the bombastic, pedantic elevation isn't really a community), but in lieu of such an answer, in lieu of that kind of grand identification, the stranger offers Peacham a witty rejoinder that makes them friends. (His answer isn't an answer to the question but an answer to a problem behind, and perhaps badly expressed by, the question.) You don't really get, of course, the kind of answers that students look for when they comb old books in their hungry searches for 'wisdom,' but sometimes you get to use what's jotted down in your notebooks to make jokes that give you what you may really have been asking for anyway: less an answer to your question than someone who answers, a place to spend the night, a host who becomes a friend. When traveling, when reading, the chance to share a joke seems a fair substitute for the failure to get a straight answer.

Walking invisibly

They meet across the arc of a shared literary language, classmates so to speak. Latin is perhaps uniquely indexed to reading in early modern Europe; it is the language of literacy and reading, the skill on which bureaucracies depend to function and bureaucrats to define themselves. This scene would not be possible without those sociological contexts, but I don't think its interest is exhausted, or its force fully registered, by seeing it as a moment of identity formation or class consolidation. Rather this is a moment of recognition in which the work of scholarship, properly a ticket to fame and fortune, is redirected towards other ends – either a misuse of such studious reading or perhaps an extension of it, an occasion for a kind of ordinary recognition that could be a further point of reading. Reading is used here, as someone who must speak a language learned from books, for ends that may exceed the original study or may be the whole point of it.

Here's one more line from Peacham's 'Of Travel' (by way of essay), some advice to a traveler: 'To help you in conjugating your verbs you may use the help awhile of a grammar of that language, but in general you must expect your perfection from conference. For hereby the true accent and native grace of pronunciation, which no book can teach, is only attained.'[21] There is, of course, a gap between the models of language in books and the native use of language in conversation. The essay, says Adorno, is organized by the latter:

> The way in which the essay appropriates concepts is comparable to the behavior of a man who is obliged, in a foreign country, to speak the country's language instead of patching it together from its elements, as he did in school. He will read without a dictionary ... It is not so much that the essay ignores indisputable certainty, as that it abrogates the ideal. The essay becomes true in its progress, which drives it beyond itself, and not in a hoarding obsession with fundamentals.[22]

Abrogating the ideal of certainty, reading without a dictionary, using another language as one travels in a foreign country, the essay offers a way of reading that doesn't hoard or accumulate, but rather, in Certeau's phrase, moves across lands belonging to someone else.

> Far from being writers – founders of their own place, heirs of the peasants of earlier ages now working on the soil of language, diggers of wells and builders of houses – readers are travelers; they move across lands belonging to someone else, like nomads poaching their way across fields they did not write, despoiling the wealth of Egypt to enjoy themselves. Writing accumulates, stocks up, resists time by the establishment of a place and multiplies its production through expansion of reproduction. Reading takes no measures against the erosion of time (one forgets oneself *and* also forgets), it does not keep what it acquires, or it does so poorly, and each of the places through which it passes is a repetition of a lost paradise.
>
> Indeed, reading has no place ... [the reader's] place is not here or there, one or the other, but neither one nor the other, simultaneously inside and outside, dissolving both by mixing them together, associating texts like funerary statutes that he awakens and hosts, but never owns. In that way he also escapes from the law of each text in particular, and from that of the social milieu.[23]

Reading is like wandering, like walking in cities, in 'an imposed system,' but one that is not claimed as one's own, nor approached in those kinds of terms ('The reader takes neither the position of the author nor the author's position').[24] Reading is finding a place in language, making a home, one that is not defined by ownership but by use – like renting, poaching on someone else's land, just passing through.[25] The essay offers a register of this kind of moving, one that doesn't work like a dictionary or map (a schematic discourse that can neither explain nor contain these operations). Essays enable a way of reading that neither escapes from nor is beholden to the grid of analysis, but rather offers a way of engaging that cannot be reduced to the dynamics of production or consumption. Not an alternative, or a strategy, that recoups what was lost – not elegiac, or nostalgic, or bitter, or triumphant – but a way through one's texts, renting; 'the task of making oneself at home in existence without fixed points of support.'[26] In essays one makes a way through one's readings, and they offer a register of a trial and a trail that records one's particular way of moving through these tracts: a signature, a style.

We're no longer practiced in reading this way, and Cowley's *Essays*, once a paradigmatic example of the essay form, have become, it seems, hard to read.[27] Alan de Gooyer tells a story about Cowley's retirement that presents his literary activities as the result of his boredom in the country.

> Not long after taking over his 'country cottage,' he fell ill, then later injured himself severely, and, insofar as his talents as a gentleman farmer went, he was unable to collect his rents or protect his lands from the intrusions of his neighbor's livestock. Moreover, he discovered that his rustic labors were unable to keep him amply entertained, and when he turned to himself, he found his own mind inadequately 'furnisht with sufficient Materials to work upon.' In other words, he was bored.[28]

This is not a story Cowley tells. The lines to which this refers make suggestions about what one should do if one wants to lead a retired life. They are pitched in the key of advice familiar from other works of moral philosophy in the century.

> The first work, therefore, that a man must do to make himself capable of the good of Solitude is the very eradication of all Lusts, for how is it possible for a Man to enjoy himself while his affections are tyed to things without Himself? In the second place, he must learn the Art and get the Habit of Thinking; for this too, no less than well speaking, depends upon much practice; and Cogitation is the thing which distinguishes the Solitude of a God from a wild Beast. Now because the soul of Man is not by its own Nature or observation furnisht with sufficient Materials to work upon; it is necessary for it to have continual resource to Learning and Books for fresh supplies, so that the solitary Life will grow indigent, and be ready to starve without them; but if once we be thoroughly engaged in the Love of Letters, instead of being wearied with the length of any day, we shall only complain of the shortness of our whole Life.[29]

This passage can, perhaps, be read as thickly veiled autobiography, but even so the causation is backwards in Gooyer's version. He makes the kind of story Cowley tells about his past (he was a solitary boy who liked books more than playground activities) into a story about his retirement as an adult. Here is a story from Cowley's childhood.

As far as my Memory can return back into my past Life, before I knew or was capable of guessing what the world, or glories, or business of it were, the natural affections of my soul gave me a secret bent of aversion from them, as some Plants are said to turn away from others, by an Antipathy imperceptible to themselves and inscrutable to man's understanding. Even when I was a very young Boy at School, instead of running about on Holy-daies and playing with my fellows; I was wont to steal from them and walk into the fields, either alone with a Book, or with some one companion, if I could find any of the same temper.[30]

This account of the child Cowley could plausibly be read as his choosing books over the playground because he was 'bored' by the latter, and Gooyer's point explained by overlaying the passage of moral sententiousness onto this piece of autobiography: stealing away to the fields prefigures, and explains, the retirement to the country. But even if we took such liberties (and I see no reason to reduce the text to a single dimension – when Cowley tells a story, he tells a story, when he gives advice, why read it as a story?), this reading of the passage reverses its point, narrating the story of his literary activities as the *effect* of his retirement. But the *Essays* are an account of his retirement as an effect of his literary activities. Cowley doesn't turn to books because of his boredom in the country, but turns to the country because of his love of books. He doesn't turn to books in the fields but takes them there.

I read Cowley's *Essays* as an account of reading and within the tradition of moral philosophy that used essays as a tool of reading. In Gooyer's terms, I'm emphasizing the familiar litany more than 'the natural affections': 'Despite the litany of moral justification that animates his case for retirement … in the end Cowley offers us a motive for retirement that is of an altogether different quality. Ultimately, he supplements the well-worn arguments he offers on behalf of retirement by calling upon his own sense of personal authenticity and asserting his moral precedence.'[31] Explaining 'the priority of personal inclination' as looking forward to 'new modes of interiority,' Gooyer makes Cowley's retirement an expression of his 'secret bent of aversion,' an 'inscrutable' affection that is most his own, perhaps, because it is 'imperceptible' even to himself.[32] It's just who he is. But in the same way books (and their arguments) are skimmed to get to the sentiment (boredom, natural affection), this account elides the full story. Cowley isn't driven into the fields to feel more like himself; he goes to read.

Rather than featuring a new focus on interiority and sentiments, Cowley's *Essays* are organized by the interaction of sentiments and the well-worn arguments of books. Cowley's account of his 'natural affections' even suggests that, far from following a natural bent, the plant was carved by reading.

> You may see by it [the preceding verse] I was even then acquainted with the poets (for the conclusion is taken out of Horace), and perhaps it was the immature and immoderate love of them which stamped first, or rather engraved, these characters in me. They were like letters cut into the bark of a young tree, which with the tree still grows proportionably. But how this love came to be produced in me so early is a hard question. I believe I can tell the particular little chance that filled my head first with such chimes of verse as have never since left ringing there. For I remember when I begun to read and to take some pleasure in it, there was wont to lie in my mother's parlour (I know not by what accident, for she herself never in her life read any book but of devotion), but there was wont to lie Spenser's works; this I happened to fall upon, and was infinitely delighted with the stories of the knights, and giants, and monsters, and brave houses, which I found everywhere there (though my understanding had little to do with all this); and by degrees with the tinkling of the rhyme and dance of the numbers, so that I think I had read him all over before I was twelve years old, and was thus made a poet as immediately as a child is made an eunuch. With these affections of mind, and my heart wholly set upon letters, I went to the university, but was soon torn from thence by that violent public storm which would suffer nothing to stand where it did, but rooted up every plant, even from the princely cedars to me, the hyssop.[33]

Personality here is an effect of accident acting on one. In an overdetermined – completely appropriate – way, this is figured as an effect of reading. Cowley's life as a writer is determined by a primal scene of reading, one that defines him as absolutely as if he were selected for the political service of the harem. He can no more cease to be a poet than a eunuch can reattach his balls. The cut is made, and he's grown into it, as a tree continues to express in its bark the cut that was made when it was young. His affections and his 'immature and immoderate love' do mark him and inscribe his sensibility, which indeed 'supplements reason and experience with instinct and feeling,' and allows the essay to become 'a more supple and responsive instrument, better able to convey a faithful rendering of inner life.'[34] However, Cowley's concern with tracing this 'particular little chance' seems different from the exigencies of authenticity ('After all, any ethical judgment is not going to be contingent upon society's values and, in fact, becomes less compelling insofar as it is contrived and conditioned by the world around him').[35] Cowley's ethical judgment and his sensibility are formed, indeed, by engagement with books, and this informs both his retirement and the record of that retirement. His desire for solitude is an effect of his love of reading and this love was marked by a chance encounter: boy meets book, book makes boy bookish, bookish boy becomes bookish man who wants to find a way to replant himself not just so he can live authentically, but so he can get back to what his 'heart is wholly set upon' – 'the Love of Letters.' The *Essays* don't so much render an inner life as an affair with reading.

Cowley's account of his motivations involves a kind of historical reasoning, tracing the accidents that made him what he is, but the history that accounts for his choices is not the kind of history that David Hill Radcliffe says explains Cowley's motives for retirement: 'Failing to win the patronage he felt he had deserved for his services to the king, the man who thought of himself as "the Muse's Hannibal" dissevers his vocation from public life: he "was thus made a Poet as immediately as a Child is made an Eunuch."'[36] In a move that mirrors Gooyer's, Radcliffe makes Cowley's remark about his childhood (how he became a poet) into a statement about his adulthood (his political castration). This makes his retirement into a political statement. He's pushed into the country by political failure, he chooses texts over history because history's failed him. His writing is compensatory in a world (or at least an analytic imaginary) where all motives are finally political.[37] By creatively misappropriating Cowley's line about his childhood to figure his adult retirement, however, this reading erases the *kinds* of motivations Cowley is exploring in his *Essays*. Referring Cowley's motives to the socio-political plane from which he disengages, Radcliffe's argument places him within a debate about 'the heroic ideal of public service' that was a feature of Restoration heroic drama and poetry.[38] But to do so adopts the terms of one side of that debate, tipping the scales and effacing Cowley's position in the very presentation of it. Historicism assumes the same starting point as the discourse of civic duty: one must participate in history and one's historical identity is primary. Choosing terms other than these looks like 'opting out,' a choice against rather than a choice for something.[39]

Such a method is organized by the terms of one side of the debate (motives are political), stacking analysis against Cowley's terms (any motives that aren't political are elided).

One needs Gooyer's sense of Cowley's personal motivation to answer Radcliffe's overly political account, but one then needs Radcliffe's generic account to answer Gooyer's model of the self. Locating the *Essays* in the traditions of sylva, georgic, and Pindaric odes, Radcliffe characterizes Cowley's structure as 'a promiscuously Pindaric structure with centers everywhere and nowhere' and as 'the familiar georgic structure of repetition and variation.'[40] Such a decentered structure organizes Cowley's motivations as well. These are indeed personal but the model of 'person' that accounts for this is not organized by concerns for authenticity, a nascent romantic selfhood, but by a structure (or dynamics) of 'repetition and variation.' Cowley's account of becoming a poet is carefully traced to an accident, a contingency that inscribes him as a product of his history (in both senses; this is the particular private encounter with a particular public text that at once gives him his own history and makes that an effect and aspect of history more generally). But the terms of that history are thoroughly literary, organized by his engagement with texts. Cowley's history is private, and his self is fully mediated.

Generically, 'by way of essays,' Cowley announces his project as a 'draught of reading,' a tool that enables better reading, and better thinking, by running them through the page. Cowley retires to the country to read, to get back to the kind of life that was interrupted by the wars, the kind of life he was made for (when books made him into their carrier). It is in the fields that he can practice 'the habit of thinking,' the 'cogitation that distinguishes the solitude of a god from a wild beast.' Books supply the materials that supplement the insufficiencies of one's 'own nature' and 'observation,' and allow one to indulge one's 'love of letters.' Cowley says this habit of thinking, a practice of reading, will allow one to enjoy 'the good of solitude.'[41] I take the *Essays* to be the effects of that kind of work, a record of the act of loving letters – reading and its attendant practices. Cowley's *Essays* offer a glimpse of the formation of this reader, a tracing of the effects of reading, which wind through the *Essays* as a kind of transfer, inscribing as he was inscribed, not because he wants to be more, or more authentically, himself, but because this habit of thinking and the reading integral to it are what makes him most himself.

Cowley's sensibility is organized by his movement through texts, by his working through his readings. This is not a sensibility that's prior to these texts, but one that's an effect of them. If the shape of his *Essays* offers a sense a self, it's not because Cowley's faithfully rendered an authentic inner life, but because he presents a self in terms of a practice of reading – one that may, or may not, echo in the reader's own experience.

> The meaning of all this is no more than that most vulgar saying, *Bene qui latuit, bene vixit,* He has lived well, who has lain well hidden. Which, if it be a truth, the world (I'le swear) is sufficiently deceived: For my part, I think it is, and that the pleasantest condition of Life, is *in Incognito*. What a brave Privilege is it to be free from all Contentions, from all Envying or being Envyed, from receiving and from paying all kind of Ceremonies? It is in my mind a very delightful pastime, for two good and agreeable friends to travail up and down together in places where they are by nobody known, nor know anybody. It was the case of *Æneas* and his *Achates*, when they walkt invisibly about the fields and streets of Carthage, *Venus* her self
> A veil of thickened air around them cast,
> That none might know, or see them as they passed.[42]

Cowley reads in the commonplace a truth that's hidden in plain view, on everyone's lips (most vulgar) but in no one's heart; if the saying is true it proves 'the world' is deceived, but the saying gets repeated – that's what makes it a saying – without being attended to. This offers an example of Cowley's procedures. He's not concerned with originality, or authenticity, but with thinking through commonplaces, and it's these engagements that define both the space and the style (the signature) of the *Essays*. In this, of course, they are well-named as trials or experiments, though to recognize that they are what they say they are is only to repeat the gesture they enable, an occasion to recognize the commonplace and think through it. In this particular instance, as he thinks through the vulgar saying, Cowley offers a figure for the pleasures of retirement in terms that resonate with his own history. If in 'Of My Self' the child prefers the company of a book or a like-minded friend to the playground ('I was wont to steal from them and walk into the fields, either alone with a Book, or with some one companion, if I could find any of the same temper'), here the adult describes the pleasures of retirement with an image from a book that has two friends traveling incognito through strange fields and streets. I read this figure of retirement as Cowley's figure for reading as well – the two cannot be distinguished, each is an occasion for the other. An image read in a book of two friends secretly traveling figures the act of reading, a little retirement into a field with a book. It's not important whether the book figures a trusted friend or the friend the safety and intimacy of the book, or whether the friend's a friend because she also likes books. It's rather the pleasure of sharing of this activity – with a friend found in a book or a friend found via a book – that's registered by the *Essays*. And if you recognize that pleasure, if you also walk in strange cities under a veil of obscurity through which your secret mission cannot be seen by the citizens going about their business and dreaming heroic dreams, then the point is made and nothing more need be explained. Essays are at once the effects of that kind of recognition and invitations to it, modeling and enabling the kind of retirement into fields (whether in or with books) that can't be explained in any other terms.

Not that it – the space of moral reflection, or the space of a practice of reading on which that has come to depend – will necessarily be in the country (though it may be), or anyplace else for that matter. Rather it will be 'there' as it is in Cowley's *Essays*, in the no-place of reading that they record, model, and enable. One takes one's book into whatever fields and streets are nearby, and it's only from the position of the playground that it seems the point of such reading is to be in the countryside. But to account for the reading by the place of the reader is to miss Cowley's point altogether. That kind of mist is certainly useful. It provides the kind of anonymity that Cowley, at least, desires, and that may be bound up with his desire to read.[43] The cloud of Venus, the cloud of comforting obscurity within which readers pursue their pleasures and undertake their rigors, seems at once a fit and perhaps even a necessary image.

Certeau refers to this same Virgilian scene – 'The goddess can be recognized by her step' – to make a point about how movements are lost in the writing of them.[44] Any action becomes legible only in its trace, as writing serves as a mechanism of forgetting, a map: 'Surveys of routes miss what was: the act itself of passing by.' Writing is a way to 'transform action into legibility,' but as Certeau well knows (as I learned from him), the story of writing is only part of the story.[45] What happens on the other side of 'the scriptural economy' is reading: 'readers are travelers; they move across lands belonging to someone else.'[46] The goddess who disappears behind the writing, the trace of her passage, enables, by that very obscurity, a different kind of movement – one Cowley uses the remainder of Virgil's scene to figure as two friends secretly walking within her cloud. In strange fields, on borrowed streets, we pass in turn, retracing those footsteps with friends, reading along by way of essay.

What reading is is something that may, perhaps, only be undergone and not described. Essays, perhaps, can finally only be read and not fully written. Draughts of reading, they're only the temporary shape of one's movement through books, through the fields and ways of texts, and they await their reader in turn. Essay is the name of this activity of engagement, and to call it another name, to put it into another kind of story, is to mistake the peculiar movement the genre models, to refuse the skill it exists to enable and lose the practice it passes on. I can't tell you what I mean by reading – but I recognize the idiosyncratic strain of Cowley's temper in his use of Virgil's image. As if a goddess kindly shrouds us in mists, 'That, thus unseen, their Passage none might stay.'[47] And perhaps it is undertaking that activity of poaching, of obscurely wandering, of reading through books to other readers and other books, that gives me that shock of recognizing another who is not like me because we're the same, but rather like me in that he is making his own way through his fields as I am making my way through mine. At that moment my host becomes a friend.

I wonder, further, though, if Cowley's Virgil's Venus' cloud conveys more than a distant memory, or dream, of founding a world. I wonder if it holds a key not just to that epic moment but to a different kind of activity, if it doesn't refer but instruct. What allows you to make hosts into friends is a moment of recognition, seeing the other not as a figure for, or representative of, a system or an economy, but as a singularity; seeing beyond example to style.[48] Not just a way for you to move (though you must get this in order to get the other), but the trace of a particular movement, a signature, for you to respond to. This may be how God talks to us, not as a voice preserved, one hopes authentically, in the pages of books, as an echo of a heroic or sublime power that we either submit to or claim for our own, but rather as echoes of responses, notes of readers, moments of attention that can't precisely be answered but only answered in kind. Such attention, as it flows through history, may be the trace of the holy, reports of goddesses once sighted, or suspected, which, when read, turn out to be occasions to undertake the work of response that is our way of passing on what we've learned to work through. What we learn in essays is that such work – the practice that is required to learn the art and get the habit of thinking, the work of reading – is the point of these works. Essays may be 'provisional hardenings' of a flow of energy, human attention and recognition, that in a world of print flows through texts.[49]

A road traveled again and again

Salt of course preserves as well, and at the same time as they aid digestion these essays offer a mode of conservation (which may be too close to conservatism for some, but to each her own taste). I think finally they serve as a mechanism that conserves this art of digestion – this mode of attention and recognition – encoded in their textures: the work, or working through, that serves as the necessarily secret project of culture. (The secret must be kept because the secret is just the effort and energy of figuring it out, and that can't be given away but only discovered, each for herself.) This mode of reading, and writing as a 'draught of reading,' enables a skill that is, I think, worth practicing, but that is effaced in recent accounts of the genre.

Essays are not writerly, but 'readerly' in a sense that Barthes's phrase elides. In *S/Z: an Essay*, Barthes says while 'the goal of the literary work (of literature as work) is to make the reader no longer a consumer, but a producer of the text,' the literary institution leaves the reader 'with no more than the poor freedom either to accept or reject the text: reading is nothing more than a *referendum*. Opposite the writerly text, then, is its countervalue, its negative, reactive value: what can be read but not written: the *readerly*. We call any readerly text a classic text.'[50] Barthes does have other words for this writerly practice, rereading for example, but he construes it differently than I do; 'rereading is no longer consumption, but play.'[51] Barthes's fantasy about how the institution works gives him the terms with which he resists it. Construing the options as passivity (reading, acceptance, consumption) or production (writing, rejection, play), he chooses the latter. He rewrites the texts he reads so he won't be written by them:

> the writerly text is *ourselves writing*, before the infinite play of the world (the world as function) is traversed, intersected, stropped, plasticized by some singular system (Ideology, Genius, Criticism) which reduces the plurality of entrances, the openings of networks, the infinity of languages. The writerly is the novelistic without the novel, the essay without the dissertation, writing without style, production without product, structuration without structure. But the readerly texts? They are products (and not productions).[52]

By escaping the system in this way, though, Barthes seems to have internalized it, transforming a fantasy of the system's untrammeled production, and a consequent anxiety about being played by it, into a desire for such productivity as one's own, realized as untrammeled play.

I don't buy this either as a dream of freedom or an account of reading, and I want to look back from Barthes's text to one of his sources, a passage from Bataille he says inspired his *Essay*.

> The narrative that reveals the possibilities of life does not necessarily appeal, but it reveals a moment of *rage*, without which its author would be blind to its *excessive* possibilities. I believe it: only suffocating, impossible trial provides the author with the means of attaining the distant vision the reader is seeking, tired of the tight limitations conventions impose.
>
> How can we linger over books to which obviously the author was not *constrained*?[53]

Bataille describes a relay from an author's trials and the excess they enable to the reader's search for that excess by lingering over the books that register those trials. The answer to Bataille's rhetorical question is contained in his previous statement: one reads the books that are the effects of impossible trials and through which one sees the rage one hopes will answer those tight limitations. One lingers, that is, over the constraining books not to be constrained but to see what can only be seen by means of those trials. One reads and undergoes a similar trial, reading the author's rage, and perhaps reading with rage. If Barthes's play is supposed to answer Bataille's rage, it does so by changing its dynamics. The difference between the excess that is an effect of work for Bataille and the work (or play) that is the effect of '*excess*' for Barthes – the former what you get when you linger over books, rereading, the latter what you get when you rewrite – is the difference between undergoing the trial that enables the excess and grasping immediately for it.

I have doubts whether starting from that excess (writing as play) yields the same results. Barthes's desire to escape from systems and products, a striving for essays as pure play, seeks an immediate 'vision,' as if one could short-circuit the constraints that Bataille says enables that.[54] Barthes's *Essay* is writerly, organized by pleasure, pleasing, pleasant. Given his choice between constrained reading and free writing one might choose as he does. But I don't agree that reading is just consumption, or that a lover's discourse does the same work as reading. There's no violence in his sex.

Recent accounts of the essay have followed Barthes's lead, construing it as a mechanism of resisting commonplaces, a 'refusal to submit discourse to the laws of ancient models,' and as a way of expressing the excess beyond such defining discourses.[55] Claire de Obaldia writes: 'The *Essais*' confrontation with the authority or "truth" of tradition is intimately linked to the examination and subversion of given discursive structures or forms.'[56] Here the essay is presented as a romantic genre, one Obaldia uses a phrase of Kauffman's to categorize as embodying 'the perennial dialectic between individual and established thought system.'[57] We know how such stories go (does the individual ever question and endorse the system?), and Obaldia's account stresses the essay's 'creative and emancipative potential' and its 'authenticity' in guarding against 'the bad faith of ideology.'[58]

Réda Bensmaïa sees the essay as organized by a logic of complication rather than mastery or systems, 'tactics without strategy,' concerned with 'arranging ... without totalization.'[59] But if essays resist systems they also seem to internalize their rationale, offering a purer form of production. Stressing the 'intrinsic productivity of the form' and its generative alterity and excess, Bensmaïa calls the essay 'the moment of writing *before* the genre, before genericness – or as the matrix of all generic possibilities,' an example of the 'as such' moment to which critics inevitably seem to drift (even as they recognize the essay as 'an essentially supplementary discourse').[60] This production is not, of course, the system's but rather the writerly reader's, a pleasure or 'bliss' in which one is utterly self-defined.[61] The experience of orgasm organizes essays for Bensmaïa – a space in which I am fully myself because there is no one there (neither myself, finally, nor another) in a pleasure that I, nevertheless, get to have for – and as? – myself.[62] The essay here is discourse bucking its customary limits, a genre offering access to an excess that can't be constrained. Defined either as authenticity or pleasure, as a voice or a moan, and offering a way to recoup a realer identity (or difference), essays, according to such accounts, transcend the limits of the common, the shared.[63] They are a chance to turn reading into writing.[64]

These are the terms of what Stanley Fish calls 'dialectic,' a mode of discourse to which he opposes the 'Experience of Bacon's *Essays*.' Bacon's essays, in Fish's account, are 'instruments of inquiry and examination' that do not issue in transcendence but in further reading.[65] Fish reads the *Essays* not as a way to escape *doxa* but as a process of examining it: 'The magisterial moralisms which open and often close an essay are severely qualified by what transpires in the interim, yet they are never abandoned.'[66] Fish contrasts this procedure with 'dialectic,' exemplified by Plato's dialogues and Donne's sermons, which works not by polishing but 'purging' the mind, not making it capable but 'unmaking' it.[67] Bacon's essays are like 'seeds' that will

> flower in other words rather than in a vision, and in words which do have the referential adequacy that is presently unavailable. For all their provisionality the *Essays* are finally objects; they are not used up in the reading but remain valuable as source material for future consultation, for they reflect quite accurately the partial (not irrelevant) understanding of the mind that fashioned them and of the minds that read them.[68]

Fish notes that the change wrought by dialectic is 'profound' while that of the essays is 'superficial' or 'unfinished.'[69] That is, essays do not enable fuller self-possession (or self-annihilation or ecstasy; other kinds of writings aspire to and perhaps enable that). Rather they remain resources for rereading. Essays are not instruments of transcending texts but tools of returning to them. What you get at the end of undergoing their experience is not a new or even renewed self, but better attention to the same old thing right there, still, in front of you on the page.[70]

The essay's mode of engagement is not organized by a simple choice between being interpellated by a system (becoming a number, a statistical marker) or abandoning the grid for your own private Idaho. In those terms, one's moves are defined by the power dynamics of systems, the stark terms of the sublime – surrender to or appropriation of the power that abjects you. But the essay doesn't construe the options by which we face *doxa* and culture in terms of one's facing a system. There's nothing wrong with writing (or with love) but I wonder whether all reading needs to be construed in terms of its exigencies, as either production or consumption, either a system writing you or you stealing its fire. There are, of course, plenty of genres organized by those sublime dynamics, tools for that kind of work. But essays work differently; they're more like readerly writing than writerly reading. And they sponsor a way of reading that is neither passive nor productive, but a process of thinking through, a work without end.

This at least is Lukács's account of the essay, and his essay on the form remains the best exploration of the puzzle at its heart. An essay is a draft, a preparation, the genre of Schopenhauer as he writes *Parerga* in anticipation of *The World as Will and Idea,* and of John the Baptist as he awaits his savior:

> And if that other does not come – is not the essayist without justification? And if the other does come, is he not made superfluous thereby? Has he not become entirely problematic by thus trying to justify himself? He is the pure type of the precursor, and it seems highly questionable whether, left entirely to himself – i.e. independent from the fate of the other for whom he is the herald – he could lay claim to any value or validity.[71]

Lukács's question mines an issue contained within the very name of the genre and articulated in the first account of the newly minted English essay, Cornwallis's 'Of Essaies.'[72] This account of 'a maner of writing wel befitting vndigested motions' dismissed Montaigne's essays as 'able to endure the sharpest trial' and therefore not rightly termed essays; his own are properly essays because they are just trials, like a maid or 'prouidence that tastes before she buys.' But once she buys, once you eat, does the taste have any value of its own? Do we care about the tasting once we've digested, or Schopenhauer's juvenilia once we've read his mature works (if we do isn't it only because of those latter works)? Only once providence has fulfilled its mission, once dinner's on the table and Jesus has come, does its enabler, the maid or John the Baptist, matter, and then only for reasons that are subsumed in the redeemed promise. So what good are essays, promissory notes, if left entirely to themselves, independent of the fate of the other for whom they are only the servants?

It comes as a surprise, then, when Lukács wants to redeem the genre: 'But this longing for value and form, for measure and order and purpose, does not simply lead to an end that must be reached so that it may be cancelled out and become a preposterous tautology ... the end is unthinkable and unrealizable without the road being traveled again and again; the end is not standing still but arriving there.'[73] Essay names the traveling not the getting there, and, even if there were an end to this process, it is literally unthinkable without being thought 'again and again,' the road traveled again, the work undertaken again. The essay enables the undertaking, endlessly, of one's participation in any thought, any end that may be realized. In a paradox like Zeno's, essays have no end, not because they're infinite, but because they offer occasion to claim what you think you know for yourself – realize the significance of what you think by doing the thinking entailed in the thought, retracing the process congealed in the product, reawakening the energy temporarily condensed into form, and vice versa, re-forming the energy to realize it again.[74] Essays are a way of digesting, undertaking the work of realizing what everyone already knows, thinking through the commonplace, again and again, riding its train of thought for oneself. This attitude wouldn't be necessary in a redeemed or finished world, in which thoughts do your thinking for you, or you realize you are, or yours are, the thoughts of God, but that's not the point of essays, that's not the kind of thinking they enable.

When Lukács says this is 'a fact of the soul with a value and existence of its own: an original and deep-rooted attitude towards the whole of life, a final and irreducible category of possibilities of experience,' he's cancelled out his earlier question but from the opposite direction.[75] The answers to the questions about the point of essays if they don't lead to anything, and so are aborted drafts, or if they do, and so are absorbed into the finished work they announced, turn out to be ones that have nothing to do with either of these results. Not the work but the reward has vanished. Rather than waiting for the final form that will redeem it, the essay turns against that kind of end. This is not to say that the maid frees herself from her duties, but that she serves even without a master. For Lukács the essay offers a return to the work that is all you ever have, not a way out of a false or fallen world, but a way through its forms. There may be no call, but there are responses.

Lukács ends up with a discipline of working through, again and again, a maid without a master, a John without Jesus. Here the essay has moved beyond the romantic fragment, beyond intimations of immortality, a move that is similar to Lyotard's well-known remark that the fragment is modern and the essay postmodern, but with a significant distinction.[76] Lyotard distinguishes between modern 'regret' and postmodern 'assay.'[77] The latter can't be judged by familiar categories and doesn't entail a determining judgment but rather is the work of looking for such categories. This caps, and names, the search for local, temporary, and provisional rules that has been Lyotard's recurrent concern throughout *The Postmodern Condition*.[78] Essay is the shape of postmodern knowledge, inventing momentary contracts in the face of doubt about the given ones, and refusing to indulge the modern melancholy of a compensatory formalism.[79] Lytoard construes the essay as a celebratory modernity, a fresh start, and the choice seems to be between an aesthetics of nostalgia and one of invention, a choice between looking back and being happy.[80] But I don't think essays require that choice; they look back happily. Lyotard's 'essay' suggests if Jesus doesn't come we're all gods, freely playing, freely inventing. But Lukács's 'essay' suggests we're all Johns, and our 'longing for value and form' is not construed in those terms: 'the essay always speaks of something that has already been given form, or at least something that has already been there at some time in the past; hence it is part of the nature of the essay that it does not create new things from an empty nothingness but only orders those which were once alive ... it orders them anew and does not form something new out of formlessness.'[81] Lukács's essay offers a work of response instead of a play of invention; it comes late but without the cant of belatedness.

Harrison critiques Lyotard in similar terms. Rather than seeing the essay as offering a new aesthetic beginning, a renewal of confidence in expression and hermeneutical experimentation, Harrison sees the essay as the last chapter in modernism: 'essayism is a symptom not of happy relativism but of skepticism at odds with its own despair.'[82] If one fully believed one's skepticism about (false) expectations, despair – a hangover of those expectations – wouldn't exist. Harrison's essay is an attitude that understands both that skepticism and its costs. 'The only certainty attending this new subjectivity without a subject is neither a feeling nor a goal but, rather, an on-going need to take a stance in the world, a need for openness, endurance, and the management of conscious perplexity, a stance that is therefore no stance at all, at least not in the sense of firm position.'[83] This presents a version of Lukács's position as an ethics, one that focuses on how, not what, one believes, 'a messianism, without eschatology, serving no utopia but that of the motivated life.' Meaning is located in the activity of looking for meaning *as if* that were possible (while recognizing it is not), 'a condition of alertness and wonder in which the Spirit is felt in its absence.'[84] Harrison arrives where Bacon's reader arrives for Fish, in a condition of increased alertness, but this time without the books, trading those 'moralisms' for an ethical practice that moves beyond them: 'essayism accompanies the juncture where reason abolishes truth but not the will to truth.'[85]

I think this is backwards. Essays accept *truth* precisely as provisional, conventional, and commonplace, as occasions for thinking, but suspend the *will* to truth. Essays direct you not to 'knowledge' or to questions that yield those kinds of answers, but to 'use,' to a different kind of response. The answers they give are the same ones you started with, the same old horse, but now freshly ridden, arrived at again and newly appreciated. Essays offer a transfer from answers to questions, but also from something that yields truth to something that yields work, and which in turn offers a different way of construing texts. The kind of answer essays give you, the chance to undertake the activity congealed in texts, also enables a different kind of recognition, one that takes such 'truths' in a different spirit altogether, not as fragments of a will to (absent) truth but as occasions to use them in a different way.[86]

I want to return to Lukács's question, 'it seems highly questionable whether, left entirely to himself – i.e. independent from the fate of the other for whom he is the herald – he could lay claim to any value or validity.' For Lukács the essay is both response and draft, at once secondary, in relation to other works, and anticipatory, in relation to 'the fate of the other for whom he is a herald.' Against Lukács's point, or at least against his rhetoric, I want to superimpose these two relations onto each other. As essays offer occasions to do your own work, they also offer occasions to recognize someone else's doing hers, a recognition not of another who will guarantee, or redeem, your thought but only another John, another maid tasting before she buys. Essays forgo the messianic altogether, and instead of thinking of texts as fragments of larger systems (or hints towards one), they read them for use and as registers of prior uses. Essays guide you to think through the commonplace, not as examples that interpellate you in a culture (though they may do that too), but as a chance for you to undertake your own work which no one else can do for you. In the same way they offer occasions to recognize another, not as an example of a culture (though she may be that too) but as someone who's done what you're doing – another singularity whose own work you recognize in the response you make to hers. If the other doesn't come, your work was the point anyhow. If another does come, that work is continued, but only in kind. As a work is an opportunity for thinking through, so that thinking through is an opportunity to recognize that others mediate our responses just as works mediate our thinking.

Essays are a way to transfer from the exigencies of knowing to those of acknowledging.[87] If essays move from answers to questions (questioning the possibility of certain knowing), they also let one move from asking questions to hearing answers, even if those responses are as questionable as one's own. If we redeem essays by thinking their thoughts along with them (reading along), we also recognize them as formed by that same work. It's work, as they say of turtles, all the way down, and recognizing that offers a different kind of answer – a response – in place of the kinds of answers expected by other ways of reading. Essays trade the desire for the kind of spirit Harrison describes ('a condition of alertness and wonder in which the Spirit is felt in its absence') for a different kind of relation, a condition of attention in which a presence is felt by its work of attention. Essays direct you to recognize an other not as defined by the exigencies of writing (creation, authenticity, possession, knowing), but by the exigencies of reading, revisiting, acknowledging the familiar – a neighbor recognized as strange. Santner distinguishes between a 'global consciousness' in which 'every stranger is ultimately just like me, ultimately familiar' and a 'conception of universality' in which 'every familiar is ultimately strange.'[88] In these terms, essays don't map global systems, but register the work of a stranger as he moves through his texts in his own particular way – one who is recognized not by his identity but by his style, the way he walks. Such essayers direct us to walk this way, not in the light of a providential truth, or even the internalization of such an aspiration as will and commitment in the face of the impossibility of that end, but as the working out of one's responses in relation to others doing the same.

I see the essay neither as postmodern, with Lyotard, nor as modern, with Harrison, but rather as premodern, or amodern, outside the exigencies of the modern (only in the terms of modernity does this look residual). If the modern is defined by economic relations, visibility, and maps of cognition, the essay offers a practice that is neither defined by those terms nor escapes from them (reinventing their dreams in its innocence), but works its way through the 'strangeness' of the everyday.[89] This is not, I've argued, a practice of writing, a trace of a lost divinity – or a promise of a coming one. Rather, essays enable reading by modeling readers reading at a certain pace and scale, a practice of reading on this side of eschatology but not organized by messianic anticipations.

From the beginning of the genre of 'Essayes' in English, a distinction between knowledge and ethical practice was operative. The essay offered an alternative to knowledge, a kind of writing that was organized not by questions of authorship or self, authority or power, originality or origins, innovation or creation, but rather by the exigencies of reading, engaging, and responding to the ordinary and to others doing the same. This practice of reading was not, of course, something new in seventeenth-century Britain, but an updating of a classical practice, one beautifully described by Hadot.

'A truly new and original book would be one that made people love old truths.' Yet for their meaning to be understood, these old truths must be *lived*, and constantly reexperienced. Each generation must take up, from scratch, the task of learning to read and re-read these 'old truths' ... And yet we have forgotten *how* to read: how to pause, liberate ourselves from our worries, return into ourselves, and leave aside our search for subtlety and originality, in order to meditate calmly, ruminate, and let the texts speak to us.[90]

The patient relation enabled by this kind of reading, neither being claimed by another nor using another for one's own pleasure but rather sharing a way with her, is likewise very familiar and has an old name that has traditionally been associated with the essay. In 'Of Friendship,' Montaigne writes of la Boëtie, 'If you press me to tell you why I loved him, I feel that this cannot be expressed, except by answering: Because it was he and it was I' [Par ce que c'estoit luy; par ce que c'estoit moy].[91] The refusal to know, to define, the other in any other way than his name – indeed in any other way than his presence, 'he' – is a transfer from identity to singularity. Essays sketch a response to another that neither absorbs you into him (as John will be made superfluous by Jesus) nor him into you (as John would be by becoming Jesus-like). They ask you to do your own work on texts, your own reading and digesting, your own thinking through, and in the same way they offer a way to recognize texts as effects of that same process. The mechanism that allows you to digest a text also allows you to recognize that text as an effect of the same kind of work, and so potentially enables a recognition of others, and their strange texts, as friends.

If essays don't help you address the big problems, '*humanum est errare*,' they do, as in Peacham's story, give you occasion to recognize strangers, not because you can identify with them under some category, but because such categories are occasions, sometimes, for another kind of work. Peacham's friend in 'Of Travels' may be the one he refers to in 'Of Friendship' when he contrasts 'The common and ordinary friendship of the world' which is 'measured by the benefit that one man reaps by another' with that of a stranger.

> And this [ordinary] friendship for the most part lives and expires with men's lives and their fortunes, and indeed merits not the name of friendship. I confess myself to have found more friendship at a stranger's hand whom I never in my life saw before, yea, and in foreign parts beyond the seas, than among the most of my nearest

kindred and old acquaintance here in England, who have professed much toward me in empty promises.[92]

The actual mechanism of this encounter, as I discussed above, consists of trading commonplaces, but not for their truth content or taken at face value. Instead, such commonplaces are occasions to forge relations outside a calculus of exchange and benefit. The answer to 'I'm lost' isn't 'that's human' (that's just a joke) but rather a local, contingent, convenient use of that commonplace of global identity. In Peacham's story, you need a common language, not to tell you who you are, or even who you refuse to be, but to have material to work with. The essay offers a way to both record and recognize that kind of adaptive work, and Peacham's story of this kind of travel, this kind of reading, offers as good an example of the essay as any. A genre in which being secondary is not a way to recoup primacy through an improved self or self-awareness, essays allow readers recursively to think through the thoughts of others (who did the same). The relation to work encoded in these texts is also a way to relate to others, a way to practice hearing one's books not as one hears a divine voice (or voices that claim such originary or creative power) but as one hears a neighbor through her response to what you always thought you knew. That skill in hearing is what I think they finally register and enable.

This is a practice of reading that doesn't need to be redeemed as writing. It is not a knowledge, a way of knowing, but a practice, a way of undergoing. I don't know my books or neighbors any better, but I recognize them. And in the space of that refusal to know, that abdicating of certainty and the need to name and fix them, in that space of recognition and distance and waiting is the condition of friendship (it may never happen), a relation that enables the art of listening without needing to speak, a way to 'let the texts speak to us,' and respond without needing to answer.

Provisional hardenings

To situate the essay in a discursive or historical frame to which it offers an alternative isn't so much wrong as a missed opportunity.[93] An opportunity to practice and think about a mode of literacy – a way of reading – that isn't organized by the exigencies of writing, production, or possession. Such reading does have a history, it happens for contingent reasons, emerges from specific confluences, and is used for local occasions. But the actual procedures and operations that are invited, enabled, and modeled by the genre offer a different way through the categories of history and a different way of using its texts. That skill, that practice, is worth recognizing, using, and passing on, not as a historical curiosity, or a promised alternative to history, but as a habit that has its own worthwhile exigencies, ones worth thinking through again.

The story I've told cuts across both the post-structuralist accounts of reading that organize genre studies and the historicist accounts of readers that organize cultural studies. If my story of the essay and the practice of 'writing as the draught of reading' it enables isn't part of those kinds of stories, how does it fit? Or: what kind of story does it enable? If my account is one of how a particular skill, or competency, comes to organize a genre that, in turn, enables, encourages, and models it (allowing its users to learn and practice that skill), how do you account for a competence? To offer a model of the larger story I think the essay's generic evolution is part of I want to borrow a phrase from Manuel de Landa, 'provisional hardening,' an echo of a standard description of the essay.[94] The phrase captures the sense of essays emerging from the traces of one's reading, tentative orderings of reading notes that enable better reading and wait to be re-used and re-read in turn.

What is flowing through the world of print? What is the energy that flows through books as we read them, write them, write them as efforts towards reading them? Essays seem particularly susceptible to this kind of question, as they have historically been considered nodes or nexuses of energy.[95] Essays transmit the use and the practice of reading they're effects of. They are tools and models of a practice of reading that can only be realized in the actual reading of them, writings put out in order to again 'looke vpon them.' Essays enable a kind of work, what I've been calling thinking through, a way of reading for use, a way of engaging the commonplaces and books of commonplaces – the essays – that make up some of the world of print. It is this skill, a classical practice of philosophy translated into the terms of print and literacy (not the face-to-face pedagogy of oral models) that the essay enables, translating into reading that skill of thinking through the ordinary in a world that disseminates its energies, and its lessons, through the media of texts. And it is this competency, finally, in a kind of thinking – not owning thoughts or being possessed by them, but practicing them, thinking them through, and thinking through them, using them as vehicles for your own movement even as you learn how they move and how they allow you to move – it is this kind of *attention* that I think essays provisionally harden, and which I've tried to explicate by undergoing my own draughts of reading, my own trial through these trails.

Attention, the effect of this kind of reading, is not only a chance to participate in the feedback loop of print culture through which this energy flows, but also offers an opportunity to understand, or model, print culture in these terms: constituted by texts legible as essays, a world of prose organized by texts of a certain scale, size, and scope. If this doesn't explain the entire range of literate practices of early modern print culture, any account of it that doesn't include such works will, likewise, be incomplete. The history of print culture, though, may be part of a larger, more layered and 'geological' story of evolving practices of literacy, the skills of reading and the tools that enable them, that print culture itself is a provisional hardening of. I offer this account of the essay, then, less as part of the story of the emergence of early modern print culture than as a frame for it. The genre of the essay offers a way to explain – understand, model, and enable – the energy that drives the culture that is its remains.

Part 2
Essay Exapted

3
Boyle's Essay

Robert Boyle's 'Proemial Essay' (1661) attaches his epistemological reformation to a shift in literary form, and places the genre of the essay both at the center of his natural philosophy and at the cusp of the emergence of modern science. This chapter considers the implications of that choice, exploring Boyle's adoption and adaptation of the essay. Boyle's 'Essay' is both a significant moment in the history of early modern science and a chapter in the story of the essay's evolution; I argue that the latter is integral to the former.

Historians of early modern science have rewritten the neat stories of heroically modern innovators to include the messy details of laboratory work, the assistance of servants, the material tools, and the emergence of modern practices out of – not just against – purportedly residual practices. A literary history organized as a study of genres offers one more strand to this complex story, another way to trace the myriad local adaptations that are the actual texture of change. A history attuned to genres offers a means of specifying the contemporary categories that organized ways of knowing. By recognizing the work of these categories in the production of knowledge – the particular practices they enabled, the skills they solicited, the ways they named and structured specific conceptual possibilities – we will be able to see one site of interplay between innovation and convention, adaptation and continuation, and begin to appreciate the knotty loops of use, re-use, and even misuse, that define at once how knowledge is practiced and how knowing works.

Scholars have recognized Boyle's 'Proemial Essay' as an important methodological statement, describing it as the 'rules for the literary technology of the experimental programme' (Shapin and Schaffer), and a 'general defense of his approach' (Sargent).[1] But while the importance of the 'Essay' has been generally noted, the significance of Boyle's choice of the genre hasn't been adequately characterized or fully contextualized. By situating the 'Essay' and its advocacy of essays in their local literary context, I argue that Boyle's adoption of the genre enables a practice of reflection that is indispensable to his natural philosophy. In *The Sceptical Chymist* (1661), Boyle expresses a wish that his work provoke both further thinking and further experiments:

> whether the Notions I propos'd, and the Experiments I have communicated, be considerable, or not, I willingly leave others to Judge; and This only I shall say for my Self, That I have endeavour'd to deliver matters of Fact, so faithfully, that I may as well assist the lesse skilful Readers to examine the Chymical Hypothesis, as to provoke the Spagyrical Philosophers to illustrate it.[2]

Essays were integral to the work of assisting 'readers to examine,' underwriting Boyle's willingness to 'leave others to judge,' a central condition of his epistemological reform.

In locating Boyle's 'Essay' within the generic context sketched above in Part 1, a practice of writing in the service of reading, I argue that Boyle adopted an available tool rather than invented a new one. In doing so, I join those recent scholars who focus on the continuities between Boyle's work and earlier, 'pre-modern' practices.[3] Such work puts early modern natural philosophy more squarely within a continuous stream of adapted ideas and evolving practices – philosophical, experimental, social, and, I want to add, literary – a site of an amodern flow, not a modern eruption or rupture of the kind imagined by both seventeenth-century moderns and contemporary post-moderns alike.[4] Instead of a break, I see a bridge across which what Boyle calls 'a way of thinking' spans his moral and natural philosophies. Boyle construes this mode of reflection as a kind of reading, which he transfers from books to the world and from devout to 'physical' uses. In doing this, he participates in a larger evolutionary shift, and shows one route (though certainly not the only one) through which humanist moral philosophy is transformed into experimental natural philosophy. The particular hinge of this emergence, or perhaps just merge, is Boyle's adoption of an old tool, the essay, for a new way of knowing.

It was not an obvious choice. One might expect essays from his brother, Francis (according to a tutor 'not soe much giuven to his booke as my most honored and affectionate Mr Robert'), as essays were lazier and looser than scholarly modes of writing.[5] In his *Moral*

Essays (1690), Francis Boyle rehearses the genre's typical rationale, calling them 'the small Issue and Recreation of my own private Thoughts and Meditations, during my two Years Retirement in the Country, where I spent much of my Time in serious Reflections upon the various Changes and Instability of Sublunary Things.'[6] The generic repertoire of the essay had been well established for a century: a short, private, recreational form for writing leisurely thoughts and reflections. Earlier in the century (1628), Owen Felltham professed himself a gentleman, not a scholar, and thereby excused himself to write essays instead of studious and strict – and pedantic – works.[7] John Hall calls his *Horae Vacivae, Or, Essays* (1646), 'Faint breathings of a minde burthened with other literary employments, neither brought forth with Care, nor ripened with Age'; they employ a 'cursory and imperfect manner (for hee that expects exactnesse and method in an ESSAY, wrongs both the Author and his owne expectation).'[8] Throughout the century such writing, 'by way of essay,' named a way of recording, as Gethin's *Misery's Virtues Whetstone* puts it, 'private undigested Thoughts and first Notions hastily set down, without Method or Order, and designed only as Material or a Foundation for a future structure to be built thereon.'[9] A cursory, inexact, and imperfect kind of writing – private, leisurely, and even undigested – this genre seems an inauspicious ground on which to base an epistemological reformation, yet this is precisely what the more scholarly and more famous Boyle advocates.

Boyle explains 'why I have cast [my works] into Essays, rather than into any other form' in the 'Proemial Essay': 'I must freely acknowledge to you, that it has long seem'd to me none of the least impediments of the real advancement of true Natural Philosophy, that men have been so forward to write Systems of it, and have thought themselves oblig'd either to be altogether silent, or not to write less than an entire body of Physiology.' Systems require writers to address every part of a subject, even those about which they have nothing to say, making them 'idly ... repeat' others, or 'say any thing on them rather than nothing, lest they should appear not to have said something to every part of the Theme, which they had taken upon themselves to write of.' You have to fill in the blanks even if you have nothing to add. And, further, if systems make writers do things they do not want to do, they discourage readers from doing anything at all, inhibiting further inquiry because they speciously suggest that natural philosophy has been 'sufficiently explicated' and there is nothing left to do but passively 'learn what [philosophers] have taught, and thankfully to acquiesce in it.' In contrast, a more imperfect form of writing solicits a more active kind of reading as writers are free to write only 'Thoughts and Observations' based on their own experience and experiments, and readers, in turn, are free to do the same, reflect on those experiments for themselves.[10]

Boyle makes a point of saying his own 'Essay' models as well as describes 'that form of Writing which (in imitation of the French) we call Essayes.' In adopting this established form, Boyle hopes to revalue it, 'bringing so usefull a way of writing into the request it deserves,' and offering a rationale for the genre: the 'great Conveniency of Essayes' makes for less bored readers, who need 'not be clogg'd with tedious Repetitions of what others have already said,' and less boring writers, who are not obligated to write more than they understand, or more than they can write well.[11] The writer's 'liberty to leave off when he pleases,' and take things for himself, is matched by the reader being 'left at liberty' to do the same.

> And if such Essayes be but as they should be competently stock'd with Experiments, 'tis the Readers own fault if he not be a learner by them: for indeed when a Writer acquaints me only with his own Thoughts or Conjectures, without enriching his discourses with any real Experiment or Observation, if he be mistaken in his Ratiocination, I am in some danger of erring with him ... but if a Writer endeavours, by delivering new and real Observations and Experiments, to credit his Opinions, the case is much otherwise; for let his Opinions be never so false, his Experiments being true, I am not oblig'd to believe the former, and am left at liberty to benefit my self by the latter; and though we have erroneously superstructured upon his Experiments, yet the foundation being solid, a more wary builder may be very much further'd by it in the erection of more judicious and consistent Fabricks.[12]

Boyle describes the exigencies of the essay as a process of thinking. Because such essays require a writer to 'credit his Opinion' with 'real Observations and Experiments,' they allow, and even encourage, readers to do the same in turn and think through the experiments for themselves. Essays raise questions they do not claim to answer, offering a space for first thoughts, not final words. And they invite further revision, suggesting that if you have to do it for yourself, you do not do it by yourself.

Boyle's adoption of the essay as the genre for his natural philosophy solicits a practice of thinking through trials that, in turn, encourages and enables further thinking. It is worth stressing this process of interactive reflection because Boyle's essays recently have been explained in terms of representation. Though Boyle hopes to engage his readers 'to cast their Physiological Observations and Reflexions into Experimental Essayes,' historians have paid more attention to the former, the observations, than the latter, the reflections. Shapin and Schaffer construe Boyle's essays as a 'literary technology' of representation that solicits readers as 'virtual witnesses' to experiments.[13] Their account presents this literary technology as representational in two senses: it represents the facts isolated in the laboratory as a kind of word picture, and it portrays a trustworthy narrator who stands for the reliability of those facts, a representative to guarantee the representations.[14] Such writing offers the 'expository means by which matters of fact were established and assent mobilized,' an abstraction of the activities of the lab, the work of observation and experiment.[15] Boyle's literary technology is said to have been crafted to secure the assent requisite to constituting matters of facts, an account that reduces reading to simple validation.[16]

Recent historians have argued that this literary technology was neither as new nor as strategic as Shapin and Schaffer suggest.[17] Principe argues that the style of Boyle's experimental reports can be explained by his early interest in French romances and their epistemological claims situated in a tradition of alchemical 'transmutation histories.'[18] But if he suggests local contexts that provide Boyle the means to do the work of Shapin and Schaffer's literary technology, Principe gives no account of the genre specifically named by Boyle. Similarly, Sargent has resituated Boyle's experimentalism within several traditions – philosophical, legal, Christian – and offers a nuanced account of Boyle's 'writing' as part of the 'dynamic learning process' of his experimental philosophy.[19] But she too overlooks Boyle's particular generic context. Principe's contexts do not include the one named by Boyle, and Sargent's 'writing' is not contextualized; the literary context of Boyle's 'Essay' has fallen through the cracks.

When critics do think about the genre, they think in French. Paradis, for instance, argues that Boyle models his experimental essays on the 'French familiar essay.' Like Shapin and Schaffer, he explains Boyle's essay as a 'mechanism designed to create and sequester facts.' In this account, Boyle shifts the focus of Montaigne's 'authentically individualist' *Essais* from the internal to the external, transforming

Montaigne's 'uniquely personal speculations' into 'a passive instrument of observation.'[20] While I agree that Boyle adapts the essay for his own purposes, I do not think Montaigne is as expressive, nor Boyle as representational, as Paradis says. He seems to abstract Montaigne's reflections from the dense thickets of quoted passages to which they respond, an account that drastically empties the *Essais* of most of their actual content and misconstrues Montaigne's project of thinking through his voluminous, and voluminously cited, reading. In contrast to Paradis, I read Montaigne's *Essais* as a record of his responses to texts, a commonplace book gone wild. Boyle's essays are like them in this sense, registers not just of facts but of reflections as well.[21] It is this practice of response that the genre of the essay facilitates.

Boyle's 'Essay' has been mischaracterized and miscontextualized. Paradis situates it exclusively in a French milieu, Montaigne's *Essais*, at once suggesting a generic context (the French essay) that is dubious and eliding the one (the English essay) that is in fact most relevant. Boyle recommends 'that form of Writing which (in imitation of the French) we call Essayes' – not a French genre but one that is called by a French word.[22] (Culpeper echoes this ten years later in his 'Of Essais': 'The word *Essay*, we have From the French, in which Tongue it signifies a tryal or probation.')[23] Seventeenth-century French writers did not write 'essays' – the title was too closely identified with Montaigne to be claimed by others – and actually considered the genre an English one.[24] Further, one of the few French writers who did call his work *Essais*, Pierre Nicole, sounds more like Boyle than Montaigne, or at least articulates a generic expectation that Boyle also shares. Nicole offers an account of 'what's marked out by Essays': a practice of writing various matters as they present themselves 'without undergoing the trouble of disposing and ordering them according to Method' and without the 'necessity of filling methodical Works with an infinite number of things, which have no other benefit, than that of being requisite to *Order*.'[25] For Nicole (or his editor: the 'Advertisement' is unsigned), as for Boyle, the essay is a way of addressing complex fields on one's own terms, and without having to answer the demands of method, saying things you do not want to say while leaving out things you do.

There was not much of a seventeenth-century French genre of the essay, but there was a large and thriving English one. The genre, though, did not, as Paradis claims, 'create and sequester facts.' Indeed while the Royal Society's early *Philosophical Transactions* evidence many literary technologies that sought to secure facts ('observations,' 'experiments,' 'relations,' 'accounts,' 'inquiries,' and 'descriptions'), the 'essay' is not one of them. And when one does find an 'essay,' it is used to do something else. 'An Essay of Dr. John Willis, exhibiting his Hypothesis about the Flux and Reflux of the Sea' (number 16, 6 August 1666), is called an essay because Willis offers a hypothesis without experiments to back it up. Willis says he does not have time for 'prosecuting the inquiry and perfecting the Hypothesis' and so he gives 'some general account of my present imperfect and undigested thoughts,' 'an Account of my thoughts, as to this matter, though yet immature and unpolished.'[26] Essays are not a genre in which one reports experiments but rather in which one offers 'conjectures' (as Oldenburg says in his preface to Willis's essay) and solicits responses and assistance from others.[27] Willis's essay is a response to Galileo's hypothesis about the tides, which Willis calls an essay because it is to be adjusted as more particular information becomes available.[28] And he asks others to respond in kind to his:

> And what I say of Galileo, I must in like manner desire to be understood of what I am now ready to say to you. For I do not profess to be so well skilled in the History of the Tides, as that I will undertake presently to accommodate my *general Hypothesis* to the *particular cases*; or that I will indeed undertake for the certainty of it, but onely as an *Essay* propose it to further consideration; to stand or fall, as it shall be found to answer matter of Fact.[29]

Rather than a literary technology of representation that solicits facts, essays name here a tool of hypothesis and conjecture that facilitates 'further consideration.'

Situating the 'Proemial Essay' in its generic context reorients Boyle's 'literary technology' from representation to reflection, and it also reorients his 'social technology' from identity to skills. Shapin and Schaffer's account of Boyle's literary technology neglects one side of his 'Essay' and that practice of reflection is the (absent) literary aspect of the 'social technology' of gentlemanly codes that Shapin later explores. Explaining that 'the English experimental community had relocated gentlemanly codes into the practice of natural philosophy,' he writes:

> It was common in early modern society to contrast the society of gentlemen with that of scholars according to the different values they respectively placed upon truth and good manners. Polite

writers condemned traditional scholars because they would sacrifice the good order of conversation to the imperious demands of truth and accuracy, while the scholar might justify himself through variants of the ancient trope used to identify oneself as 'a friend of Aristotle but more a friend of truth.' Yet changed conceptions of the nature of scholarly practice in the seventeenth century – especially in England but also elsewhere – increasingly reordered and respecified the characters of the scholar and the gentleman. It was now urged that the end of philosophy – the search for truth – might best be acquitted by deploying features of conversational practices that had traditionally belonged to gentlemanly and not scholarly society. Lowered expectations of philosophical accuracy, a more reserved way of speaking, a less passionate attempt to claim exact truth for one's claims were justified on explicitly epistemic as well as explicitly moral grounds.[30]

Shapin argues that a social practice reorders epistemology as the practices of 'polite writers' serve to ground the new science on gentlemanly conversation, which produces a truth organized by 'a more reserved way of speaking.' Experimental science was, of course, as much a textual as a social project; when Shapin slides from polite writing to a reserved way of speaking, then, he is not making an exact, scholarly claim, but employing a loose, gentle locution. What he means is a more reserved way of *writing*, but the slip is instructive, signaling a missing dimension to Shapin's story: a way to explain how social practices answered epistemological problems. Rather than the precise and pedantic models of truth of scholars (and mathematicians and logicians), the experimentalists' approach was organized by the civil conversation of gentlemen.

> The unwarranted 'confidence' and quarrelsomeness of the school-philosopher were juxtaposed to the humility and modesty of the experimentalist. 'Diffidence' in asserting truths and the professed willingness to alter one's views were mobilized into emblems of disinterestedness. The presentation of claims as certain and exact, by contrast, was identified as the mark of a scoundrel. One was invited to recognize the genuine experimental philosopher by his civility, decorum, and display of Christian virtues.[31]

Shapin's concerns are centered on 'emblems,' 'marks,' and 'displays' of identity and authority, on philosophers instead of philosophies.[32] But in tracing the ways social solutions are given to epistemological problems, he replaces the latter with social problems.[33] Social solutions, though, are solutions because they provide epistemological answers to epistemological problems.

Social motivations are only part of a complex story. I want to follow Sargent's suggestion that 'the epistemic dimension of a social practice could provide a valuable resource for the introduction of an innovative idea in science' by arguing that gentlemanly practices underwrote experimental natural philosophy by installing a practice of reading at its core, not just a means of self-fashioning as its context.[34] Essays enable a practice of reflection, and this practice is at the heart of the 'gentlemanly codes' that define Shapin's social technology. From Cornwallis (1600), through Feltham (1628) and Culpeper (1671), as I discussed above, essays were a 'Gentleman-like Learning': 'A cursory Knowledge, [which] though it be not exact enough for the Schools, is more pleasant, and perhaps more useful then to over burthern the Brain with Books, which may be called a Gentleman-like Learning, or one who is in *Omnibus aliquid.*'[35] In essays, writers and readers are 'left at liberty' to think for themselves, not bound by the exigencies or exactitudes of systems, but only by their own interests, pleasures, and uses. Writers are at liberty to write only what they know, 'a little bit of everything,' modeling and enabling an inexact but also unconfined skill of reflection which is not only an 'emblem' of disinterestedness, an identity that does social work, but a practice of thinking.

Rather than a social technology of gentlemanly identity that guarantees facts secured by a literary technology of representation, the essay enables a gentlemanly practice of reading – a particular tool of literacy. Boyle makes the practice of inexact and unconfined reading that Culpeper calls 'a Gentleman-like Learning' – a gentlemanly skill, not just the sociological fact of being a gentleman – the motor of his reformed epistemology. In essays you must do it for yourself, if not by yourself, and this skill of participatory reading and collaborative exploration was as integral to Boyle's project as the reporting and witnessing of experiments. Within their local generic context, experimental essays look less like a technology of writing and representation than a tool of reading and reflection. Rather than a way to secure facts or fashion identities, they are a way to solicit the practice of reflection on which Boyle's project equally depends.

Accounts of Boyle's writing have been governed by the classical debate between philosophy and rhetoric, between language as exposition and language as persuasion. At a certain level of abstraction, Shapin and Schaffer's account looks rhetorical (focused on questions of authority and ethos), and Sargent's philosophical (focused on epistemic questions) – though Sargent does recognize the public, social aspects of Boyle's project and Shapin its epistemic ones.[36] But at the same time, they share an emphasis on the 'philosophical' side of the 'Proemial Essay' and construct their accounts around Boyle's 'matters of fact' – though they understand these in different ways.[37] In their discussions, each neglects the rhetorical aspect of the 'Proemial Essay': 'the "florid" style to be avoided was a hindrance to the clear provision of virtual witness: it was, Boyle said, like painting "the eye-glasses of a telescope."'[38] Boyle does say that rhetoric hinders virtual witnessing, but he does not say it should be avoided. Rather he recommends it as one aspect of his experimental essays:

> as for the style of our experimental Essays, I suppose you will readily find, that I have endeavour'd to write rather in a Philosophical than a Rhetorical strain, as desiring, that my expressions should be rather clear and significant, than curiously adorn'd ... certainly in these Discourses, where our design is only to inform Readers, not to delight or perswade them, Perspicuity ought to be esteem'd at least one of the best Qualifications of a style; and to affect needless Rhetorical Ornaments in setting down an Experiment, or explicating something abstruse in Nature, were less improper, than it were (for him that designs not to look directly upon the Sun itself) to paint the Eye-glasses of a Telescope, whose clearness is their Commendation, and in which even the most delightful Colours cannot so much please the eye, as they would hinder the sight.

I read the phrase, 'in these Discourses, where our design is only to inform Readers,' as indicating particular places in these discourses (not the whole of them). In such places of 'setting down an Experiment' or an observation, clarity is more effective, and language serves as a lens. You do not, of course, look at but through a lens, and any pleasure given by colors painted on it distracts you from its purpose, to see through. But having made this point about the proper use of philosophical language, Boyle shifts gears. Perhaps with an awareness of how he has made his point, employing a vivid and effective figure to recommend a slim-figured use of language, Boyle catches himself and steers clear of a pedantry he does not want to slip into:

But I must not suffer myself to slip unawares into the Common place of the unfitness of too spruce a style for serious and weighty matters; and yet I approve not that dull and insipid way of writing, which is practis'd by many Chymists, even when they digress from Physiological Subjects: For though a Philosopher need not be sollicitous, that his style should delight its Reader with his Floridnesse, yet I think he may very well be allow'd to take a care, that it disgust not his Reader by its Flatness, especially when he does not so much deliver Experiments or explicate them, as make Reflections or Discourses on them; for on such Occasions he may be allowed the liberty of recreating his Reader and himself, and manifesting, that he declin'd the Ornaments of Language, not out of Necessity, but Discretion, which forbids them to be us'd where they may darken as well as adorn the Subject they are applied to. Thus (to resume our former Comparison) though it were foolish to colour or enamel upon the glasses of Telescopes, yet to gild or otherwise embellish the Tubes of them, may render them more acceptable to the Users, without at all lessening the Clearness of the Object to be looked at through them.[39]

At times language should strive for clarity, the servant of things, a lens, but it is no contradiction to recognize that, even in recommending this, one does not have to be so rigorous, or dull, as to avoid figures altogether. Boyle does not prefer philosophical to rhetorical language in reporting experiments because he thinks language should just be philosophical, but because when using it in this way it should be. Language does many things. There are times when figures darken lenses (when one should be looking through language). And there are times when it adorns, when it is fit 'to delight or perswade' readers. This is one of those latter times. Boyle's 'Essay' on the essay is, of course, a 'reflection.' By his own account it is appropriate here to take the liberty of employing the ornaments appropriate to reflections. And indeed he finishes his point with a surprising and witty extension of his figure, taking up his telescope and looking at it again – though not through it. This engaging use of rhetorical language, though, does more than adorn; it makes the point. Sometimes ornaments are mechanisms too, and the figure may do more than Boyle here says. Perhaps he means what he does as well as what he says.

Boyle turns to the figure, and to figures more generally, not just because it does not matter if tubes are painted but because ornaments can clarify. At the end of the passage, Boyle opposes 'darkening' to 'adorning,' suggesting that rhetoric be used only to delight when it can do no harm. But the image that colors also explains. That is, figures give 'strength' as well as 'light' to passages.[40] Instead of imagining language as a lens that does its real work by getting out of the way as much as possible, Boyle's figure here suggests that language is a complex tool. Lenses are no less crafted than tubes, but they are constructed to do a different kind of work, to make possible a particular ability. One does not have to choose between a lens grinder's diagram and a tube-engraver's wit and whimsy to explain what a telescope really is. Rather one must see how they work together to allow it to do the complex things that it does.

Just as telescopes are complex tools with several parts, lenses and tubes, so experimental essays are complex tools with several parts, experiments and reflections. Boyle does not banish rhetoric but recommends it as one aspect of his experimental program. You use rhetoric for reflections, which do a different kind of work than lenses; a writer 'may be allowed the liberty of recreating his Reader and himself' when he makes 'Reflections or Discourses' on experiments. This 'liberty of recreation' repeats Boyle's characterization of the essay, the genre in which readers are 'left at liberty' to think for themselves, and writers to write only what they understand and 'can write well.' The essay sponsors this work of literacy, of reading and reflection, not the work of representation, securing either facts or identities.

Reflections are as integral to Boyle's project as experiments; 'when once a Man is in the right way of making Inquiries into such Subjects, Experiments and Notions will reciprocally direct to one another.'[41] In *The Christian Virtuoso* (1690) Boyle more fully explicates this relationship between experiments and reflections.[42] He situates his experimental philosophy between 'School-Philosophers' and 'mere Empiricks.' The former 'in the framing of their System, make but little use of Experience ... superstructuring almost their whole Physicks upon *Abstracted Reason*.' In contrast,

> those, that Understand and Cultivate Experimental Philosophy, make a much greater and better use of Experience in their Philosophical Researches. For they consult Experience both frequently and heedfully; and, not content with the *Phaenomena* that Nature spontaneously affords them, they are solicitous, when they find it needful, to enlarge their Experience by Trials purposely devis'd; and ever and anon Reflecting upon it, they are careful to Conform their Opinions to it; or, if there need be just cause, Reform their Opinions by it.[43]

If reflecting on *experiments* distinguishes experimental virtuosi from systemizers, *reflecting* on experiments distinguishes a virtuoso from 'a mere Empirick, or some vulgar Chymist ... who too often makes Experiments, without making Reflection on them, as having it more in his aim to Produce Effects, than to Discover Truths.'[44] The Christian virtuoso brings experiments and reflections together.[45] A 'true Naturalist' combines an uncommon 'curiosity and attention' and 'competent knowledge,' which together make one an 'attentive and intelligent Peruser' of the world.[46]

When Boyle recommends the essay, then, it is to solicit a skill of attentive reflection that is construed as reading. Such reading serves as a hinge between Boyle's moral and natural philosophy, both of which depend on a 'way of writing' that evolved out of a humanist practice of reading. This process involved two shifts, one of the objects of reading (from books to the world) and one of the ends of reading (from moral to natural philosophy). Boyle neither began nor completed these long-term conceptual shifts, but his *Occasional Reflections* (1665) offers one point of transfer in which a practice of Protestant reading begins to develop into a desacrilized natural science (an end-point Boyle's own work neither reaches nor aspires to).[47] 'I have endeavoured to Display the Usefulness of that *way of thinking* I would invite to,' Boyle writes, 'an attentive frame of mind,' 'an attentive observation of the Objects wherewith [one] is conversant.'[48] Such attention transfers a skill of reading from books to the world. An occasional reflector makes 'the world both his Library and his Oratory';

> whereas Men are wont, for the most part, when they would Study hard, to repair to their Libraries, or to Stationers Shops; the Occasional Reflector has his Library always with him, and his Books lying always open before him, and the World it self, and the Actions of Men that live in it, and an almost infinite Variety of other Occurrences being capable of proving Objects of his Contemplation.[49]

Boyle argues that this fosters an even more active kind of reading. Reading explicit instructions in books only requires an ant-like docility, while reading the world requires an extraordinary bee-like and transformative – perhaps even chymical – attention.[50]

In addition to this shift of the objects of reading from books to the world, Boyle also opens a space for various kinds of reading, a transfer (not fully undertaken by Boyle himself) from devout to secular reading.

He recommends occasional reflections as a pious practice, training 'Heavenly Mindedness, which is a Disposition and a readiness to make Spiritual Uses of Earthly things.'[51] But he also says that devotion is not the only purpose of such reflections: 'there is no necessity of confineing occasional meditations, to matters Devout, or Theological.'[52] In a remark that is refreshingly clear-eyed, especially in this context, Boyle notes that it may be the insistence on theological or moral uses that has kept such reflections so little cultivated: 'I would not confine Occasional Meditations to Divinity it self ... but am ready to allow mens thoughts to expiate much further, and to make of the Objects they contemplate not onely a Theological and a Moral, but also a Political, an Oeconomical, or even a Physical use.'[53] Here Boyle anticipates his natural philosophical work, which applies the skill of reflection originally articulated as a practice of moral philosophy to reflect on new objects in new ways.[54]

The particular link between the two is a 'way of thinking' that *Occasional Reflections* construes as a practice of reading – one modeled and enabled by a 'way of Writing' that is characterized, implicitly and explicitly, in terms of the essay: 'immature Productions,' 'far short of being an Exact and finish'd Piece,' 'written for my own private Amusement,' and requiring 'not any other than a loose and Desultory way of writing.'[55] The *Occasional Reflections* are 'Green Fruit' of the sort Boyle names, in his exemplary 'Occasional Consideration of a Fruit-tree,' 'green and immature Essays.'[56] In a blueprint, or an echo, of his advocacy of essays as the tool for his natural philosophy (the *Occasional Reflections* were written before the 'Proemial Essay' though published after it), Boyle recommends them in the same terms he uses in the 'Proemial Essay': 'such Reflections, being of the nature of short and Occasional *Essays*, may afford men the opportunitys, of saying the Hansomest things they know, on several Subjects, without saying any thing Else of them, or filling above a *Sheet*, or perhaps a *Side* of Paper at a Time.'[57] Such short and sweet (honey-like, transformative) writings form at once the link between Boyle's moral and natural philosophies and the core of each.

In calling this means of reflection 'essays' Boyle uses a contemporary term in a standard way and situates his text in a well-established generic context. 'Essays' signifed a collection of reading notes, as in Uffley's *Wits Fancies* where he 'endeavours to write truly those things that (by his own Experiences) he knows.'[58] Throughout the century, 'essay' named this practice of writing in the service of reading, a way to register raw and undigested thoughts. William Master's *Logoi eukoiroi*,

Essayes and Observations Theologicall and Morall (1653) are thoughts out of school, 'unstudied thoughts' that are 'committed to paper' to help him 'recall' his occasional considerations more profitably (and Master is unabashed about the kind of profit he hopes to reap from his essays, financial not moral).[59] Similarly, though with a higher tone, Lady Chudleigh describes her 1710 *Essays Upon Several Subjects* as her way of processing the 'new and useful Hints' provided by her thoughts: 'the Notices they give me, I strive to improve by Writing; that firmly fixes what I know, deeply imprints the Truths I've learn'd. / The following *Essays* were the Products of my Retirement, some of the pleasing Opiates I made use of to lull my Mind to a delightful Rest, the ravishing Amusements of my leisure Hours, of my lonely Moments.'[60] Essays were part of a practice of moral philosophy, a way to improve thoughts by 'firmly fixing' and 'deeply imprinting' what one thinks in order to reduce 'knowledge into practice, and live those truths we have been learning.'[61]

Essays, then, do not enable the transmission of a body of knowledge as much as the diffusion of a skill of attention that is relayed by readers through books to other readers. Such essays can not tell you exactly what to do (that would defeat their purpose – to allow your own engagement with the material). Instead they offer necessarily particular examples of that work of reading both books and the world, a skill of close attention which is as much the point of Boyle's project as the observations and experiments through which it must pass. The 'Essay on Nitre,' with its 'Experiments and considerations tending to countenance or illustrate the Reflections therein set down,' offers a rationale for regarding the essay as the proper form of such reflections.

> I am sufficiently sensible of my having not yet been able to look into the bottom of it; and that very sense of my own ignorance, help'd to keep me from lengthening your trouble in this Essay, lest by solemnly endeavouring to countenance my Conjectures, I might be thought Dogmatical in a hasty Scrible, where 'tis much more my design to awaken and engage your Curiosity, than acquaint you with my opinions.

In writing essays, 'hasty scribbles,' one announces one's own ignorance, one's inability to see to the bottom, in order to solicit help, 'to awaken curiosity.'[62] Boyle says he publishes such 'unpolish'd and unfinished' work not to claim knowledge but to affirm its absence and to seek assistance in pursuing it.[63]

Forgoing authority, essays at once model and enable a 'naked way of writing' that solicits the habit of careful attention at the core of Boyle's new way of knowing, a practice of writing articulated in terms of the essay in *Occasional Reflections* and put at the center of Boyle's experimental program in the 'Proemial Essay.' In both works, essays underwrite Boyle's desire for a community of knowers bound by a practice of attention:

> they that would compleat the Good Fortune of these Papers, may do it more effectually, by Addicting themselves, (as considerable Persons have been of late induc'd to do) to Write Occasional Reflections (how excellent so ever they may prove) then by being Kind to These; since having written them, not to get Reputation, but Company, I cannot but be Unwilling to travel alone: and had rather be *out-gone* than *not* at all *follow'd*, and Surpass'd, than not Imitated.[64]

A similar statement ends the 'Proemial Essay': 'And you will easily pardon me the injury which for your sake I do my own Reputation by this naked way of writing, if you, as well as I, think, those the profitablest Writers, or at least the kindest to their Perusers, who take not so much Care to appear Knowing Men themselves, as to make their Readers such.'[65] It may be, of course, that Boyle means exactly the opposite of what he says, and performs a pose of modesty that disguises an actual interest in reputation. But to believe what he says costs exactly the same as to question his disinterest. And even if we choose distrust over trust, we have done exactly what Boyle asks, undertaken the work of reading his claim for ourselves, not just endorsed his authority. This does not, it seems to me, refer to another, hidden level of authority, or a further trick of authorship, but rather trades both for a different kind of knowing, one organized by a chain of readers reading other readers, or, same thing, writing essays.

The continuity within Boyle's work is part of a larger continuity. Principe has argued that experimental reports were 'a locus of continuity, not of disjunction' between a less modern Boyle and a less ancient alchemy.[66] The same is true of Boyle's adaptation of the essay, his use of a 'residual' humanist practice of moral philosophy for his 'emergent' experimental science. Anthony Grafton has argued that the old story of humanism eclipsed by science masks a considerable and interesting complexity. Rather than a history of ruptures and radical epistemic breaks, Grafton tells a story of co-existing practices that build bridges across the dubious gaps introduced by modern stories, both seventeenth-century ones and our own.[67] Among such continuities, Grafton names the notebook method – a practice of reading with pen in hand, writing in the service of reading: 'the student, armed with a notebook and a set of *loci*, places, or categories, in which to store material for rapid retrieval, set out as confidently in 1630 as his counterparts had one or two centuries before to break up the classics into bite-sized segments and organize them for aggressively confident re-use.'[68] The essay evolved out of this humanist method of reading, 'a draught of reading' organized by the peculiar exigencies of one's own needs, uses, and pleasures. The practice did not fade away. It was as integral to experimental natural philosophy as to humanist moral philosophy, as can be seen in Henry Oldenburg's preface to the third installment of the Royal Society's annual *Philosophical Transactions*.

> Neither have we discouraged or refused Essays of some famous Philosophers, learned Philologers and Antiquaries; whose Disquisitions, Readings, and Reasonings, have extended farther than their Experiences; since by such bold Excursions and Sallies many valuable Truths may be started out of their recesses. *Architects* do require some variety and store of Materials for the further satisfaction of their Judgment in the Choice: And the *Sculptor* must pare off somewhat his richest Marbles, Onixes, Diamonds, &c. before he can perfect the Portraiture. Such liberty an exact Philosopher must claim in his Extracts from Men of much Learning.[69]

The essay was one hinge between the practices of humanism explicated by Grafton and those of experimental philosophy illustrated by Oldenburg. It was an old tool that names the 'liberty an exact Philosopher must claim in his Extracts' and was much a part of the public *Transactions* as a student's private notebook.

The essay underwrote a practice of reflection that was as important to Boyle's natural philosophy as to his moral philosophy, and as integral to his natural philosophy as experiments. Placing Boyle's use of the essay more exactly within its contemporary generic context reminds us that 'literary technologies' are not only ways of writing, but also ways of reading. Boyle makes the skill solicited by the genre – a particular literacy defined as responsive and not foundational, interactive and not self-fashioning, open-ended and not conclusive – the motor that drives his experimental philosophy. He uses the essay to organize his new way of knowing as a form of literacy instead of logic, and to replace reason with reading.

Boyle's 'Essay' offers not only a representational literary technology that guarantees facts and identities, but also a tool of literacy, specifically a practice of gentlemanly *reading* that is as indispensable to Boyle's project as the 'social technology' of gentlemanly identity. I'm suggesting that literary history should not be only a subset of sociology, bottomed exclusively on categories of social authority and identity, nor a subset of intellectual history, organized by abstract models of writing and discourse. Rather, the precise historical specificity of thoughts and practices may be best located in a study of the particular genres that self-consciously organize historical practices. If we are looking for continuities, they will be mediated by adaptations of available tools, somewhat like Shapin's model of a relocated gentlemanly practice. At the same time, as Sargent argues, an account of social practices needs to address the way they answer, not just replace, the problems they were adapted to solve. Gentlemanly practices provided epistemological solutions because they solicited a skill, not just an identity, around which to orient a new way of knowing. A literary history organized by genres – the co-evolving tools and skills of literacy – may offer a way to mediate histories of ideas and their social contexts by offering a history of the tools of ideas that enable the skills named by particular local identities.

In following the essay's evolution from a practice of humanist moral philosophy into an instrument of experimental natural philosophy, I have tried to explore one of the ways that this history unfolds. Boyle's adoption of the essay works more like a Rube Goldberg machine than a great leap forward across epistemic chasms. It is best explicable in terms of small, local, and convenient readjustments and adaptations – in terms, I suppose, of the essay itself. The 'history' of the essay, that is, recursively takes the form of the very evolutionary process the genre makes possible. Essays are the registers and effects of evolving uses, variously re-used and even misused by many people exploiting the genre for their own myriad exigencies. From the perspective of the history of science, the essay is the name of a tool available to be picked up, one that fit, and was fitted to, its procedures of experiment, participation, and perpetual correction. From the perspective of the evolution of the genre, experimental natural science newly applies the skills enabled by the essay, ones that emerge from a humanist practice of reading and that, in turn, are redeployed to support a new way of knowing – a new chapter in an old story.

The essay's evolution offers a mediate link across the epochal divides proposed by stories of modernity (in which Something Happens that Changes Everything). 'Emergent' scientists were 'residual' humanists, and the practices of the latter informed the former, not paradoxically but integrally. 'Residual' skills enable 'emergent' practices. This kind of development looks like a contradiction only from the perspective of a progressive history organized by gaps and fissures that, one suspects, are introduced by historians so that they can be bridged by their histories. But one could start with the fact of crossing and recognize that if thinking stitches patterns across even the most rigorous conceptual separations, it may best be conceived as a practice of literacy, less a problem of writing things down than taking them up.

4
Social and Literary Form in the *Spectator*

In *Occasional Reflections*, Boyle makes a fascinating remark that announces not only a shift from devout to secular uses, as I discussed in the previous chapter, but also a shift from pastoral to urban places: 'And if we should lead our Reflector from the Garden to the Woods, or to the River side, or into the Fields, or to the Street, or to a Library, or to the Exchange, or, in a word, to I know not how many other places I could name, I have some reason to think, that each would supply him with the variety of Occasional Meditations.'[1] This sounds like a prescription for the periodical essay, which relocates the essay form, and the skill of reflection it enables, precisely to such places. Boyle's general cluster of concerns here, novelty, variety, curiosity – all associated with the essay – may belong to a genealogy of the *Spectator*. I hear a presage of Addison's 'man of polite imagination' in Boyle's promise that 'which way so ever he [the reflector] turns his eyes (not onely upon unobvious things, but even upon the most familiar ones) [he will] behold something that instructs, or delights him' with 'Innocency and Pleasure.'[2]

Addison and Steele described the *Spectator* (1711–12) as a 'Diurnal Essay,' at once applying the rhythm of the daily newspapers to the genre and re-forming the metropolitan press in its terms.[3] In turn, the periodical essay offered a new way to understand a sphere of social relations mediated by that periodical technology, and so enabled a public space distinct from both church and state.[4] By applying the 'Method' of an 'Essay Writer' to the modern 'Art of Printing' and the 'Penny Papers,' Addison and Steele offered a mode of literary reflection for the modern city, using the form of the essay to represent – reflect, understand, explain, and define – its urban dynamics.[5]

In this chapter I present a reconstructive account of the *Spectator*'s internal logic, formal and developmental, to argue that its particular – literary – history is integral to understanding its place in broader historical and cultural developments. I explain the *Spectator* as written at the convergence of three early modern phenomena, a new use of print technology, a new literary form, and a new social space. I argue that the daily press, the essay, and the city were mutually defining; that is, each was defined in terms of the influence of, and its own effect upon, the others. A new literary form was developed at the intersection of the city and the press; a new urbane ethos emerged from this meeting of literary form and technology; and finally that structure of politeness offered an indigenous form with which to explain the modern city to itself.

While recent accounts of the *Spectator* have complicated the once-standard Whiggish story of the rising middle class that featured Addison as the prophet of the bourgeoisie, those complications have not so much changed the terms of discussion as reversed them.[6] Now Addison is read as the ideologue of the bourgeoisie, an agent of 'class-consolidation' or the 'disciplinary regime' of modernity.[7] The effect of such criticism has been to focus on the persona of Mr. Spectator as a model of modern subjectivity, a 'prosthetic person' or 'a disembodied public subject' that makes readers 'recognize and accept his public prose as a comprehensive account of oneself.'[8] The suggestion that literature has its effects because readers simply imitate texts – compelled either to follow the leader or to question authority – underlies the urgent questioning of such texts. But our own practice of criticism belies this simple conception of reading, and we are routinely able to recognize the text's efficacy without falling prey to its seductions. While critics read texts like the *Spectator* as enforcing ideological subjection, they demonstrate their own more complicated responses in those readings, raising questions – and kinds of questions – that are supposed not to occur to readers. Similarly, I suggest that the interest of the *Spectator* is not exhausted by insisting on its 'mystification' in grounding authority in a consensus it helps create, or by noting that its 'mode of free, apparently random discourse is used to disguise an ideological program' and remarking that its 'cultural achievement' is 'deeply political and ideological.'[9] In these terms, what else could it be? The study of ideology, though, often slips, in Raymond Williams's words, from considering 'the general process of the production of meanings and ideals' into an accusatory unmasking of 'a system of illusory belief.'[10] When critics who study 'ideology' slide from the former sense to the latter and make their points by uncovering 'ideology,' they belie their critical assumptions by suggesting a pathos of discovery that could only mean something if there was a discourse somehow not ideological.

This chapter is less concerned with evaluating bourgeois subject formation than with understanding its formal preconditions, and such a question cannot be answered in the terms of identity without begging a further question about how the forms that were internalized came to be. I offer an account, then, of how a particular literary form, the essay, was used to organize one of the first and most influential articulations of the nascent social formation, civil society. I take as axiomatic that this social formation was – as all social formations necessarily are – an ideological construct, serving to make (or allow) people to think of themselves and their world in particular ways. And instead of remarking what it was, I ask how this structure developed and how it was imagined to work. The answer I offer traces the development of the *Spectator* from its predecessor, the *Tatler*, through its own statements about its workings and use. Some readers may be disturbed by my failure to interrogate the claims of the work, to note that its assertions of inclusion actually excluded many people, that the equality of the coffeeshop was underwritten by a set of highly unequal assumptions, or that the 'conversational voice' was merely 'fictional.'[11] But I hope that an account of how these social and literary forms interacted will enable the reader to decide what they therefore meant.

In the *Tatler* a confluence of the new technology of the newspaper and the ancient literary form of satire produced a new kind of representation, one that provided a way to depict a modern public sphere in indigenous terms. As he was starting the *Tatler*, Steele was editing the London *Gazette*, an organ of the ministry that shows the range of the government's concerns in both content and form.[12] If the referential geography of the *Gazette* were mapped, something like the ministerial imagination emerges as a formal shape: a world with centers of gravity in Paris and Rome, lines of strong attraction from Harwich to Barbados strung through Guinea, weaker lines to Calcutta strained by the voyage around the Cape. A technology that at once shapes and responds to the substantive worries of the government, the *Gazette* offers a sketch of the political imagination of Steele's ministerial employers. And when Steele, editor of the *Gazette* and man about town, turned the technology of the newspaper to the Town with the *Tatler*, he mapped an imagination defined by London's social geography.[13]

Steele's new paper records the different topics of conversation heard in the different coffeehouses under their appropriate bylines, 'From Will's Coffee-house,' or 'From St. James's Coffee-house' – 'under such Dates of Places as may prepare you for the Matter you are to expect.' The first number, for instance, includes a story of unlucky love under 'White's Chocolate-house' (the site of 'Accounts of Gallantry, Pleasure, and Entertainment'); a review of Mr. Betterton in 'Love for Love' under 'Will's' (the place of 'Poetry'); reports from Flanders about troop movements and peace negotiations under 'St. James's' ('Foreign and Domestick News'); and a satiric account of the death of Mr. Partridge, the hoax of Swift's from which Steele borrowed the character of Bickerstaff, under the heading, 'From my own Apartment' (where he presents 'what else I have to offer on any other Subject').[14] Steele organizes his paper by 'the Passages which occur in Action and Discourse throughout this Town,' and in doing so he carefully matches the style of particular 'Discourses' to the topics of 'Action.'[15] So the language of 'White's' is that of the beau, while 'St. James's' is written in the idiom of the *Gazette*. The paper brings the variety of the city together, as both the actions and the discourses appropriate to each space are presented in jostling juxtaposition. The concerns of 'White's' stand next to the voice of 'St. James's,' at once distinct but joined by a topographical form that lets each place speak to and be heard by each other – and lets all be heard by a general public defined by this formal innovation. In so transforming the practice of the press by structuring the *Tatler* around London's civil society, offering an epitome of its distinctive concerns and particular languages, Steele produced a way to represent a public sphere defined by those associational spaces.

Over the course of its two-year run, the *Tatler* developed from a paper structured by the social geography of London into one that offered a new kind of discourse – an urbane voice formed from the urban voices represented in its pages. This development of a polite style that incorporated the particular characteristics of the various social spaces of London into a flexible medium able to mediate their differences is epitomized by Bickerstaff's evolving style. In the first number, Steele opens the section from Bickerstaff's 'Apartment': 'I am sorry I am so oblig'd to trouble the Publick with so much Discourse upon a Matter which I at the very first mentioned as a trifle, *viz.* the Death of Mr. *Partridge.*'[16] Starting with an apology that bows humbly to the audience but only in order to keep the speaker in view ('I' is repeated three times before we even know what he's talking about), the 'Apartment' is the space of Bickerstaff's satiric critique on miscellaneous topics, 'what else I have to offer on any other subject.'[17] The univocality of satire is central to Steele's initial project, and echoes the preface to the paper, where Bickerstaff says he will 'consider all Matters of what Kind so ever that shall occur to Me.'[18] First and foremost the site of a voice – one defined as 'writing in an Air of Common Speech' – the 'Apartment' is the self-conscious place of style itself, where topics become subordinated to tone.[19] Other sections match style to topic, but the 'Apartment' subordinates topic to style, miscellaneous folly to satire.

The medley of subjects of the 'Apartment' is at once contemporary and literary. The 'Graecian' coffeeshop (the site of 'Learning') is not represented in the first number, but it perhaps hovers at the edges. The paper's Juvenalian motto, 'Quicquid agunt Homines nostri Farrago Libelli' [whatever people do will form the mixed subject of my paper], refers to the classical form of satire, a farrago or medley that judges vice and folly by measuring it against an ideal.[20] With the press, Steele applies the satirist's classical prerogative of publicity to the new public space.[21] The stated purpose of the paper ('from Time to Time [to] Report and Consider Matters of what Kind so ever') is echoed by the satiric threat at the end of the paper: 'I therefore give all Men fair warning to mend their Manners, for I shall from Time to Time print Bills of Mortality,' bills that announce the public death of mere 'pretenders' to 'Being.'[22] Appearing 'from Time to Time' – using the technology of the periodical press – as the means of his satire, Steele connects one of the most classical of literary practices to the most modern of social technologies, the 'Bills of Mortality' that count populations and the newspapers that mediate those populations. In doing so, Steele develops a literary practice at the nexus of ancient literary forms and modern social formations.

Initially the *Tatler* applied the new mechanisms of publicity to the ancient project of satire, but gradually Steele synthesized these strands into a new project. The paper started out mimetic of London – its form shaped by the geography of the coffeehouses whose discourses it represented – but over the course of the first year, the dialogic variety of its subjects and spaces – 'the different Tasts that reign in the different Parts of this City' – begins to affect Bickerstaff's voice.[23] A shift from representing particular urban voices to presenting a more general urbane voice occurs as the site of Bickerstaff's satire, the 'Apartment,' gradually becomes the focus, and eventually the sole content, of the paper.[24] As more general topics come to occupy a greater part of the paper, Bickerstaff's voice undergoes a corresponding shift, losing much of its satiric edge as it not only subsumes the subjects but also integrates the styles of the other departments.

The variety of satire's topics becomes a variable voice as Steele folds his two representational modes together and places them within a club, the space of a sociable style. Described as the place to 'relax and unbend [my Mind] in the Conversation of such as are rather easy than shining Companions,' the club is the space of a different voice. There 'Conversation ... takes the Mind down from Abstractions, leads it into the familiar Traces of Thought.'[25] The club is the locus of the easy style, and I read the shift from Bickerstaff's satiric commentary to a civil voice of criticism as figured by his inclusion in a club of 'easy ... Companions.' A single discursive locus comes to dominate the *Tatler*, but that language is correspondingly simmered and reduced, able to represent the variety of the mundane with a mundane discourse. This marks the shift from the ancient literary mode of satire to a modern ethos of politeness. The satiric regulation of the self-conscious variety and lash of the 'Apartment' is smoothed out into a kinder, gentler style, grounding a literary form geared not to the threat of pain, but to the promise of friendship, mutuality, and pleasure. In the last number of the paper, Steele said he was most proud of this aspect of the *Tatler*: 'it has been a most exquisite Pleasure to me to frame Characters of Domestick Life, and put those Parts of it which are least observed into an agreeable View ... In a Word, to trace Humane Life thorough all its Mazes and Recesses.'[26] Steele's social periodical becomes a sociable paper, developing into a tool that represents the previously unremarked spaces of civil society in their own terms by offering an 'agreeable' voice able to negotiate its variety – that is, by articulating a discourse of civility.[27]

Steele and Addison further develop the *Tatler*'s formal and stylistic innovations in the *Spectator*. What had been peripheral in the former becomes the organizing structure of the latter, as Bickerstaff's club is given a defining role in the new paper. The *Spectator* club is explicitly a 'Representative' sociological portrait of England:

> The Club of which I am a Member, is very luckily composed of such Persons as are engaged in different Ways of Life and deputed as it were out of the most conspicuous Classes of Mankind: By this Means I am furnished with the greatest Variety of Hints and Materials, and know every thing that passes in the different Quarters and Divisions, not only of the great City, but of the whole Kingdom.[28]

The *Tatler*'s representational spaces become representational figures in the *Spectator*. Its topological variety and its critical voice are combined into a typological variety, in which the spaces and topics of the public sphere are represented not only by a variety of styles, but also by a variety of commentaries. The *Tatler* was organized in part by miscellaneous topics matched to miscellaneous voices, and in part by a single voice commenting on various topics. The *Spectator* takes this one step further and provides a means to represent a variety of commentaries to match the variety of topics and voices. Instead of a monologic commentary by the satirist, the *Spectator* is organized by a civil space of mutually-defining critical conversation that replaces the private center of criticism of the 'Apartment.' A new critical voice, a condition for the modern public sphere, is thus enabled through the articulation of a style formed from that space.[29]

The *Spectator* club members incorporate various aspects of the *Tatler*'s style and form. The extra-legal locus of politeness is embodied in a lawyer who studies the theater, figuring the shift from law to manners (and replacing 'Will's'). Will Honeycomb, who 'is very ready at the Sort of Discourse with which Men usually entertain Women' and whose 'Way of Talking ... very much enlivens the Conversation,' replaces 'White's.'[30] And the concerns of 'St. James's' are split between Captain Sentry (a figure of post-chivalric virtue) and Sir Andrew Freeport (a figure of modern commerce and its virtues).[31] An ill-defined clergyman, a shadowy presence here and practically non-existent in the rest of the papers, marks the absence of ecclesiastical concerns, stressing the mundane nature of the space of the club. Ironically, one of the few things the clergyman does say announces his own marginality; he gives the purpose of the paper: 'the great Use this Paper might be of to the Publick ... [is] reprehending those Vices which are too trivial for the Chastisement of the Law, and too fantastical for the Cognizance of the Pulpit.'[32] With the *Spectator*, the periodical press becomes a technology through which a mundane public can see itself in extra-legal and extra-theological terms, and the form used to so represent itself was the essay.

The *Spectator* completes the *Tatler*'s experiment, perfecting the literary mode the earlier paper had developed. In the *Spectator*, the satiric Bickerstaff becomes the politely comic Roger De Coverly. This marks a shift in genre. The gradual abstraction of the form and the style of the *Tatler* away from satire evolved into a new kind of representation that was structured by the variety of the mundane, but not based on the classical literary mode. The development of Bickerstaff's voice in the direction of the discourse of his club – into a style informed by the dynamics of polite conversation – allowed Steele and Addison to separate the 'Apartment,' the site of 'what else I have to offer on any other Subject,' from its origin as the site of satire. In doing so they arrived at the 'irregular' form of the essay, as exemplified by Sir Roger's 'conversation': 'he entered into the Matter, after his blunt way of saying things, as they occur to his Imagination, without Regular Introduction, or Care to preserve the appearance of Chain of Thought.'[33] Sir Roger's easy, essayistic style is the end point of the mellowing of Bickerstaff's satire, marking the full development of the civil form that mediated civil society through the press.

The terms Addison uses to describe Sir Roger's conversation are those of the essay, and the exigencies and structures of this literary form characterize the project of the *Spectator* as a whole. The 'Office of a faithful Spectator' is to record the 'singular' and the new, and its method is therefore casual and unmethodical.[34] In treating subjects 'which I have not met with in other Writers,' Addison sets 'them down as they have occurred to me, without being at Pains to Connect or methodise them': 'When I make Choice of a Subject that has not been treated of by others, I throw together my Reflections on it without any Order or Method, so that they may appear rather in the Looseness and Freedom of an Essay, than in the Regularity of a Set Discourse.'[35] Representing the contingent and the new, the essay here becomes a means by which the modern, as such, could apprehend itself. Rather than an abstraction based on disinterest, an abstraction *from* the world, the essay offers a kind of abstraction *of* the world. Mimetic of the quotidian dynamics of friendship and conversation, the essay offers a way to represent the activities of the world without recourse to extra-mundane structures.

George Savile, Marquis of Halifax, offers a context for Addison's terms. In his 'Vindication' of Montaigne's *Essays*, prefaced to the third edition (1700) of Charles Cotton's popular translation, Halifax explains them as 'justly ranked amongst Miscellaneous Books: for they are on various subjects, without order and connexion; and the very body of the discourses has still a greater variety.'[36] Halifax suggests that variety is the organizing principle of the essay, not through 'inadvertency' but because Montaigne 'did not intend to make a regular Work': 'the odd, or rather fantastical connexion of his discourses' and their 'digressions' are modeled on the 'Liberty' of 'common Conversations,' 'set[ting] down in writing' the form of conversation between 'two or three

Interlocutors.'[37] Essays are organized by the horizontal structure of 'conversation,' by the mutually defining relationship between two agents, and they offer an alternative structure to that of law (the relationship between a subject and law). Halifax's comments refer to the essay 'Of Friendship,' where Montaigne discusses essay-writing and friendship as mutually defining activities; both have no exterior point of reference or value, and both are defined only by choice and desire, not by duty, obligations, or by reference to anything except their own performance.[38] A friend allows one to measure oneself through one's relation to another human being, not to a regulatory God or state, and essays are organized by this kind of relationship, offering a kind of literary reflection organized by the mutuality and interactivity of such 'conversation' and – its exact cognate in the eighteenth century – 'commerce.'[39]

By attaching the essay to the daily press, Addison gave Montaigne's literary form a new use.[40] In *Spectator* #101, in a fantasy about what a future historian might say about the literature of the reign of Anne, Addison suggests that his 'little Diurnal Essays' may be deserving of a paragraph alongside 'men of Genius and Learning.'[41] If on the one hand Addison suggests that such 'little Diurnal Essays' exist in the interstices of the day – they are themselves daily diversions like the ones they record – on the other hand, he says such ephemera will be preserved in the essays: the historian will turn to the *Spectator* for accounts of the 'Diversions and Characters of the English Nation in his time.'[42] The manners that Addison anticipates being incomprehensible to a future audience except as 'the Mirth and Humour of the Author' – in this better future things like incomprehensible music or party politics will only be recognized as ancient 'Follies' – are later repeated as the domain of the essay.[43] In #435, Addison distinguishes two forms of writing: his 'more Serious Essays and Discourses' treat of 'fixed and immutable subjects,' while his 'Occasional Papers ... take their Rise from the Folly, Extravagance, and Caprice of the present Age.'[44] While in his earlier fantasy Addison hoped for enduring fame based on the latter, lighter papers, here he claims that most of his papers are of the former, more serious kind. But in both #101 and #435 he roots the point of the *Spectator* in the 'Occasional Papers': 'I look upon my self as one set to watch the Manners and Behaviour of my Countrymen and Contemporaries, and to mark down every absurd Fashion, ridiculous Custom, or affected form of Speech that makes its Appearance in the World, during the Course of these my Speculations.'[45] The *Spectator*'s claim to correct 'Manners and Behavior' depends on its ability to 'mark down' – to represent – such contingencies, and the ability to do so depends on developing a form at once of and about them. Such 'Occasional Papers' comment on the 'Irregularities' of the day by matching its vagaries with a literary form organized precisely by such irregularity.[46] This new form redeems the occasional, making such irregularities themselves its model, and validates the experience of the mundane world, offering it as worthy of serious attention, worthy of being noted, represented, understood.

In describing the *Spectator* as an 'Essay,' Addison was referring to a form that is structured by mutuality, interdependence, and quotidian desire, one that offered a civil and secular alternative to the republican political formations and Puritan literary forms with which the journal has recently been identified. Michael Warner uses the *Spectator* to illustrate his claim that the periodical press was constitutive of a new form of public identity (republican disinterestedness), while Stuart Sherman reads it as a vehicle of a new private identity (structured by the diary), and Lawrence Klein as an example of a new kind of culture (Shaftesburyan politeness). These interpretations do not fit together to offer a coherent account of the *Spectator*. Placing the text against mutually exclusive backgrounds that only explain selective aspects of it (its significance in the development of a new political formation, literary form, or culture) leads to a paradoxical composite picture of the *Spectator* as proffering a Puritan model of the self within a republican politics (whereas a public of diary-writers would look more like a community of saints than the *polis* of the republican imagination). Instead of using the *Spectator*'s terms to explain the background, terms from the background are imported to explain Addison and Steele's own statements.

For Warner the *Spectator* is an example of a 'republican text' located at the nexus of the press and 'republican rhetoric,' and organized by Mr. Spectator's 'Country posture of disinterested examination.'[47] Crossing Pocock's account of civic humanism with Habermas's account of the public sphere, Warner explains the mechanization of print as offering a kind of blind behind which one's social identity is hidden, enabling a form of political participation that depends on forgoing such identity.[48] The disembodying abstraction of print becomes a necessary condition of the disinterested virtue that is required in republican politics, as the press is said to offer, in its mechanical impersonality, the means by which to participate in such politics.[49]

While Warner's account is part of a history of a shift from 'a technology of privacy underwritten by divine authority' to a republican 'technology of publicity,' Sherman reads the *Spectator* as an example of the former technology.[50] Rather than a new form of republican public identity mediated by the technology of print, Sherman explains the *Spectator* as providing a new form of private identity organized by the literary form of the diary. He describes the 'diurnal form' of the periodical essay as an extension of the Protestant form of the diary, and by focusing on Mr. Spectator as 'the embodiment of a profoundly secretive self,' characterizes the *Spectator* as a new kind of 'reflective' paper that 'presents itself from the start more as monad than miscellany.'[51] Reading the paper as 'one voice delivering one discourse, usually on one topic,' Sherman presents the *Spectator* as providing the means to produce a model of the person based on passive reading, not republican activity: 'To read Mr. Spectator's daily self-rendering will be in some sense to compose it, to inhabit it, and even to recognize and accept his public prose as a comprehensive account of oneself; Mr. Spectator's public journal becomes a surrogate version of, or substitute for, the reader's private diary.'[52] While one could quibble about whether diary writing was in decline during the *Spectator*'s run (probably just the opposite), Sherman's larger point is that the *Spectator* should be understood as a vehicle of a new kind of identity, one based on a literary technology of 'self-recording prose.'[53] But though the diary certainly defined a form of modernity, it was not the only one. Reading the *Spectator*'s regular publication and eidolon as 'features of a diary, but of a diary turned inside out,' Sherman is perhaps being too clever: 'The *Spectator* read like an essay, came out like a daily newspaper, and looked like one too in its typeface and general design.'[54] The question that should follow this seems to be not, how is an essay like a diary, but what does it mean that the *Spectator* is an essay and one that looks like a newspaper?

Instead of a register of republicanism, organized by the ancient *polis*, I understand the *Spectator*'s social imaginary as informed by a modern civil society. And rather than the Puritan form of the diary, organized by the relations of a person to God, the *Spectator* explained itself as an essay, a form organized by the relations between two agents in conversation. Addison and Steele used the genre of the 'miscellany' to articulate a 'technology of publicity' structured by social dependencies, and articulated the terms of a civil, urban, and secular public structured by the essay, a literary form adapted to grasp a modernity defined by the associational dynamics of the city.

The mutually conditioning developments of a public sphere structured by commerce and sociability, and a civil ethos informed by conversation and politeness, depend on the experience of the modern city, as David Shields notes in his use of the *Spectator* as an example of 'Belles Lettres and the Arenas of Metropolitan Conversation': 'When Addison and Steele adopted a club as a mask for the *Spectator*, the friendly, conversational intimacy of belles lettres became the means by which an anonymous readership was recruited into a sense of print fellowship.'[55] Shields offers a compelling account of *what* happened, but his terms do not explain *how* it happened. He argues that the technology of print mediated the new ethos of sociability through a literature of Shaftesburyan 'private society.'[56] Yet in his discussion he recognizes the limits of this account: 'The possibility that conversation can be an open-ended exercise of social play is advanced in Shaftesburyan aesthetics, yet Shaftesbury envisions this occurring only in private companies when sociability is grounded in friendship.'[57] Shaftesbury's formal imaginary refers to ancient ideals that he uses to present an alternative to, and an argument with, the modernity that informs Addison and Steele's. His writing is organized by what Klein calls 'a gentlemanly scene of conversation,' one imagined in the country, a metonym for a conception of human relations formed by the polis, classical virtue, and their eighteenth-century ideological equivalent, landed property.[58] This was a republican project in the fully classical sense, based on an ontology informed by ancient stoic philosophy, a politics structured by land, and a resistance to (even repugnance for) modern philosophy. A remarkably pure version of ancienneté – 'post-courtly' and 'post-godly' but premodern – Shaftesbury's were the politics and philosophy of nostalgia, preserving a version of ancient ontology in the coolly abstracted air of the fading country Whigs.[59]

Klein discusses 'the language of politeness' as providing 'conceptual organization to various forms and levels of social and cultural life,' and with this hinge of Whiggish politeness, he connects Shaftesbury's project to Addison and Steele's.[60] But for Shaftesbury 'politeness' expresses a classical order of real Forms: real estate is guaranteed by an ideology based on a realist ontology, which in turn provides the terms with which to critique the associational epistemology that structures mobile property. And it is these latter dynamics that organize Addison and Steele's modern and urban conversational ethos. Formed not by ancient virtue but by modern politeness, not by the structure of the *polis* but that of the city, not by real estate but by commerce, and not with reference to a real condition of value but one derived from the processes of exchange – the mode of the periodical essay is structurally cognate with the spaces that distinguish it from Shaftesbury's political imaginary. Shaftesbury's *Characteristics* appeared during the *Spectator*'s initial run (March 1711) and the two works present contemporary but differently conceived versions of the meeting of new technologies, literary forms, and political imaginaries. Rather than considering Shaftesbury's project one of modern politeness, I understand Shaftesbury as a good example of the uses of print to express the conditions of republicanism. Shaftesbury does what Warner says the *Spectator* does: he defines a conception of the virtuous gentleman based on the abstract independence guaranteed by the disembodiment of print. The significance of this republican use of print, though, is not bound up with the periodical press. Rather, the nexus of republicanism and the press in early eighteenth-century England is marked by Shaftesbury's highly crafted, exclusive, and expensive editions of the *Characteristics* – a use of this technology distinct from, and opposed to, the *Spectator*'s widely disseminated and self-consciously inclusive papers.[61]

For Shaftesbury the 'summit of polite philosophy was the dialogue.'[62] His form depends on a mimesis of bodies in order to create the conditions for disembodied thought, while Addison's form is mimetic of an abstract form of relations in order to create the conditions for social negotiation between real people. In contrast to Shaftesbury's employment of the dialogue, Addison used the essay to develop a modern form based on the *structure* of friendship, but not necessarily the *fact* of it. The essay provided the mechanism by which a private ethos of friendship could become a public discourse of sociability. Shields comments that 'Coffeehouses had in their own aestheticization displaced nobility from persons and located it in manners and things ... Nobility transmuted by sociability became gentility.'[63] In a similar way, I understand Addison and Steele to have displaced conversation from the form of Montaigne's *Essays*, which imitate the dynamics of friendship, to an ethos of politeness by displacing it from persons and locating its structure in manners: friendship transmuted by sociability became urbanity. The essay assumes a relationship between reader and writer structured by an *ethos* of friendship, but this does not necessarily require the *event* of friendship. Politeness is an abstraction of the dynamic of friendship, a way to treat strangers as friends, and urbanity construes this as the *formal* condition of living in the city, the formal means with which to understand these new urban relations.[64]

With the *Spectator*, what had been private for Shaftesbury becomes public, what had been 'retired' is 'canvass'd in every Assembly,' and what had been based on a formal structure of independence and classical virtue, comes to be based on a modern form structured by dependence, interaction, and pleasure.[65] Through the 'Method' of an 'Essay Writer,' the *Spectator* articulated a kind of abstraction through which to understand the social person, a model of the self defined not by the private spaces of 'closets,' but by a public of 'assemblies':

> I am amazed that the press should only be made use of in this Way by News-Writers, and the Zealots of Parties; as if it were not more advantageous to Mankind to be instructed in Wisdom and Virtue, than in Politicks; and to be made good Fathers, Husbands, and Sons, than Counsellours and Statesmen. Had the Philosophers and great Men of Antiquity, who took such Pains in order to instruct Mankind, and leave the World wiser and better than they found it; had they, I say, been possessed of the Art of Printing, there is no Question but that they would have made such an Advantage of it, in dealing out their Lectures to the Public. Our common Prints would be of great Use were they thus calculated to diffuse good Sense through the Bulk of the People, to clear up the Understanding, animate their Minds with Virtue, dissipate the Sorrows of a heavy Heart, or unbend the Mind from its more severe Employments with innocent Amusements.[66]

Using the press to provide a 'Knowledge' no longer 'bound up in Books, and kept in Libraries and Retirements,' but 'obtruded upon the Publick,' 'canvass'd in every Assembly, and exposed upon every Table,' the *Spectator* both defines the structure and fills in the content of that 'Publick.'[67] Articulating an ethos based on making the 'common Prints' more common – one based on the roles of 'Fathers, Husbands, and Sons,' not 'Counsellours and Statesmen' – Addison describes the public in terms of the manners of 'Assemblies' and 'Tables,' the interactions of the civil and domestic spheres, not those of the solitary spaces of 'Libraries and Retirements.' This public is secular but not republican, and it involves a mode of privacy but not one based on Protestant structures. The *Spectator* gives the terms with which to understand a self defined by its relations with other people, and that structure of mundane interdependence grounds what the divine or virtuous structures of religion and politics had grounded before.

The infrastructure of the press was a condition of articulating a civil model of personhood defined by its participation in a network of social relations. And it is the exigencies of this new technology, the need to sell papers to readers, that offer the terms with which to begin to define that new ethos. Pleasure, curiosity, the restless desire for novelty, and the imagination are explained as the social glue – the terms of participation – by which a public defined by the reach of the press is held together. Instead of understanding social roles in terms of virtue (either classical or Christian), Addison makes a virtue out of the limitations of his literary form, defining a new ethos in terms of the essay's model of reading. The imperatives of the press – 'that [readers'] Virtue and Discretion may not be short transient intermitting Starts of Thought, I have resolved to refresh their Memories from Day to Day'[68] – suggest a new kind of reading, and a new kind of reader to be addressed:

> Those who publish their Thoughts in distinct Sheets, and as it were Piece-meal ... must immediately fall into our Subject, and treat every Part of it in a lively Manner, or our Papers are thrown by as dull and insipid: Our Matter must lie close together, and either be wholly new in itself, or in the Turn it receives from our Expressions ... notwithstanding some Papers may be made up of broken hints and irregular Sketches, it is often expected that every Sheet should be a kind of Treatise, and make out in Thought what it wants in Bulk ... The ordinary Writers of Morality prescribe to their Readers after the Galenick Way; their Medicines are made up in large Quantities. An Essay Writer must practice in the Chymical Method, and give the Virtue of a full Draught in a few Drops.[69]

With its 'lively manner' and promise of novelty, such 'irregular' writing is directed to the reader's curiosity and pleasure, and it invites – depends on – the participation of the reader in piecing together what is not fully said, reconstituting the thought from 'broken hints.' Addison is repeating here a dynamic that he had described in an earlier essay on Virgil's *Georgics* (1697):

> Virgil ... loves to suggest a truth indirectly, and without giving us a full and open view of it, to let us see just so much as will naturally lead the imagination into all the parts that lie concealed. This is wonderfully diverting to the understanding, thus to receive a precept, that enters as it were through a by-way, and to apprehend an Idea that draws a whole train after it. For here the Mind, which is always delighted with its own discoveries, only takes the hint from the Poet, and seems to work out the rest by the strength of her own faculties.[70]

This 'indirect' form is directed to the restlessness of the imagination; the motive of such reading is simple curiosity and its effect is 'discovery' and 'the strength of [the mind's] own faculties,' perhaps even a discovery *of* the mind's faculties. A mode of reading that depends on the reader's active participation, the 'Chymical Method' works with (and on) the reader's own proclivities and experiences. Coded as modern, based on experimental knowledge, and not on the authority of the ancients like 'the Galenick Way,' Addison's 'Chymical' 'Morality' works like the epistemology of empiricism, depending on the reader's own experience to confirm and validate the text.

As with Montaigne's parallel between the 'commerces' of reading and friendship in 'Of Three Commerces,' Addison describes the exigencies of his form in terms of the structure and pleasures of conversation between two human agents. Oriented to an interdependent exploration of the world and oneself, and articulating an alternative to forms defined by the republican ideal of independence and the formal structure of the 'Religion of the Closet,' the *Spectator* is structured by a formal imperative of mutual dependency that depends on the passions and curiosity stimulated by the press.[71] In turn, through that network of interaction between text and audience, new terms are developed with which to explain what's unique in that public sphere.

At the beginning of this chapter I discussed the emergence of a new literary form out of the mutually defining innovations of the metropolitan press and the modern public sphere; the *Spectator* emerged as an effect of social developments and offered the modern city an indigenous form of representation. In turn, a new social form developed out of this literary innovation. The periodical essay offered 'a new way of Thinking,' a new way to understand those metropolitan spaces. In 'The Present State of Wit' (1711), John Gay writes that Addison and Steele have

> indeed rescued [Learning] out of the hands of pedants and fools, and discovered the true method of making it amiable and lovely to all mankind. In the dress he gives it, it is a most welcome guest at tea-tables and assemblies, and is relished and caressed by the merchants on the Change ... his writings have set all our Wits and Men of Letters on a new way of Thinking.[72]

Gay emphasizes a particular *way* of thinking, and, along these lines, I read Addison's famous comment about taking philosophy 'out of closets,' the spaces of privacy, and bringing it 'into assemblies,' the spaces of conversation, as a comment on analytic method as well as social function: 'It was said of Socrates, that he brought Philosophy down from Heaven, to inhabit among Men; and I shall be ambitious to have it said of me, that I have brought Philosophy out of Closets and Libraries, Schools and Colleges, to dwell in Clubs and Assemblies, at Tea-Tables, and in Coffee-Houses.'[73] Addison's truncated history of philosophy offers the *Spectator* as a continuation of Socrates' project, as philosophy was moved down from 'Heaven' to 'Men' it is now moved out of 'Schools' and into 'Assemblies.' This double movement suggests that Socrates' original humanizing of knowledge has been highjacked by scholars and in turn needs to be freed from their exclusive haunts. Addison hopes to be remembered as a Socratic figure, reclaiming philosophy, if not from heaven, then from those who claim an undue authority, who speak with divine voices.

Addison's claim to supercede 'colleges and schools' marks him as an heir to humanism, and his humanist ambition inscribes itself in the statement of it, couched in a buried quotation from Cicero's *Tusculan Disputations*.[74] Addison quotes Cicero's claim to be Socratic, mimicking his method in the citation of it. (Humanist pedagogy works by making models one's own.) In Addison's source, as in Cicero's sources, Socrates taught how to ground philosophy in conversation, in civil exchange, precisely by applying philosophy to the spaces of such association:

> from the ancient days down to the time of Socrates ... philosophy dealt with numbers and movements, with the problem whence all things came, or whither they returned, and zealously inquired into the size of the stars, the spaces that divided them, their courses and all celestial phenomena; Socrates on the other hand was the first to call philosophy down from the heavens and set her in the cities of men and bring her also into their homes and compel her to ask questions about morality and things good and evil.[75]

Cicero describes a change of topic that entails a change of method. In turning from what Cicero's Greek sources described as 'speculation' about 'the so-called "Cosmos" of the Professors,' Socrates is said to have introduced a new mode of philosophy, a particular kind of inquiry with a limited set of possible claims.[76] Because speculation on the heavens is unresolveable, as illustrated by the endless debates about cosmology, Socrates' 'conversation was ever of human things.'[77] This new method implies a new space, a human world that is understood neither in relation to the cosmos nor by 'divine' methods of speculation, as Plutarch writes: 'He was the first to show that life at all times and all parts, in all experiences and activities, universally admits philosophy.'[78] Likewise for Cicero's Socrates, the human world becomes the object of a knowledge that is formed by the experience of that world alone, displacing the methods of speculation – 'numbers and movement' – that had been the province of earlier (Pythagorean) philosophy. For Socrates, the ontological commitment of knowledge is grounded in the process of dialogic exchange, and there is no privileged knowledge outside the process of knowing (or trying to know). The *Spectator* construes this dynamic in terms of the modern city, as Addison updates Cicero's Socratic method and adopts his 'many-sided method of discussion' with 'varied' subjects – a varied method to match its various subjects – to explain the new urban spaces and their ideal urbane voice.[79] Philosophy is redefined as the mutually correcting and confirming process of communication, offering a knowledge organized by the dynamics of mundane conversation that define the modern city.[80]

The ancient Socratic imperative is to look at where one is, a classicism that enjoins one always to be modern. Addison and Steele develop a new way to understand the emerging urban spaces based on this Socratic method. Directed not only *to* the practices of the modern city, but also structured *by* such practices, the *Spectator* provides a new mode of reflection. The movement from 'Closets' and 'Schools' to 'Assemblies' and 'Coffee-Houses' is at once an institutional and a methodological shift from the places and methods of solitary thought to those of sociability, crossing the space between two conceptions of knowledge and authority. The former, the institutional and formal locus of theology, imagines knowledge on a model of the relation between person and general (divine) law – with particulars distant shadows of the real; the latter, a secular site and form, imagines knowledge on a model of the relation between person and contingent event – with generalizations distant shadows of the real. This alternate form, articulated by Addison and Steele in the *Spectator*, comes to serve as the structure with which to challenge ontologies of divine – or natural – law, and offers the formal conditions with which to express an epistemology grounded in the interactive dynamics of human association, 'commerce,' and 'conversation.'

In 1714 Joseph Collet wrote to his daughter of the *Spectator*: 'Next to the Bible you cannot read any writings so much to your purpose for the improvement of your mind and the conduct of your Actions.'[81]

Collet's comments suggest that the *Spectator* starts where the Bible stops, articulating a distinct sphere of *social* relations that are not defined by the duty of religion or the obligation of politics, but by an ethos formed in the new public sphere.[82] The essay provided a formal structure for this new ethos, the means by which it could be represented, a literary methodology with which to explain a social world coordinated by the 'looseness and freedom' of 'conversation.'

To claim that the essay provided the formal conditions by which the public sphere could be understood seems to suggest that literary form has some necessary relation to its content or its ethos. There were of course Protestant and republican periodical essays; and to say that the form inherently contains an ethic is surely to misunderstand both form and ethics.[83] My claim is, rather, that the relations between this particular literary form and this particular social formation were mutually defining. To echo Alastair Fowler's statement that 'kind tends to mode,' the essay form tended to the mode of politeness, an ethos of conversation that defined the conditions of participation in the emergent urban spaces.[84] This was an accidental confluence, a contingent meeting, but one that had an inherent historical logic – a logic that can be explained as a way of showing, not the unfolding of history along a determined track, but its specific unfolding along the track it did take. I understand this to be a three-part process, one that evolves along the axes of interaction between the city and the press, the press and the essay, and finally between the essay and the city. Located at the nexus of the mutually defining technology of the press and the emerging social spaces of the city, Steele and Addison developed a distinctly modern literary form that they characterized as an essay, offering a new use of this literary form. The formal imperatives of the essay were then used to explain the distinctively *social* structure of relations of the modern city.

This new form of social coordination (politeness) is usually interpreted as an effect of a new systemic coordination, a function of ideology greasing the tracks of the market's development. In these terms literature is seen as a functionary of the system, and the pathos of modernity is that systems' functions replace the organic ones of everyday life; people become cogs in the machine and agency becomes the effect of systems. But what's asserted as a historical fact is perhaps only a result of a methodological assumption, a choice about the process, content, and meaning of modernity. Literary critics have embraced a strategy of critical analysis that understands modern reflection as defined by a limited conception of instrumental reason.[85] But throughout the history of modernity, claims have been made for a different form of reflection, one like that of Montaigne's essay, based on a communicative dynamic of mutuality and a shared assumption of agency – one organized by a mode of reading in which both text and reader are accorded agency. Our critical choice to privilege the formal imperatives of systems (the market's structure) over the formal imperatives of the social makes such claims immediately suspect, topics for a suspicious hermeneutics. But we may have it backwards. We depend on an abstraction of system to explain social relations, but it may be that a social abstraction of human relations is required to understand the abstract system of the market at all.

I'm arguing that it is productive to draw a theoretical distinction between the structures of politeness and those of the market, one that accounts for the self-understanding of the early eighteenth century. Our critical habit of collapsing the period's broadly social category of 'commerce' into a restricted economic sense mistakes a crucial historical evolution. A systemic theory of the market was an *effect* of post-traditional social thinking. The history of the development of a market system passes through a post-traditional articulation of a sphere of mundane relations in which social bonds are articulated as distinct from theological (Protestant) and political (republican) commitments.

Only when the logic of *pre*-systemic social structures is grasped can their *proto*-systemic place in the histories of systems development be understood. First society was reimagined as a distinct field of relations with its own dynamics and methodological imperatives – the moment of the communicative form of the essay I have discussed in this chapter – and then a subsequent articulation of an economic system took off through the development of distinct analytic tools, ones that were derived from the models used to explain those new social relations. The purpose of post-traditional social thinking was not, first, to explain the mystery of new economic relations, but to comprehend the new social relations of the modern city, and literary history is integral to explaining this because the formal tools of 'commerce' and 'conversation' that were used to do this had a specific provenance in the essay.

The essay offered the formal conditions of an alternative to a political imaginary construed in terms of the spaces of the country, the *polis*, or the *res publica*, and structured a different model of identity than one construed in terms of the relations of a subject to God, to law, or to a model of reason defined in those terms. I read the *Spectator*, finally, as humanist but not republican, as commercial but not capitalist, and as modern but not structured by a Protestant ethic.[86] Providing the formal condition by which the metropolitan world became self-reflective, the periodical essay offered the dynamics of the modern city itself as a model of understanding the modern world.

5
Fleeting Habitations in *Tom Jones*

Ford Madox Ford abhorred Fielding and bitchily remarked, 'In the case of *Tom Jones*, the story is so negligible and the incidents are invented with such listlessness that we have to regard the tale as a mere string on which are threaded the pearls of Mr. Fielding's – cousin to the Right Honorable the Earl of Denbigh, Mr. Fielding, the man about town's, wit.'[1] If his evaluation of the story is not shared by most critics, Ford's sense of the relative lack of weight given to it in the novel remains a critical annoyance. Critics tend to find the significance of *Tom Jones* in the order of its tale, whether construed in Christian or neo-classical or conservative terms, and they consequently also tend to regret, or at least need to justify, the 'pearls of wit' cast throughout it.[2] The intrusive witty voice indicates Fielding's failure to adopt the formal realism and historical referentiality that characterize novels for many critics.[3] And those critics who have not resisted that voice outright have sought to manage it by personifying it or taking it as a crib sheet on the themes of the story, redeeming what made *Tom Jones* objectionable to Ford by folding the 'wit' back into the 'tale' and reading the former in terms of the latter.[4]

I think Ford's right. I don't agree with his insinuation that Fielding's social position governs his authorial choices or share his disdain for the kind of novel Fielding writes, but I too find that the overwhelming force of the wit – the intelligence, the banter, and the humor – in *Tom Jones* does indeed swamp the narrative to such a degree that the story seems occasion for the wit rather than the opposite. Lockwood has a nicer way of saying this: Fielding 'retains the essayist's privilege of talking freely in his own person' and is perhaps writing something as much like an essay as a novel.[5] Fielding himself remarks that the 'initial Essays which we have prefixed to the historical Matter' are 'essentially necessary to this kind of Writing.'[6] If this has caused trouble for historians of the novel, it also suggests that *Tom Jones* belongs in a history of the essay. In this chapter I approach *Tom Jones* from this perspective, another example of an exaptation of the essay in – or indeed as – a new genre. In the previous chapters I examined two distinct ways the essay, originally a tool of humanist reading, was adopted to serve new purposes. Boyle recommended the essay as a tool of experimental natural philosophy that would enable a skill of participatory reflection and open-ended exploration, and Addison and Steele used the genre to mediate a social and sociable public defined by commerce, conversation, and association. In each case, the literacy modeled and enabled by essays – a 'digestive' and adaptive mode of reading – drives a new project. Similarly, Fielding puts the essay at the center of *Tom Jones*, periodically punctuating the narrative with essays and more generally making the literacy enabled by the genre integral to his novel.

Throughout the seventeenth and early eighteenth century in Britain, the essay served as a tool of reading. Essays enable the feedback loops that drive print culture as readers register their engagements with the texts and commonplaces of their culture in a form that invites further readers and further readings. The essays in *Tom Jones* do the same thing, offering a space in the novel dedicated to that kind of response. Fielding glibly compares his essays to the Latin tags that served as epigraphs for each *Spectator*. As the latter guaranteed that imitators would know at least 'one Sentence in the learned Languages,' so, he writes, 'I have secured myself from the Imitation of those who are utterly incapable of any Degree of Reflection, and whose Learning is not equal to an Essay.'[7] Anxious to distinguish it from the other 'Romances, Novels, Plays and Poems, with which the [book] Stalls abound,' Fielding says his work is distinguished, 'marked' or 'stamped,' by essays and the learning and reflection associated with them.[8] An examination of the essays in the novel, then, must start with the work of 'learning' in *Tom Jones*.[9]

Fielding lays out four 'qualifications' for his 'Order of Historians': genius (invention and judgment), learning, conversation, and a good heart.[10] These form an interlocking chain: learning trains genius, while conversation finishes learning. 'Learning' is the art by which one develops one's capacities or, in Fielding's figure, by which one learns how to use the 'tools' of one's 'genius.'[11] Learning 'fits tools for use' by offering writers rules to guide them and materials to work on. Fielding says it shouldn't be necessary to prove that Tools are of no Service to a Workman, when they are not sharpened by Art, or when he wants Rules to direct him in his Work, or hath no Matter to work upon. All these Uses are supplied by Learning: For Nature can only furnish us with Capacity, or, as I have chose to illustrate it, with the Tools of our Profession; Learning must fit them for Use, must direct them in it; and lastly, must contribute, Part at least, of the Materials. A competent Knowledge of History and of the Belles Lettres, is here absolutely necessary; and without this Share of Knowledge at least, to affect the Character of a Historian, is as vain as to endeavour at building a House without Timber or Mortar, or Brick or Stone.[12]

There's a dense and interesting knot in this account: a book is like a building constructed, or perhaps reconstructed, out of the available materials of its culture, and those materials train one in the use of the tools necessary to that construction. It's like saying the board teaches the hammer how to be a hammer by being hammered. This seems less redundant if the 'tool' is reflection; the capacity to reflect is learned by engaging the materials that register other reflections, other texts of 'History' and 'Belles Lettres.' In these terms, Fielding's work doesn't seek to replace or cancel out the other books on the stalls but rather models a practice of engaging them, a practice that realizes a process embedded in them. *Tom Jones* is self-consciously built of books, like Homer's and Milton's, that are in turn informed by 'all the Learning of their Times.'[13] Fielding's account of learning as both providing 'Materials' and fitting capacities for 'Use' reminds us that such buildings are not simply built but inhabited – at least fleetingly, as when Molly fights a mock-Homeric battle or Tom's expulsion is registered momentarily as a second Fall (or, more exactly, invokes Milton's rewriting of that originary text).[14] Such fleeting habitations, to adapt Alter's nice phrase, at once use, or re-use, those old forms and self-consciously enact, or re-enact, their skill in learning, sharpening one's 'tools' as one negotiates the echoes that reverberate through the layered texts.[15] *Tom Jones* faces both backwards and outwards, reassembling the materials of its printscape in order to transmit to its readers a skill that is encoded in those materials. It offers readers an opportunity to learn in turn, to practice in a text densely layered with 'all the learning of its time' the skills required to engage a world densely layered with texts of all kinds, all ages, and all pedigrees.

The chapter that introduces Sophia (book 4, chapter 1) offers an example of this kind of self-conscious building with the materials of learning. Fielding rehearses a wide range of his culture's resources, and provides a kind of map of his culture, or perhaps an x-ray – and, as with an x-ray, seeing the hidden structure doesn't inhibit the functioning of the mechanism. The chapter self-consciously explores the question of what's behind the scenes as well as the efficacy of forms that function even after, or perhaps even via, such demystification. Fielding distinguishes his work, on the one hand, from unnatural romances, 'Productions, not of Nature, but of distempered Brains,' and, on the other, from the unformed facts of 'modern Historians' whose works, like newspapers, are merely true, tiresome, and soporific.[16] Between these extremes of the unnatural and the unformed, Fielding's work offers sections that relieve the boredom of the latter without the extravagance of the former: 'That our Work, therefore, might be in no Danger of being likened to the Labours of these Historians, we have taken every Occasion of interspersing through the whole sundry Similes, Descriptions, and other kind of poetical Embellishments.' In this particular case, such special effects are deployed to introduce the heroine and 'prepare the Mind of the Reader for her Reception, by filling it with every pleasing Image, which we can draw from the Face of Nature.'[17]

Of course nothing is ever quite so direct in *Tom Jones*, and before we actually get to the promised images in the next chapter, our minds are prepared with a short dissertation on precedents for this kind of thing, starting with playwrights, who introduce their heroes with drums and trumpets, and moving to the theater owners who are 'in on this Secret' and add 'a large Troop of half a dozen Scene-shifters' to the aural flourish – a clever conflation of the effect (caused by a troop) with its workings (caused by a stage crew). This is illustrated by a story from the theater, behind-the-scenes gossip about an old colleague of Fielding's playing King Pyrrhus, which in turn is used to explain the political practice of the Lord Mayor's annual procession in which 'several Pageants precede his Pomp' to add a sense of 'Reverence.'[18] The theatrical monarch leads to a remark on the theatricality of majesty, and at this point Fielding comments on the power of such effects, even for those, like him and now like us, who are let 'in on the secret' and see behind the scenes:

> Nay, I must confess, that even I myself, who am not remarkably liable to be captivated with Show, have yielded not a little to the Impressions of much preceding State. When I have seen a Man strutting in a Procession, after others whose Business was only to

walk before him, I have conceived a higher Notion of his Dignity, than I have felt on seeing him in a common Situation.[19]

This complex series of moves rapidly shifts the grounds of reference from writing to theater to politics and all in order to isolate and grasp an effect that will be redeployed in writing. Fielding may offer his own testimony about the power of such shows to subtly underline (or undermine) the effect he's creating. By inhabiting it, he naively (or ironically) models the kind of response he wants his reader to have too, performing the force of even a deconstructed show and challenging us perhaps to deconstruct his performance in turn, or perhaps to take his point. The rhetoric assumes a personified voice within an examination of the power of personifications. But even noting the effect (and taking the lesson), I do take that testimony at face value; such performances do have a power within them, an 'office,' that works even when recognized as such. (You aren't married by the woman who serves as the judge but by the office of the judge.) The effect works, the voice says, even if the secret is known, and seeing how the strings move doesn't preclude being moved.[20]

Fielding's testimonial about the effect shows have even on those in on the secret frames the figure of Flora, a basket-woman or a goddess, or a figure that demonstrates how easily the one can morph into the other.

But there is one Instance that comes exactly up to my Purpose. This is the Custom of sending on a Basket-woman, who is to precede the Pomp at a Coronation, and to strew the Stage with Flowers, before the great Personages begin their Procession. The Antients would certainly have invoked the Goddess *Flora* for this Purpose, and it would have been no Difficulty for their Priests or Politicians to have persuaded the People of the real Presence of the Deity, though a plain Mortal had personated her, and performed her Office. But we have no such Design of imposing on our Reader, and therefore those who object to Heathen Theology, may, if they please change our Goddess into the above-mentioned Basket-woman. Our Intention, in short, is to introduce our Heroine with the utmost Solemnity in our Power, with an Elevation of Stile, and all other Circumstances proper to raise the Veneration of our Reader.[21]

That an account of 'poetical Embellishments,' or flowers of rhetoric, ends with flowers strewn by a basket-woman who personifies a goddess, is just the last in a long series of transferals, and it sums up the chapter's rapid-fire switching of rhetorical, theatrical, and political registers, each of which gives way to the others but never fully. The effect of the flowers finally *doesn't* depend on the success of the impersonation. Fielding's figure is prepared in the same way, the mechanism exposed in order to both remark and reuse its effect. Telling doesn't disrupt showing here. The quick gloss of 'Priests' by 'Politicians' works in the standard enlightenment way, seeing through the 'priestcraft' to the politics and recognizing the efficacy of theology, or superstition, in mundane terms. (Similarly, Fielding speculates that Homer may not have believed the theology of the figures he used, which could be read as either a subtle Christianizing of the poet – he sees through false religion – or a subtle philosophe-izing of him – he sees through all religion.)[22] Old goddesses survive as political devices and literary tropes. Like the ancients, Fielding will invoke a goddess, Flora, to introduce his heroine in the next chapter, but in using this admittedly dated figure (dated, though, as both past and present, an occasion to mark a continuity of literary as well as political uses), he suggests that 'preparing the mind' of the reader is less a kind of mystification than a series of exposures that demonstrates the workings of a still-functioning mechanism.[23] Explicating these effects in instrumental terms doesn't dispel them, and this essay about how they work gives way in the next chapter to an actual staging of them. Such effects do indeed introduce the heroine to a reader now well-positioned not just to see through her pomp but to appreciate it and so recognize her role – a precipitate of goddess and basket-woman who will act in the novel as the object of a devotion (Tom's, the author's, perhaps ours) which is no more reducible to one of those referents, goddess or woman, than love is reducible to hunger.[24]

The next chapter starts with a self-consciously flowery passage about Flora.[25] I'm not sure if 'the lovely Flora' who is called forth by Zephyrus here is a heightened, 'Sublime,' version of the Sophia of the next paragraph, 'breathing Sweetness from her rosy Lips, and darting Brightness from her Sparkling Eyes, the lovely *Sophia* comes.'[26] If so, Sophia is momentarily personified by the sublimed rhetoric (she's introduced as the sublime Flora in a passage that serves as an ironic reminder of the power of such rhetorical flowers), and she inhabits her role as fully as the actor of the previous chapter inhabits his (he's described simply as King Pyrrhus). In this case, the demystifying, modernizing, or satirically deflating dynamic of replacing the goddess by the basket-woman would be directly echoed in the description of Sophia; she finally steps out of the figure simply as flesh and blood, the woman behind the special effect of a theatrical (or theological) goddess. Another way to read Flora would be as figuring the morning, or perhaps as the morning flowers that Sophia is like. If this is so, there'd be a further transformation between the two chapters, a shift from the goddess who spread the flowers to flowers themselves, or from the divinization of the natural phenomenon to the naturalization of the divine. In this case, when 'the lovely *Sophia* comes' she is associated with the flowers themselves (like those the goddess/basket-woman throws) in a way that finally bypasses both personifications by focusing on the natural phenomenon they figure: Sophia is as colorful, bright, and sweet as flowers. (This could also figure her as the flowers of rhetoric – she's figured as figuration, or perhaps as the way flowers grow from ground to figure.) Whichever way the elaborate invocation is parsed, the effect is announced, 'So charming may she now appear,' and we appreciate at once the 'Show' and how it's done – and perhaps the former more for recognizing the latter.[27]

After we've received this lesson about moving through old texts, old forms (and old formalizations), seeing both how they worked and reusing them for new versions of that kind of work, Fielding continues with a quick series of references to beauty that at once map his culture's conventional terrain of the beautiful (in both art and women) and ironically surpass it. We're given a list of representations of famous beauties and famous representations of beauty (the latter of course guaranteeing the former; famous beauties are so because there are representations of them). But this naturally fails to capture Sophia's beauty, and after all this false compare, the passage proceeds to a novelistic blazon that describes Sophia both in novelistic terms, only daughter of Western, and in poetic ones, a self-aware blazon that piggy-backs on others by Suckling and Donne.[28] Rothstein suggests that Fielding stages his allusions in order to dispel their authority and claim it for himself; the novel 'frees itself from tyranny of the pre-established' and 'Fielding proffers his own world alone as the "real."'[29] I don't think, though, that we're supposed to imagine Sophia as *really* more beautiful than all these representations, or indeed as realer than them, but rather to think about both the power and limits of representing beauty – the power and limits of which suggest something about the necessity of a response to realize the effects of representation, and perhaps the necessity of love to realize beauty.

In all of this comically overloaded description, Fielding toys with us by offering less a description than a catalogue of ways of describing.

I take this as both a realization of the poetic embellishments announced in the previous chapter and a continuation of the lesson on how to use them. Sophia emerges at the end of this long string of descriptions as a vanishing point beyond all description and against which all descriptions pale. This is most noticeable when Fielding, in a lovely homage, compares Sophia to his dead wife: 'most of all, she resembled one whose Image never can depart from my Breast,' a line that points to (and can only point to) a limit beyond which expression cannot go, and that undercuts all the other descriptions by reminding us that beauty is finally housed in the heart, not the eyes.[30] If there's a hint of haunting here – Sophia haunted by Charlotte or Fielding haunted by her memory – it's finally as fleeting as every other momentary reference. I read the effect of these rapid passages in terms of the work, the speed, and the care of reading they require instead of any given step they take. The chapter ends on such a note by refocusing attention from the outside frame to the 'Inhabitant' within, praising Sophia's 'Mind' and noting that no amount of description will help you know this. You'll have to find out about it, like love, for yourself: 'Nay, it is Kind of tacit Affront to our Reader's Understanding, and may also rob him of that Pleasure which he will receive in forming his own Judgment of her Character.'[31] (There's a generous impulse in refusing to submit Sophia's mind to anatomization and in suggesting that all her beauty is only the starting point of recognizing her.) At the end of her long introduction Sophia is thoroughly framed by pomp and poetical embellishments that finally add up only to the opportunity to do what we do with every other character in the novel, judge her by her actions. But along the way she has accumulated, let's say, the scents of all these flowers (and the sense of all these figures), which not only do suggest a grandeur appropriate to her role as the beloved, but also remind us of the power of such roles. An instrumental understanding of the effects of such figures doesn't cancel those effects. And likewise, the preparation for the role Sophia will play in the novel not only exposes the conventions of tradition but harnesses their effects, renewing them by using them and indeed even by remarking them.

Sophia is like a flower. She's like Flora, or the flowers that Flora spreads, or the basket-woman who spreads them. (Or perhaps even like the basket itself, woven of many fabrics, reweaving their strands into the texture of another text.) Or at least her description suggests how seamlessly all these possible descriptions can transform into each other simultaneously to uncover *and* realize the effect of Sophia. Rather than describing Sophia, or explaining an effect, or performing it, Fielding does all of these at once by overlaying many descriptions, many explanations, and many versions in a series of fleeting habitations. The style offers us a quick series of steps that leave us breathlessly running upstairs; we don't fully inhabit any single one of those steps but they do get us somewhere. The net effect is to tap the power even of what is superseded. Sophia, like Tom and like *Tom Jones*, is perhaps less a character than an occasion to try on and test out the culture's particular cluster of representational resources. These don't so much hide reality as, in their overwriting and undercutting of each other, reveal the many faces of a reality irreducible to one representation, or one kind of representation. In this spirit, *Tom Jones* doesn't finally choose between any of the representations it cycles through, and it only ironically dismisses what it comically amasses. But it does so only after the figures have served to introduce the lovely Sophia through a process that may start with the demystification of traditional forms, but only in order to realize (or re-realize) their effects as appropriate to a figure made, thereby, worthy of attention and perhaps devotion.

These passages are slowed down for analytic purposes, but the effect of these chapters, like Fielding's prose throughout *Tom Jones*, is *speed*. The style is a fast and witty trade in similitudes that don't ever quite add up to a complete description as much as offer multiple approaches to the characters, their motives, and their actions. In turn the energy of our reading feeds back into the characters we read about. If the characters are defined by a series of approximations, those images are blurred and blended (like a flipbook or pictures in motion) by the speed and energy of their movement and the speed and energy of our moving through them.

The effect of multiplying references corresponds to the multiple motivations with which Fielding at once satirizes his characters and challenges his readers. Applying Empson's 'double irony' and its both/and logic, Paulson notes, 'When Fielding says that Black George, who has just stolen Tom's money, really does love Tom, he is saying a number of different things – that Black George has persuaded himself by rationalization that he loves Tom, but also that there is a sense in which Black George really does love him, even if at the moment he loves money more.'[32] When we're ironically offered multiple motives to explain an action, the ones we pass through don't disappear completely: 'the very recording of multiple motives and qualifying clauses invites the reader to embrace them in his assessment.'[33] We don't simply reject what we see through.[34] When Sophia swoons 'from the

Sight of Blood, or from Fear of her Father, or for some other Reason,' the 'other' reason is the right one: seeing Tom bleeding.[35] But the stated reasons, a general queasiness about blood or fear of her father, are not completely wrong, just not exactly right. It's Tom's blood that scares Sophia, and the reason she can't admit that is because she doesn't want to contravene her father's wishes. We're immediately reminded of Western's prohibition against Sophia's marrying beneath her station, and his own mixed desires: 'He called [Tom] the Preserver of *Sophia*, and declared there was nothing, except her, or his Estate, which he would not give him; but upon Recollection, he afterwards excepted his *Fox-hounds.*'[36] Western *does* love Tom, *and* his estate (and even his daughter) and if he doesn't bring these all together it's because they're not fully compatible, but no less individually true for all that. The novel continually sustains this kind of complexity, and one of its ironies is that we do have to use the 'sagacity' that we're ironically invited to use. (Such 'sagacity' is the sarcastic compliment offered to our ability to place the last piece in the puzzle.)[37] As with the recognition that demystifying figures doesn't denude them of their power, the force of rationalizations isn't dispelled by correctly addressing their suppressed need. (Rationalizations are often constructed out of good reasons.)

At every level, *Tom Jones* is concerned with the multiple resources available to define a character or explain an action, and not with a final referent or a 'real' representation. In another well-known critical *topos*, Tom passes through a landscape of romance; it's springtime and he finds himself in 'a most delicious Grove' with breezes, murmuring waters, and nightingales.[38]

> In this Scene, so sweetly accommodated to Love, he meditated on his dear Sophia. While his wanton Fancy roved unbounded over all her Beauties, and his lively Imagination painted the charming Maid in various ravishing Forms, his warm Heart melted with Tenderness, and at length throwing himself on the Ground by the Side of a gently murmuring Brook, he broke forth into the following Ejaculation.[39]

At this moment of pause between paragraphs, the exact content of that ejaculate is perversely suspended, leaving us perhaps to imagine Tom in some ravishing forms that are analogous, as well as responsive, to those in which he imagines his beloved. But the continuation offers a sublimation of Tom's desire (though it could be that the romance rhetoric figures the orgasm rather than substitutes for it). In a paragraph of hyperbolic apostrophes, and many exclamation points, Tom recites the standard litany of devotion and constancy. And then is interrupted by Molly. I wonder if the next bit of dialogue could be intended doubly. 'Our Hero had his pen-knife in his Hand, which he had drawn for the before-mentioned Purpose, of carving on the Bark.'[40] The comma perhaps suggests a momentary, joking ambiguity about the referent of the previously mentioned purpose (the raptures that Sophia's name stimulates or the carving of the bark to which they lead), an ambiguity that raises a question about what Tom has in his hand.[41] Molly doesn't clear this up as much as continue to talk in innuendo when she 'cry'd out with a Smile, "you don't intend to kill me, Squire, I hope."'[42] If Tom's pen-knife doesn't figure his penis, it at least figures the rhetoric that at once expresses and sublimates his desire.[43] The passage has moved from a romance setting which 'accommodates' Tom's 'wanton Fancy' about Sophia to a romance apostrophe to the anti-romance of Tom's sexy encounter with Molly. Like the multiple figurations and the multiple motivations, this series of kinds of discourse doesn't resolve into a single one but plays on – and plays with – the complex overlays and undercuttings that define, in its complexity, the reality of the novel's printscape.

The recursive quality of Fielding's text has often been remarked. Van Ghent and Welsh have pointed out how sentences and descriptions can work like little versions of the plot.[44] Similarly, this passage could figure the project of the novel as it's construed by critics who see Fielding's satire as part of a modern project of deconstructing inherited forms in order finally and adequately to name the real those forms belie.[45] In these terms, sex with Molly is the real referent of the inflated discourse of romance. But I see Tom's motivations as co-existing in a meaningful complexity, an intertwining of romance and anti-romance that offers a choice we do *not* have to make. Just as Tom really does love Sophia and really is horny, the novel uses the forms of romance to do what those forms do alongside other forms that do other things. As with Flora, we can recognize the work of romance even if we no longer believe in it in the same way and choose to replace its characteristic terms with psychological ones. Tom isn't a hero from romance, but when he speaks of (and to) Sophia in the clichés of the sonnet tradition, it's because those are the terms available to say what otherwise can't be said.[46] (The claim that 'To paint the Looks or Thoughts of either of these Lovers is beyond my Power' is a cliché of romance writing that also expresses how love is experienced.)[47] Such conventions don't block expression or feeling but enable them. The realist assumption that we really speak, and understand and feel, beyond clichés – that conventions belie and don't realize sentiments – is a convention of literature, not love. I take the moments when the characters think in the conventional categories available to them – when Sophia thinks Tom heroic and angelic, and momentarily imagines herself in conventionally heroic terms – not as failures of psychological realism on Fielding's part, but as some of his truest insights into psychology.[48] When Tom speaks in romance, he expresses something more than sexual desire (though it is compounded of sexual desire too), and that other referent remains true even after realizing the sex that is one of the other ingredients of romance. Sex may desublimate the desire mystified in romance, but that doesn't exhaust romance, which expresses more than that kind of desire. Similarly, when *Tom Jones* speaks in romance, it expresses something more than a reality defined only by sexual desire (though it's compounded of that desire too). Those conventional and perhaps residual representations aren't simply superseded by a text that is looking for a truer representation. Rather they are part of a reality that cannot be reduced to a single form.

The novel's refusal to reduce the truth of romance to sex (or love to hunger) is one of its structuring dynamics. At every level, Fielding asks us to bear in mind multiple reasons and multiple expressions and not simply choose one. It is 'learning' that affords access to this variety of discourses and provides a counterweight to the force of mere genius, or, as Fielding has it, mere vanity. In his account of the uses of learning Fielding echoes his critique of the egoism of modern philosophy and the way it reduces love to hunger, discovering 'by the mere Force of Genius alone, without the least Assistance of any kind of Learning, or even Reading' that there is no truth in abstract terms (God, virtue, goodness, love) except pride and vanity.[49] Such genius only has the resources to work with, and on, itself. (In these terms the pen is always and only a penis.) The same critique is applied to modern writing and criticism.

> As several Gentlemen in these Times, by the wonderful Force of Genius alone, without the least Assistance of Learning, perhaps without being well able to read, have made a considerable Figure in the Republic of Letters; the modern Critics, I am told, have lately begun to assert, that all kind of Learning is entirely useless to a Writer; and, indeed, no other than a kind of Fetters on the natural

Spriteliness and Activity of the Imagination, which is thus weighed down, and prevented from soaring to those high Flights which otherwise it would be able to reach.[50]

(These heights are ironic; the direction is really downward or inward, a version of Swift's attack on the moderns as spiders that build their homes from their guts.)[51] The narrative itself performs an anti-modern refusal to dive into the 'Jakes' of Blifil's depths: 'it would be an ill Office in us to pay a Visit to the inmost Recesses of his Mind, as some scandalous People search into the most secret Affairs of their Friends, and often pry into their Closets and Cupboards, only to discover their Poverty and Meanness to the World.'[52] And this ironically discreet refusal to monger scandal is mirrored by what we do see of Blifil, who embodies the orientation of modern philosophy and takes the self as the only object of attention or affection.[53] *Tom Jones* suggests that both love and writing need more than a single focus and must associate with others in order to realize themselves. Writing that aspires to move beyond, and not through, the forms (and skills) of learning carries the taint of the modern reduction to self, and selfishness.

The effect of stepping into and out of forms, realizing their uses without fully inhabiting them – the effect I'm calling fleeting habitation – is a recursive mechanism in *Tom Jones*. Fielding's 'external characterization,' a long-standing and helpful critical cliché, works in this way.[54] More recently Campbell has shown how the 'adoptive' or constructed nature of Fielding's characters allows him to explore the conflict between competing models of gender identity and politics, an account that complicates the category of identity but remains organized by it.[55] I think the complication could be pursued further. If models of identity complicate the characters, it is equally the case that the characters serve as occasions to explore these models. Through the characters' enacting of conventions from many different kinds of texts, classical and contemporary, romance and picaresque, narrative and philosophical, *Tom Jones* places these various discourses side by side, in a sense animating its culture's bookstall and allowing those myriad volumes sitting side by side to speak to each other, par-ode, in parody.

When Tom passes through a romance environment he enacts the conventions of romance discourse. When he's interrupted by Molly, a character out of *'pastourelle'* or perhaps 'plain English actuality,' he both realizes and supplements romance with sex, measuring one kind of story by another.[56] Elsewhere he both realizes and supplements abstract justice with sentiment, offering a counterargument to the Man of the Hill and later a generous gift to Mrs. Miller's cousin.[57] Tom and the eponymous novel speak the same language, quite literally, with Tom reciting the lessons of the narrative. His remark to the Man of the Hill, 'many a Man who commits Evil, is not totally bad and corrupt in his Heart' repeats the lesson the narrator gives about Black George and then about books.[58] And Tom himself deploys the sentimental eloquence that worked so well on his humanity – when Mrs. Miller painted a pathetic word picture – to convince Nightingale to show the same humanity to Nancy.[59] In such cases, the appropriateness of Tom's discourse is measured less by any internally cohesive personality than by his situation in the narrative, and he seems more like a mouthpiece for a corrective discourse than a correct character.

Like the style and the characters, the narrative works through a series of fleeting habitations that are at once seen through and corrected, but also adjusted and re-used. The two interpolated stories offer possible futures for Tom and Sophia but in terms of residual narratives. Tom answers the stoic lesson of the Man of the Hill with the moral latitude of *Tom Jones*, and doubts Partridge's superstitious claim that it offers a 'warning' to them.[60] And if Mrs. Fitzpatrick's story seems at first to offer a gothic warning to Sophia (imprisonment awaits disobedient women), much of its effect is dissipated by the demystification of its romance into the banal and modern terms of bad marriage and money.[61] But if the novel doubts the efficacy, either moral or narrative, of these kinds of superseded stories it does reproduce them, and I think it does so in order to locate and harness part of their effects. The Man of Hill's story offers a Whig pedigree and a Swiftian moral to *Tom Jones*, both of which are integral to the novel's framing and provide it with another layer of political and cultural affiliation. Mrs. Fitzpatrick's story addresses another shelf of the bookstall and exemplifies some of the problems with circumstantial narration that Fielding addresses in the introductory essays' critiques of 'modern histories' and 'newspapers.'[62] Mrs. Fitzpatrick says, in self-conscious interjections: 'Think, my Dear, if you can to yourself what I must have undergone,' and 'I am afraid, my Dear, I shall tire you with a Detail of so many minute Circumstances. To be concise, therefore imagine me married; imagine me with my Husband, at the feet of my Aunt; and then imagine the maddest Woman in Bedlam, in a raving Fit, and your Imagination will suggest to you no more than what really happened.'[63] These comments direct readers to their own experience as the validation of the fictional examples (as we're instructed to do by the narrator as well), but they also indicate the limit of such empiricist reading.[64] In the next chapter, which interrupts Mrs. Fitzpatrick's story, the effects of depending on such 'minute Circumstances' are made clear when the Landlord mistakes Sophia for Jenny Cameron and she misunderstands his warning in terms of her own fears about her father. Happily he only means the arrival of a Jacobite army, and the comedy dispels the immediate fear, but only after suggesting (as the narrator remarks) how domestic dangers can loom larger psychologically than distant public troubles, and only after hinting that the Landlord isn't completely wrong – Sophia is, indeed, a substitute for Jenny Cameron, Fielding's Whig answer to Jacobite romance.[65]

Tom takes a tincture of his interlocutor, the Man of the Hill, and Sophia of her mistaken identity, Jenny Cameron, as each at once absorbs and exceeds these figures. Likewise, the narrative itself adopts and adapts the 'residual,' or at least other, narratives it passes through, at once rehearsing them, parodying them, and reanimating them in an effect like a conversation, or an argument. Bakhtin says this process defines the novel as a genre:

> The novel begins to make use of these languages, manners, genres; it forces all exhausted and used up, all socially and ideologically alien and distant worlds to speak about themselves and in their own style – but the author builds a superstructure over these languages made up of his own intentions and accents, which then becomes dialogically linked with them. The author encases his own thought in the image of another's language without doing violence to the freedom of that language or to its own distinctive uniqueness ... the parodied language offers a living dialogic resistance to the parodying intentions of the other; an unresolved conversation begins to sound in the image itself; the image becomes an open, living, mutual interaction between worlds, points of view, accents.[66]

Like Tom, *Tom Jones* is encased in others' voices, an echo chamber in which any final claim is only another voice. Bakhtin suggests that the authorial superstructure, which is analogous to Lockwood's 'essayist's privilege of talking freely in his own person,' participates in a field of many voices and in doing so enables them to be heard, and often to be heard again and heard afresh.[67] It is by adopting what could be called the essayist's privilege of digesting freely, entering into relationships in a field defined by those associations – the gathering of many voices and many texts in an open-ended, exploratory mode of readerly writing – that the novel achieves its characteristic shape and makes its characteristic demands. As the narrative and the narrator do, readers are offered occasion to think through another's (and others') thoughts. The novel becomes at once an 'image' of that process, a register of one reader's engagement with his texts, and an invitation to participate in that particular textual culture. In these terms, the novel as a genre can be defined in terms of the way it preserves, extends, and adapts its traditions, instead of the way it supersedes them. *Tom Jones* is most novelistic at the moments of its essays, when it registers the many voices and the many texts (the 'learning') of its culture and engages them in 'reflection,' another voice and another text participating in an unresolved conversation.

Like an essay, *Tom Jones* both represents and enacts a system of borrowings and adaptations. Its present isn't defined against its traditions, and it doesn't aspire to realize an authentic representation beyond those texts. But it isn't strictly defined by them either. Rather it's defined by the energy of working on or through various texts, keeping those forms alive via the energy of re-use. This conservative, or conservationist, project is routinely recognized but its mechanism often described (or dismissed) in the terms of a different kind of project of realist or historicist representation. *Tom Jones*, though, is better understood as a study of how forms survive, as well as a brief for their survival – though not just for their cultural capital (as if you get credit simply for having books, or simply for having read them, as Fielding sarcastically remarks).[68] Rather, learning to engage those forms teaches a skill of reading that is no less part of a modern public sphere than the models of identity learned from diaries or the referential transparency adopted from newspapers.

From the perspective of a history of the essay, *Tom Jones* looks like a way to extend and intensify that genre's practices of literacy. The novel represents a polytextual print culture and offers a range of self-conscious, ironic, and comic lessons on how to deal with it, how to read. From the perspective of recent histories of the novel organized by expectations of formal realism and historicist referentiality, this adoption of the essay looks distorting or distracting. Watt characterizes *Tom Jones* as 'only part novel, and there is much else – picaresque tale, comic drama, occasional essay,' and Richetti reads the 'stability and finality of the essayistic mode' as placing *Tom Jones* outside of the history of the novel, indeed a reaction against it.[69] There have been several important modifications of Watt's thesis of the 'rise of the novel' that have questioned whether the rise has been quite so neat, but there has been comparatively less attention to the other part of the phrase.[70] We now have several 'rises' but perhaps not enough 'novels,' not enough kinds of novels.[71] Bakhtin, Alter, and Mace have each noted distinct traditions of the novel, and I think that focusing on the distinct generic roots of distinct kinds of novel offers one way to grasp differences between texts that are perhaps too quickly summed up by a category 'novel' defined in terms of immersive reading and illusive representation.[72]

Watt, of course, proposed an alternative 'realism' to account for Fielding's failure to offer a 'realism of presentation,' and many critics have productively pursued the way Fielding's 'realism of assessment' both represents judgment and challenges us to judge.[73] But the original force of Watt's point may have been lost in these amplifications. 'The tedious asseveration of literal authenticity in Defoe and to some extent in Richardson, tended to obscure the fact that, if the novel was to achieve equality of status with other genres, it had to be brought into contact with the whole tradition of civilized values, and supplement its realism of presentation with a realism of assessment.'[74] One need not accept all of this to take the basic point. (I disagree with the assumption that genres exist to be something – a genre – rather than do things, and the assumption that the values of this tradition are the whole tradition of civilization.) With these caveats, I think Watt's point addresses an important aspect of Fielding's work, the intertwined relationship between assessment and contact with tradition. The judgment the novel is famously concerned with is not offered only at the level of the story, either as a way more realistically to render the world or to ask readers to judge that world in order to create a different kind of realism.[75] In those terms a realism of assessment ends up as just another kind of realism of presentation. However, I think that, rather than an exercise in a realer realism, the skill of assessment *Tom Jones* seeks to model and foster isn't defined merely in terms of the working of the plot (characters judging each other and readers judging characters), but rather in terms of plotting the work – in terms, that is, of how to tell a story and how to represent character at all. In this project it's not rendering a real that's most important, but negotiating the many representations of the real that are preserved in the culture as tradition – the novel rendering its traditions.[76] And it is this aspect of the novel that the essays address, adding something more than the testing of good nature by experience that is the substance of Tom's and Sophia's trials. The skill of reflection enabled by the materials of learning is at once something beyond Tom and his story and integral to *Tom Jones*.[77]

Tom Jones gathers and sifts the texts of its tradition and trains readers in that skill of sifting so that they too can engage those texts, participate in those traditions, and adapt those moves. This work of reading or cycling through old forms does have an analogue at the level of narrative, but I want to conclude by suggesting that finally the resolutions of the plot do not fully resolve the complexities of the novel. Price remarks that 'Fielding insists upon the difficulties' and I take the 'uses of learning,' or energy of reading, that the novel models and invites to be sustained beyond the neat resolutions of the plot.[78] A standard and useful critical account of *Tom Jones* describes it as a dialectic between form and energy.[79] But if Tom learns proper formation without excessive formalism – for instance, he must learn to 'curb and restrain' his passions but not lose them altogether by adopting the empty 'Form and Affectation' and 'Vanity and servile Imitation' that defines 'upper life' – we don't simply learn in reading about him to be like him.[80] Tom certainly learns to see beyond the blind submission to rules taught by Thwackum and Square (such rules inevitably prove to be cruel or hypocritical in the novel) and the plot replaces those rigid forms of reflection with good nature and good fortune. I don't think, though, that Fielding is offering Tom's sentimental education as an answer to the discarded structures of reflection of his early education – as if the four criteria of the novel could be reduced to two, and genius and learning simply replaced with experience and humanity. (This would make the novel finally a version of the modern claim to replace old forms with feelings and dispense with learning altogether.) Rather, *Tom Jones* is bigger than Tom's story, and, if he arrives providentially at a happy ending, we don't have it so easy.

How happy is the happy ending? The form of *Tom Jones* has been read as expressing a Christian ideal and a conservative ideology, but the confidence and stability of the final form that underwrites such readings have been questioned by recent accounts of the theology and the cultural politics of *Tom Jones*. Rosengarten reads a 'principled diffidence' in the providential order of the novel and argues that an account of Fielding's theology shouldn't conflate stated positions in the text with the position of whole text.[81] In this reading the 'order' of the providential plot doesn't resolve the energy as much as remind us of the further work we have to do. Similarly, McKeon's account of

Fielding's 'extreme skepticism' about both modern and traditional forms, and his merely instrumental deployment of the latter, suggests that Fielding doesn't offer substantial answers to the questions he raises as much as a chance to ask them again.[82] Both Rosengarten and McKeon find in the order of the plot a skeptical diffidence that I think is realized in the practice of wit with which Fielding addresses the myriad orders built into his novel.

McKeon hears a 'quiet desperation' in the merely formal, functional, or literary answer Fielding gives to the intertwined social and epistemological crises he addresses with his novels, a reading that's congruent with accounts of Fielding as inheriting the satiric mantle of the Scriblerians.[83] I don't hear such elegiac nostalgia, though, in the exuberance of *Tom Jones*, with its wisecracks, dirty jokes, skipping slippages, and massively overdetermined faith in a good humor it represents as failing at every turn. Instead of an answer to a cultural crisis that dreams of a lost purity in its deployment of archaic forms, *Tom Jones* shows how those forms remain somewhat viable. But if these forms remain useful, they're not simply secure in their own piety. Tradition doesn't answer modernity any more than modernity replaces tradition; both need to be read.

Everything about *Tom Jones* is densely and thoroughly, but not finally, mediated. The novel offers another loop through which textual 'materials' are fed back into the culture, mediated and so made available for further use. After flipping through the multiple forms offered by the novel (the many responses and reactions of the characters, the many conventions of representation that define and confuse character and plot alike, the many genres in dialogue), the final shape of the novel may be less any single form – as if one of them finally won the novel's quarrel of the books – than a dense web, or text, of many overwritten and undercutting forms. The skill of literacy adequate to such a book (and such a world) is registered, modeled, and enabled in the essays. When we take the shape of the novel to include the work of the essays as well as the workings of the plot, the novel's final shape emerges from the work we do as we cycle through the many forms that make it up.

Putting *Tom Jones* in a history of the essay highlights different aspects of the novel. The learning that goes with the essays offers both the materials and the skills out of which *Tom Jones* is built. The novel, then, as those inherited forms themselves do, offers a chance to practice the reflection trained by such learning and to negotiate the variety of texts that make up the substance of the culture. The novel is another essay in ordering those many other orderings; it is self-conscious in its recognition that such texts are cobbled together of many others. The literacy sponsored by such a novel is not organized by expectations of identification, immediacy, or immersion, but rather by engagements with the many mediations that claim, variously and quarrelsomely, to represent the real. Built of clashing old forms, *Tom Jones* also wittingly explores their various uses, and neither rejects them out of hand nor adopts any finally or without irony. It is this double project of renewing old forms, keeping them alive while using them to give shape (or shapes) to one's world, that defines a genre of novels self-consciously embedded in a world of many texts, many discourses, and many others. Such novels practice, and offer practice in, a mode of differential reading in a space that is at once artificial and artifactual.[84] They allow us fleetingly to inhabit multiple positions, as much of the pre-texts and intertexts as we know, or can keep in mind, or can bear, and so test out those various discourses for ourselves, seeing ourselves in other lights and in others' light.

We don't experience a present only in utterly contemporary terms, and the effect of a historicist criticism focused on limited notions of historical authenticity has been distorting. In its refusal to be bound to a single moment or a contemporary form Fielding's novel is thoroughly historical, registering and recording a history that isn't defined only by events or identities or even ideologies but by the work of understanding and evaluating these with all the available tools, all the texts and forms and conventions the multiplicity and variety of which define any culture. Booksellers' stalls were full of books as well as newspapers; if we're only interested in the latter, in the minimal present, we impoverish our sense of history and our own historicism. *Tom Jones* is a vastly more representative text, a better picture of the range of its culture's interests and concerns, than almost any other document of the period. What it registers, though, is a kind of response, a skill of literacy, that is dismissed for exactly what makes it historical: it's witty and witting, and it construes its sources as resources instead of hauntings. Like the essays it adapts and extends, Fielding's novel reminds us that books are tools, occasions for reading, and the challenge is to spell, not dispel, the forms that define us.

Appendix A Whitlock, from 'The Author to the Reader,' *Zootomia, or, Observations on the Present Manners of the English: Briefly Anatomizing the Living by the Dead* (1654), [A8v]–a

This why I write at all, now why I write thus: I must use Mountaignes Apology in his Essay of Books; I make no doubt (saith he) but I handle many Themes that are farre better handled in the scattered works of able Writers: But my intent was not to beat my Brains in the Acquisition even of Knowledge it selfe that was too difficult; Nor have I[:] what came easily among Authors or Observations to my understanding; what conduceth to living or dying well, that I communicate. To say true, I finde Mountaignes Pallate (and not quite without judgment) pretty generall among Readers of most Ages; and because his words are very significant, take them in his own language. Je aime en generall les liures, qui usent les sciences, non ceux qui les dressent. I love, saith he, books that make use of Sciences, not compile them into their Geneticall, or Analyticall Parcel. Authors (to say true) are more Thumb'd that are variously usefull, than those Embodyers of Arts in Cancellos suae Methodi, into the limits of their proper Method: usefull I confesse they are, but wanting the Dulce, Pleasure of variety, and convenience of more contracted brevity: the paines of reading them is seldome bestowed on them, especially if they swell into Tomes of that bignesse, that he that can have no leisure, dareth not look on them, and he that will have none, careth not. I know not, how but as Montaigne saith of himselfe, Tracts of a continued Thread are tedious to most Fancies, which of it selfe indeed is of that desultory nature, that it is pleased with Writings like Irish Bogs, that it may leap from one variety to another, than tread any beaten Path. Among many kindes of writings I finde Plutarchs most inviting Imitation for the form, (call them Discourses, Essayes, or what you will) nor behinde any for matter; if mixt sometimes with those Mucrones Sermonum, Enlivening Touches of Seneca full of smart Fancy, solid sense and accurate reason: such like Peeces compiled by able Pen-men out of Plutarchs fulness and Seneca's quickness, would undoubtedly fill the mouth of the most gaping Expectaltee among Readers.

Appendix B Cornwallis, opening of 'Of Essaies and Bookes' (1601), 190-1

I Holde neither *Plutarche's* nor none of those aunciert short manner of writings nor *Montaigne's* nor such of this latter time to bee rightly tearmed Essayes; for though they be short, yet they are strong and able to endure the sharpest tryall. But mine are Essayes, who am but newly bound Prentise to the inquisition of knowledge and vse these papers as a Painter's boy a board, that is trying to bring his hand and his fancie acquainted. It is a maner of writing wel befitting vndigested motions, or a head not knowing his strength like a circumspect runner trying for a starte, or prouidence that tastes before she buyes. For it is easier to thinke well then to do well, and no triall to haue handsome dapper conceites runne inuisibly in a braine but to put them out and then looke vpon them. If they prooue nothing but wordes, yet they breake not promise with the world, for they say, 'But an Essay,' like a Scriuenour trying his Pen before he ingrosseth his worke. Nor, to speake plainely, are they more to blame then many other that promise more; for the most that I haue yet touched haue millions of wordes to the bringing forth one reason; and when a reason is gotten, there is such borrowing it one of another that in a multitude of Bookes, still that conceit, or some issued out of that, appeares so belaboured and worne, as in the ende it is good for nothing but for a Prouerbe. When I thinke of the abilities of man, I promise my selfe much out of my reading, but it prooues not so. Time goeth, and I turne leaues; yet still finde my selfe in the state of ignorance; wherefore, I haue thought better of honesty then of knowledge. What I may know, I will conuert to that of vse; and what I write, I meane so, for I will chuse rather to be an honest man then a good Logitian. There was neuer Art yet that laid so fast hold on me that she might iustly call me her seruant. I neuer knew them but superficially, nor, indeed, wil not though I might, for they swallow their subiect and make him as Ouid saide of himselfe.

Quicquid conabar dicere versus erat.

I would earne none of these so dearly as to ty vp the minde to thinke onely of one thing; her best power by this meanes is taken from her, for so her circuit is limited to a distance, which should walke vniuersally. Moreouer, there growes pride and a selfe opinion out of this, which deuours wisedome.

Appendix C Cornwallis on Moral Philosophy and Reading

In the standard classical manner, Cornwallis says philosophy is directed to use, providing one with the tools to master one's passions and so be less affected by 'the turnings of the world'; wisdom is applying one's reading to one's own life, and knowing oneself is the proper use of knowledge.

> Man knoweth he is mortall and what he hath is transitorie. Hee is vnhappy that is not armed against the turnings of the world, with the experience of the turnings of the world ... Hee that reades to speake, ends with the commendations of an old wiue's tale; hee that reads to applie his reading to his owne life is wise; he poureth oyle into the lamp that will giue him light; the other snuffes it without supplying it. Anaxagoras made good vse of his Philosophie when his sonne's death assaulted him ... To know himselfe and the appurtenaunces to himself is the vse of knowledge, and this knowledge vnmaskes his eyes & shews him wonders in himselfe. He becomes in this like vnto God. ('Of Sorrow,' 165)

Here production, reading to speak and snuffing one's lamp, is marked as vanity and waste, and contrasted to proper application and stocking oneself. This theme is elsewhere figured in a personal register; note the shift from 'our' to 'my':

> So doth our discerning but beget Opinion; and when we haue said we thinke thus, our knowledge is at the farthest. My steps are the steps of mortality, and I do stumble and stagger for company and crawle rather then goe; yet I desire to get further and to discouer the Land of light. To this end I reade and write, and by them would faine catch an vnderstanding more then I brought with me[,] before decrepitenesse and death catch me. ('Of Ambition,' 34)

The grammar performs the absorption of what *we* say and *we* think into *my* steps. The precise practice of reading and writing is explicated in another place. Reading and writing are a way of stocking, or 'stuffing,' oneself:

> I Had no neede to teach the world new opinions, for I hold all I know, more by tradition then reason. I haue a braine like a French force that doth it [sic] best first; my incountring an argument is most vigorous at the prime opposition. I, after, fall and waxe lazie and, in truth, shallow. I doe nothing well but speake much worse then I write, and, perhaps, worse (in something) then I can doe, which, I must confesse, the fault of my braine; for I neither lispe, stutter, nor speake in the throat; Nature hath made the cariage of my wordes large and swift enough, but I want marchandize and stuffe. ('Of Trappes for Fame,' 121)

Reading gives one something to work on. But all this depends on properly digesting what one has gathered:

> Let no man think this mislike [of affectation] barres my allowance of inriching my selfe by the example of the vertuous. No, the best may want if hee bee onely stored by his owne meditation. Bookes and men are both good instructions; those wee must read and obserue; but when that is done, to make our reading and obseruation no longer theirs but our owne. I haue noted a people content inwardly to be so humble as to weare cast [off] Apparrell; but of the outward satisfaction, they would alter and trimme them to defend them from being knowne and so fit them to their bodies before they were [seen] too wide. Thus must they doe that desire to be adorned with knowledge and iudgement and vertue. Whatsoeuer I read, I vnderstand it not if my Digestion makes it not naturally mine. Thus it becommeth men and makes the constitution of the minde strong and faire and worthy of allowance, if not of Admiration. ('Of Affectation,' 68–9)

It's not the borrowed clothes that matter here, but the work one does on them to make them one's own. This work of digestion, the 'fitting' of what one's received to one's own size, is elsewhere described as a cow-like process, spitting up in order to have it stay down:

> I thought last of Fame [this is the last essay in the first volume of essays], and my thoughts haue ridden (as I thinke) ouer her whole circuite. What I haue seene in my trauaile, I will trust this peece of paper with and so ridde my braine of that carriage ... My occupation hath been vehemently bookish; I haue been councelled by Plato and Seneca for Philosophy. Writing is the draught of reading, and by this I haue disburthened my head & taken account of my profiting. ('Of Fame,' 73, 74)

'Of Essaies and Books' continues this discussion in fuller detail, fleshing out this mention of Plato and Seneca. Socrates exemplifies the process of use: 'Socrates was the wisest man of his time, and his ground for that was his turning all his acquired knowledge into morality; of whom one saide, he fetched Philosophy from heauen and placed her in Cities' (191). And Seneca provides a classical recommendation of such digestion. Finally, the same dynamic of shifting the focus from knowledge to morality is echoed in Cornwallis's account of Montaigne, who offers 'profitable Recreation' and speakes nobly, honestly, and wisely, with little method but with much iudgement. Learned he was and often showes it, but with such a happinesse as his owne following is not disgraced by his owne reading. Hee speaks freely and yet wisely, censures and determines many things Iudically, and yet forceth you not to attention with a 'hem' and a spitting Exordium. In a word – hee hath made Morrall Philosophie speake couragiously, and in steede of her gowne, giuen her an Armour. He hath put Pedanticall Schollerisme out of countenance, and made manifest that learning mingled with Nobilitie shines most clearly. ('Of Censuring,' 42)

Appendix D Culpeper, 'Of Essayes,' *Essayes or Moral Discourses on Several Subjects* (1671), 1–3

The word *Essay*, we have From the French, in which Tongue it signifies a tryal or probation: As it is applyed to things, it admits of no positive definition, which might be the reason, that neither their [the] great Essays [Essayist] *Montaigne*, nor the Lord *Bacon* our more incomparable writer in the same kind, hath thought it requisite to define the word, because it hath so little to do with the matter it handles; rather expressing a generality of knowledge, then oblig'd to any particular Science: as we see in building, there are many Artists, that may own the compleating of some parts of the Fabrick, yet not claim the perfecting, of the whole structure, so in *Essayes* there is required instructions from Philosophy, History, and what else can be usefully expressed for other observations, and moralities of life, that in them a man may read an Epitomy of himself, and the world together: neither is the wit, and eloquence, (the ornaments of the Pen and thought) more lively to be expressed in any kind of writing, then in this of Essayes, which as they treat of men and manners (the most natural imployment of our best conceptions) there ought to be in them such a pertinent ingenuity, as tends most to application and benefit. Histories may discover the actions of some perticular times and men, whilst Essayes have more familiarity with our selves and business, giving us besides an useful acquaintance both of the dead and living together.

Nor are they turned [termed] descants upon such or such pertinent subjects, (like the wit or clinch of an Epigram) or the smart sayings in Characters and Satyrs (though handling much of the same Argument) nor the sweet and elegant insinuations of Poets, and Orators, that can contain the business of Essayes, though they may gather some honey from the best flowers of wit, and learning, they have a limitation from none, and yet come nearer our selves, then these can make them; which as it is a just dignity appertaining to this kind of writing, so it needed not to have been instanced to the judicious Reader, who cannot be unknowing thereof: besides I am not to forget, that in extolling the Subject which I handle, I do in some sort prompt a greater expectation in point of performance, then I desire the Reader should have from my abilities, since howsoever this book comes now to be published, it was but the result of private thoughts, by which I endeavoured to take some prospect of the opinions, business, and manners of the world (being indeed the chief accomplishments of humane life) though not without hopes, that if these papers at any time were to be made bold, as to be seen by the world in Print, it would not be altogether without that profit, which I have reapt from them my self.

Notes

Introduction

1. Here are some examples of the uses of the phrase: William Austin, *Haec Homo, Wherein the Excellency of the Creation of Woman is described; By Way of an Essay* (1637); Abraham Cheare, *Sighs for Sion: or, Faith and Love ... In way of Essay* (1656); Edward Hyde, Earl of Clarendon, *Reflections upon Several Christian Duties – Divine and Moral, by Way of Essays* (1668); William Ramesey, *The Gentlemans Companion: or, A Character of True Nobility, and Gentility: In the way of Essay* (1672); [M. de Fontenelle,] *A Discovery of New Worlds. From the French. Made English By Mrs. A. Behn. To which is prefixed a Preface, by way of Essay on Translated Prose* (1688); Stephen Skynner, *Christian Practice described by way of essay upon the Life of our Savior* (London and Boston, 1693); W. C., *A discourse (By way of Essay) Humbly offer'd to the Consideration of the Honourable House of Commons Toward the raising Moneys by an Excise* (1695); John Savage [trans.], *Spanish Letters, Historical, Satyrical and Moral of the famous Don Antonion de Guevara, Bishop of Mondonedo ... written by way of essay on different subjects* (1697); William Sacheverell, *An Account of the Isle of Man: Its Inhabitants, Language, Soil, Remarkable Curiosities, The Succession of its Kings and Bishops, Down to the Eighteenth Century: By Way of Essay* (1702); James Clerk, *The practice of discipline, or some directions for the right managing of ecclesiastick discipline. In way of essay* (Edinburgh, 1705); *Thoughts on friendship. By way of essay; for the use and improvement of the ladies. By a well-wisher to her sex* (1725); Samuel Ashwick, *The eighth book of the Iliad of Homer; attempted by way of essay* (1750); *An enquiry (by way of essay) into the origin of feudal tenures, and the rights of eventual succession to lands in primogeniture only, as the laws of England now stand. By a member of the Middle Temple Society* (1764); Richard Preston, *An elementary treatise, by way of essay, on the quantity of estates &c.* (1791).
2. William Cornwallis, *Essays*, ed. Don Cameron Allen (Baltimore: Johns Hopkins University Press, 1946). Chudleigh's *Essays* are available in *The Poems and Prose of Mary, Lady Chudleigh*, ed. Margaret J. M. Ezell (New York: Oxford University Press, 1993). Cornwallis's first collection of 25 *Essayes* was published in 1600 and *A Second part of Essayes* (24 more) in 1601; they were enlarged and reprinted in 1606 and again reprinted in 1632. On Cornwallis as the first English follower of Montaigne, see Elbert N. S. Thompson, *The Seventeenth-Century English Essay* (Iowa City: University of Iowa Press, 1928), 34–5; Michael W. Price's entry on Cornwallis in *DLB 151: British Prose Writers of the Early Seventeenth Century* (Washington, DC: Gale, 1995), 82; and the 'Introduction' to Cornwallis's *Essays*, where Allen wittily remarks, 'he simply looked into Montaigne and wrote' (x). I take this to suggest a transfer of the issues of memory raised by Sidney's 'heart' to questions of reading, a beautifully dense and fit figure for the problems of the *Essais* and *Essayes*.

3. Philosophical essays include: Seth Ward, *A philosophicall essay toward an eviction of the being and attributes of God* (1652); John Wilkins, *An Essay Towards a Real Character and a Philosophical Language* (1668); and John Locke, *An Essay concerning Human Understanding* (1690). Poetic essays include: James VI, *The Essayes of a Prentice in the Divine Art of Poesie* (Edinburgh, 1584); *The Poeticall Essaies of Alexander Craig* (1605); John Benson, *England in its condition, briefly and most lively characterized, by way of essay* (1648); Alexander Pope, *An Essay on Man* (1733); and Benjamin Stillingfleet, *An Essay on Conversation* (1738). Essays by ancients and moderns include: William Temple, *Essay Upon Ancient and Modern Learning* (1690); John Dryden, *An Essay of Dramatick Poesie* (1668); and Joseph Glanvill, *Scepsis Scientifica: or, Confest Ignorance, the way to Science; In an Essay of The Vanity of Dogmatizing, and Confident Opinion* (1665). Essays on moral philosophy include: John Robinson, *Essayes; or, Observations Divine and Morall. Collected Ovt of holy Scriptures, Antient and Moderne Writers, both divine and humane* (1638); Walter Montagu, *Miscellanea Spiritualia: or, Devout Essayes* (1648); and Timothy Nourse, *A Discourse of Natural and Reveal'd Religion in Several Essays* (1691). Essays on natural philosophy include: Richard Brathwait[e], *Essaies upon the fiue senses* (1620); and Robert Boyle's *Certain Physiological Essays* (1661).
4. See especially the recent magisterial and field-consolidating collection of essays, Kevin Sharpe and Steven Zwicker, eds., *Reading, Society, and Politics in Early Modern England* (New York: Cambridge University Press, 2003).
5. For Barthes's famous slogan, see *S/Z: an Essay*, trans. Richard Miller (New York: Hill and Wang, 1974), 5. I discuss this passage more fully in Chapter 2.
6. Michel de Certeau, *The Practice of Everyday Life*, trans. Steven Rendell (Berkeley: University of California Press, 1984), xxi, 174.
7. Steven Roger Fischer discusses the antithesis of writing and reading: 'Writing is expression, reading impression. Writing is public, reading personal. Writing is limited, reading open-ended. Writing freezes the moment. Reading is forever' (*A History of Reading* [London: Reaktion, 2003], 8). For an account of recent research on reading as a latent faculty, what Fischer describes as a 'sixth sense,' a 'hypervision' 'parasitic yet suppletive' to sense, see 336–40. Alberto Manguel remarks, 'reading is writing's apotheosis' (*A History of Reading* [New York: Penguin, 1996], 179).
8. Cornwallis, 74, 190. I discuss this in Chapter 1.
9. Seneca is a classical source of this notion of digestion, as I discuss in Chapter 1.
10. T. C., 'Prooemium,' *Morall Discourses and Essayes, Upon Severall Select Subjects* (1655).
11. Ann Moss, *Printed Commonplace Books and the Structuring of Renaissance Thought* (New York: Oxford University Press, 1996), 255; for the relation of Montaigne's *Essais* to commonplace books, see 212–13. See also Moss, 'Commonplace-Rhetoric and Thought-Patterns in Early Modern Culture,' in *The Recovery of Rhetoric*, ed. R. H. Roberts and J. M. M. Good (Charlottesville: University Press of Virginia, 1993), 49–60; Moss, 'The *Politica* of Justus Lipsius and the Commonplace-Book,' *Journal of the History of Ideas* 59 (1998), 421–36; and Ann Blair, 'Humanist Methods in Natural Philosophy: the Commonplace Books,' *Journal of the History of Ideas* 53 (1992), 541–51.

12. Douglas Hesse calls this work of assimilation and digestion 'essayistic literacy,' and he distinguishes it from hypertext (one of our versions of commonplacing): 'Internet writers connect through juxtaposition, not commentary' ('Saving a Place for Essayistic Literacy,' in *Passions, Pedagogies, and 21st-Century Technologies*, ed. Gail E. Hawisher and Cynthia L. Selfe [Logan: Utah State University Press, 1999], 34–48, 41). Essays register that work of connecting, not just showing that there may be connections, but making them.
13. For an influential account of the essay as organized by personal voice, spontaneity, and self-expression, see Graham Good, *The Observing Self: Rediscovering the Essay* (New York: Routledge, 1988). For accounts of the essay as organized by resistance and excess, see Réda Bensmaïa, *The Barthes Effect: the Essay as Reflective Text* (Minneapolis: University of Minnesota Press, 1987), and Claire de Obaldia, *The Essayistic Spirit: Literature, Modern Criticism, and the Essay* (New York: Oxford University Press, 1995). For the essay as a different kind of 'liberation,' beyond mastery and self but also beyond all mediation (finally expressing 'the unmediated, unsocial power of liberated desire'), see Rachel Blau Du Plessis, 'F-words: an Essay on the Essay,' *American Literature* 68 (1996), 15–45, 30, 32, 36.
14. For the essay as 'discursivity as such' see John Snyder, *Prospects of Power: Tragedy, Satire, the Essay, and the Theory of Genre* (Lexington: University Press of Kentucky, 1991), 150, 200. Peter Burgand says, 'the essay reveals a characteristic of all writing' (*Idioms of Uncertainty: Goethe and the Essay* [University Park: Pennsylvania State University Press, 1992], 105). J. M. van der Laan echoes this; the essayistic text is 'writing per se' and 'epitomizes all writing' ('Essayistic Orders of Chaos,' in *Disrupted Patterns: On Chaos and Disorder in the Enlightenment*, ed. John McCarthy and Theodore E. D. Braun [Amsterdam: Rodopi, 2000], 191–202, 200). Bensmaïa discusses the essay as 'the moment of writing before the genre, before genericness – or as the matrix of all generic possibilities' (92). And Obaldia says the essay's modal excess 'concerns all texts or genres without exception' (130). Michael L. Hall connects the essay's 'examination of conventional wisdom' with 'the subversion of received opinion' as part of his thesis that 'essayists were responding to the idea of discovery, to the notion that the world was in flux and that knowledge was no longer fixed by authority but in a state of transition' ('The Emergence of the Essay and the Idea of Discovery,' in *Essays on the Essay: Redefining the Genre*, ed. Alexander J. Butrym [Athens: University of Georgia Press, 1989], 73–92, 78, 80, 89).
15. John Uffley, Gent., *Wits Fancies: or, Choice Observations and Essayes, Collected out of Divine, Political, Philosophical, Military, and Historical Authors* (1659), Dedicatory Epistle, A5, A7. For 'generic repertoire,' see Alastair Fowler, *Kinds of Literature* (Cambridge: Harvard University Press, 1982), 56.
16. Uffley, The Epistle to the Reader, A3–A3v.
17. Uffley, 31–3.
18. Two examples that bookend the century are the anonymous *Remedies against Discontentment drawen into several Discourses from the writings of auncient Philosophers* (1596) and the anonymous *Aesop Naturaliz'd and expos'd to the Publick view in his own shape and dress by way of Essay on a hundred fables* (1697). Thompson considers *Remedies* 'the first avowed English essays' (7),

and although it never calls itself an 'essay,' the work describes itself in terms that will be named by the genre: 'small discourses ... framed for mine owne private vse' (Aiiii).
19. For example, Owen Felltham cites this, in its more correct form, *'Littera scripta manet'* ('Of Trauaile,' *Resolves: A Duple Century*, 4th edn. [1631], 271).
20. Grace Gethin, *Misery's Virtues Whetstone. Relique Gethinianae. Or, Some Remains of the Most Ingenious and Excellent Lady, the Lady Grace Gethin, Lately Deceased: Being a Collection of Choice Discourses, Pleasant Apothegmes, and Witty Sentences. Written by Her for the most part, by way of Essay, and at spare Hours* (1699).
21. Gethin, 'To the Reader,' av.
22. Locke, 'The Epistle to the Reader,' *Essay concerning Human Understanding*, ed. Peter H. Nidditch (New York: Oxford University Press, 1975), 6–7. 'For the understanding, like the eye, judging of objects only by its own sight, cannot but be pleased with what it discovers, having less regret for what has escaped it, because it is unknown. Thus he who has raised himself above the alms-basket, and, not content to live lazily on scraps of begged opinions, sets his own thoughts on work, to find and follow truth, will (whatever he lights on) not miss the hunter's satisfaction; every moment of his pursuit will reward his pains with some delight; and he will have reason to think his time not ill spent, even when he cannot much boast of any great acquisition' (6). Locke says the *Essay* began when he and some friends recognized they needed to 'examine our own Abilities' and he recorded 'Some hasty and undigested Thoughts' for the others to consider (7).
23. Locke writes, in terms that echo the 'Epistle': 'Perhaps, we should make greater progress in the discovery of rational and contemplative *Knowledge*, if we *sought* it in the Fountain, *in the consideration of Things themselves*; and made use rather of our own Thoughts, than other Mens to find it. For I think, we as rationally hope to see with other Mens Eyes, as to know with other Mens Understandings. So much as we our selves consider and comprehend of Truth and Reason, so much we possess of real and true Knowledge. The floating of other Mens Opinions in our Brains makes us not the one jot more knowing, though they happen to be true. What in them was Science, is in us but Opiniatrety, whilst we give up our Assent only to revered names, and do not, as they did, employ our Reason to *understand* those *Truths*, which gave them reputation' (101).
24. Locke, 8; Chudleigh, 246.
25. S. J. Gould and E. S. Vrba, 'Exaptation: a Missing Term in the Science of Form,' *Paleobiology* 8 (1982), 4–15.
26. [Thomas Culpeper,] 'Of Essayes,' *Essayes or Moral Discourses on Several Subjects. Written by a Person of Honor* (1671). I discuss this essay more fully in Chapter 1.
27. Robert Johnson, *Essaies, or Rather imperfect offers* (1601); William Mason, *A Handfvl of Essaies. Or Imperfect Offers* (1621).
28. Maurice Blanchot, 'From Dread to Language,' trans. Lydia Davis, in *The Station Hill Blanchot Reader*, ed. George Quasha (Barrytown, NY: Station Hill, 1999), 358.
29. 'Je ne voy le tout de rien. Ne font pas, ceux qui promettent de nous le faire veoir.' [I don't see the whole of anything; nor do those who promise to show it to us.] 'Of Democritus and Heraclitus,' *The Complete Essays of*

Montaigne, trans. Donald Frame (Stanford: Stanford University Press, 1957), 219. 'For one does not say everything; there are some things which at present it is advisable only to hint. One writes for a very few people, who understand' (Virginia Woolf, 'Montaigne,' *The Common Reader. First Series*, ed. Andrew Mc Neillie [New York: Harcourt Brace, 1984], 58–68). 'Virginia Woolf's essays can be read as the autobiography of a reader, full of personal emotion and intimacy. But her life as a reader always takes the color of what she is reading and arguing with. She does not speak of herself directly' (Hermione Lee, 'Virginia Woolf's Essays,' in *The Cambridge Companion to Virginia Woolf*, ed. Sue Roe and Susan Sellers [New York: Cambridge University Press, 2000], 91–108, 106).

30. 'Instead of achieving something scientifically, or creating something artistically, the effort of the essay reflects a childlike freedom, that catches fire, without scruple, on what others have done. The essay mirrors what is loved and hated instead of presenting the intellect, on the model of a boundless work ethic, as *creatio ex nihilo*. Luck and play are essential to the essay' (Theodor Adorno, 'The Essay as Form,' trans. Bob Hullot-Kentor and Frederic Will, *New German Critique* 32 [1984], 151–71, 152).

31. 'It is the words of others which most often bring the essay into being'; 'Born of books, nourished by books ... the essay is more often than not a confluence of such little blocks and strips of text. Let me tell you, it says, what I have just read, looked up, remembered of my reading. Horace, Virgil, Ovid, Cicero, Lucretius meet on a page of Montaigne ... the context of citation. And what is citation but an attempt to use a phrase, a line, a paragraph, like a word, and lend it further uses, another identity, apart from the hometown it hails from?' (William H. Gass, 'Emerson and the Essay,' *Habitations of the Word* [New York: Simon and Schuster, 1985], 26–7). 'Considered as a literary form, the Essay is comparatively of late growth ... Long after the poet and the historian comes the Essayist. Before the stage is prepared for him, thought must have accumulated to a certain point; a literature less or more must have been in existence, and must be preserved in printed books ... Then, before he can write, society must have formed itself long enough to have become self-conscious, introspective ... there must exist a class who have attained wealth and leisure, and a certain acquaintance with the accumulated stores of thought on which the Essayist works, else his allusions will be lost, his criticism a dead letter, his satire pointless. All this takes a long time to accomplish, and it is generally late in the literary history of a country before its Essayists appear' (Alexander Smith, 'Last Leaves: Sketches and Criticisms,' adapted as the Introduction to *The English Essayists: Lord Bacon to John Ruskin*, ed. Robert Cochrane [London: William P. Nimmo, 1877], 7). Smith makes similar points in 'On the Writing of Essays,' *Dreamthorp: A Book of Essays Written in the Country*, ed. Christopher Morley (1863; New York: Doubleday, Doran, & Co, 1934), 31. For the essay as secondary, organized by response, see also Mary Lee Bretz, *Voices, Silences and Echoes: a Theory of the Essay and the Critical Reception of Naturalism in Spain* (London: Tamesis, 1992), 16–17.

32. G. Douglas Atkins comments on essays being '"in other words": essayists put it otherwise' (*Estranging the Familiar: Towards a Revitalized Critical Writing* [Athens: University of Georgia Press, 1992], 19).

1. Draughts of reading

1. Bacon, 'Dedicatory Epistle' (c. 1610–12), in *The Essayes or Counsels, Civill and Morall*, ed. Michael Kiernan (Cambridge: Harvard University Press, 1985), 317.
2. For the former claims, see Bensmaïa and Obaldia; for the latter see Good.
3. Thomas Fuller, 'To the Reader,' *The Holy State and The Profane State*, ed. Maximilian Graff Walten, 2 vols. (1642; New York: Columbia University Press, 1938), A2.
4. Thomas Goddard, *Miscellanea; Or, Serious, Useful Considerations, Moral, Historical, Theological. Together with the Characters of A True Believer In Paradoxes and Seeming Contradictions. An Essay* (1661), 'To the Christian Reader,' (a)v.
5. Ralph Johnson, *The Scholars Guide From the Accidence to the University* (1665; Menston, England: The Scolar Press, 1971), 13–14.
6. Kevin Sharpe, *Reading Revolutions: the Politics of Reading in Early Modern England* (New Haven: Yale University Press, 2000), 34, 341.
7. Ibid., 181.
8. Ibid., 184. See also 103 on arranging, selecting, translating, and weighing and gathering for one's own purposes. This is an interesting moment of a historian's noting the historical fact of dehistoricist reading.
9. Ibid., 181–2. Here is the Seneca passage: 'The primary indication, to my thinking, of a well-ordered mind is the ability to remain in one place and linger in one's own company. Be careful, however, lest this reading of many authors and books of every sort may tend to make you discursive and unsteady. You must linger among a limited number of good writers, and digest their works, if you would derive ideas which shall win firm hold in your mind. Everywhere means nowhere. When people spend all their time in foreign travel, they end by having many hosts but no friends [*ut multa hospitia habeant, nullas amicitias*]. And the same thing must hold true of people who seek intimate acquaintance with no single author, but visit them all in a hasty and hurried manner. Food does no good and is not assimilated into the body if it leaves the stomach as soon as it is eaten; nothing hinders a cure so much as frequent change of medicine; no wound will heal when one salve is tried after another; a plant which is too often moved can never grow strong. There is nothing so efficacious that it can be helpful while it is being shifted about. And in reading many books is distraction' (*Ad Lucilium Epistulae Morales*, trans. R. M. Gummere, 3 vols. [New York: Putnam's Sons, 1925], 1:7; I've adjusted the translation slightly).
10. Sharpe, 108, 185, 105, 121, 211. For another statement of this humanist cliché, see John Robinson: 'hee reads a *Booke* ill, that understands not something more either in, or, at least, by it, then the Author himselfe did in penning it' ('Of Books and Writings,' *Observations Divine and Morall for the Furthering of Knowledg, and Vertue* [1625], 239).
11. Sharpe, 278. 'Perhaps the central faultline in the early modern age was that between belief in a common hermeneutic and a growing emphasis on individual judgment'; the commonplace book is an 'example and site of that fissure' (191).
12. Ibid., 306, 307.

13. Ibid., 309.
14. Ibid., 306.
15. Ibid., 27, 57–9.
16. Ibid., 42. Sharpe also discusses Bacon's essays as emerging from his personal readings of proverbs (321), but without connecting this to the freedom Bacon exemplifies earlier.
17. Ibid., 191.
18. Ibid., 31.
19. Guglielmo Cavallo and Roger Chartier, 'Introduction,' *A History of Reading in the West* (Amherst: University of Massachusetts, 1999), 30. Chartier repeats this in his own chapter, '"Popular" Reading,' where he describes commonplace reading as a 'style of reading that proceeded by extracts, displacements, and comparisons and that invested the text read (or listened to) with the weight of absolute authority. If all lettered readers did not participate in the culture of the commonplace book (Montaigne, for one, did not), that culture none the less dictated the way the majority of lettered readers organized their readings' (282). This seems overstated. The readers who have been studied don't do that, and unless exceptionality is the condition of reading as such (a thesis worth considering), we could be more careful about asserting what humanist culture actually did, and whether what it said it did actually worked. We can be sure humanist pedagogues *said* that's how things go, but every account of actual readers reading shows fissures, complications, and resistances that belie such claims.
20. See Carlo Ginzburg's *The Cheese and the Worms* (Baltimore: Johns Hopkins University Press, 1980), 33–4, and Sharpe's comments on the 'aggressive originality' of Menocchio's reading: 'Though as far as we know, Menocchio is exceptional, there is no such thing as *a* typical reader' (270). Nevertheless, Sharpe still sounds surprised to find that 'Drake read himself into revolutionary conceptions of society and state' (211). The really revolutionary reader would be one who was so bland that she would be as thoroughly imprinted by books as cultural studies suggests readers are. Has anyone found a reader who actually reads in the ways we claim texts enforce? Is it only other people – against whom one defines one's own enlightenment – who do so?
21. See the important correction by Jennifer Andersen and Elizabeth Sauer: 'early modern books seem to have been more dynamic and fluid, less dogmatic and authoritarian than some modern stereotypes would imply. An overemphasis on concerns with authenticity and authorship may have distracted us from what contemporaries took to be the essential features of print culture: its instability, permeability, sociability, and adaptability to particular occasions and readerships' ('Current Trends in the History of Reading,' *Books and Readers in Early Modern England* [Philadelphia: University of Pennsylvania Press, 2002], 1–2).
22. Jeffrey Kittay and Wlad Godzich suggest that, with the emergence of prose, a different model of reading (exemplified by Montaigne) is required, one that assigns its readers only relative positions to inhabit as they work through a text, not a single, absolute one; prose enables a kind of literacy that 'manages the economy of its discourses' instead of 'claiming the position of a master or *auctor*' (*The Emergence of Prose* [Minneapolis: University of

Minnesota, 1987], 112, 48). Allowing no final outside position, prose is unfinished, open-ended, subject to revision, reconstrual, and rewriting (172, 174). These are characteristics of the essay, and Montaigne is the end point of Kittay and Godzich's discussion, the *Essais* a 'negotiation of the niche prose will occupy' (174), and a model of the 'operativity' of 'the prosaic world, a world supremely indifferent to categories of wholeness or autonomy' (206, 205): 'Montaigne seeks to apply a different literacy, one that is clearly based on his remarkable skills as a reader' (207).

23. John L. Lievsay, 'Introduction,' Daniel Tuvill, *Essays Politic and Moral and Essays Moral and Theological*, ed. Lievsay (Charlottesville: University of Virginia Press, 1971), xiv. For Tuvill's classical quotation and allusion, see xii; for his treating of commonplaces, see xiv. 'So little is Tuvill's originality, I am convinced, that hardly a sentence in his writings is the product of his own unaided thought' (xix). 'As usual, the slender scaffolding of Tuvill's thought is almost overwhelmed with the weight of example, quotation, and digression' (181). Lievsay calls Tuvill 'an adept follower of conventional patterns, rather than an original thinker or innovator' (217), and says he 'pillages' classical sources as well (226).

24. Lievsay, xvi. 'Obviously, Tuvill is still under the influence of the earlier essays of Montaigne: his desultory chattiness often needs a curb; his ideas often need to be drawn into a more logically coherent sequence ... His most usual technique is to "set his text" (after the manner of the sermon) and then to bring to its support a succession of detached illustrative anecdotes, dicta, proverbs, and assorted musings. At best he will divide his subject into heads and then pursue each as a separate topic, using the same unmortared pattern as with the undivided topics. If the whole lacks form and centrality, at least no one could accuse him of lacking *copia*' (xvi). For the relation between essay and sermon in Tuvill, see also 226.

25. Tuvill calls his essays 'unfashioned' in the dedicatory epistle (5).

26. Tuvill, 88, 92.

27. Lievsay, in Tuvill, 198.

28. Thomas M. Greene, *The Light in Troy: Imitation and Discovery in Renaissance Poetics* (New Haven: Yale University Press, 1982), 50; for heuristic and dialectical imitation, see 40–6.

29. Ibid., 37.

30. Ibid., 73. 'Whereas Lucretius and Horace had stressed the activity of gathering, Seneca stresses metamorphosis; movement through metaphorical space gives way to the body's invisible concoction of unlike elements into one. By reviewing theories of mellification without selecting any one, Seneca essentially allows the process of assimilation to remain mysterious. We do not, perhaps cannot, know exactly how the nectar becomes honey, how food becomes tissue and blood; analogously the assimilation of our reading is a process not to be codified, although the will is called upon to ensure the thoroughness of absorption. Seneca's analogies – for he *does* make them his own, following his own precept – may have such an extraordinarily long life because he is tactful enough to leave a space for an invisible event' (74).

31. Anthony Grafton's work on humanist reading is essential. For a recent overview, see 'The Humanist as Reader,' in *A History of Reading in the West*, ed. Cavallo and Chartier, 179–212, where he reminds us that reading is

not only a pedagogical activity, a way to teach or learn, but also a central part of our adult lives as well; any account of reading should recognize readers as adults: 'Reading, of course, did not end with schooling ... Mature individuals could make the technical skills they had mastered in school serve entirely unpredictable purposes' (205). See also: Grafton and Lisa Jardine, '"Studied for Action": How Gabriel Harvey Read His Livy,' *Past and Present* 129 (1990), 30–70; Grafton, 'Is the History of Reading a Marginal Enterprise? Guillaume Budé and His Books,' *PBSA* 91 (1997), 13–57; and Grafton, *Commerce with the Classics: Ancient Books and Renaissance Readers* (Ann Arbor: University of Michigan Press, 1997).

32. Ben Jonson, *Discoveries*, 731–41, in *The Oxford Authors: Ben Jonson*, ed. Ian Donaldson (New York: Oxford University Press, 1985), 541. The *Discoveries* were published in the 1640–41 two-volume folio of Jonson's *Works*, and probably written in the 1620s (see Donaldson's note, 735).

33. Shaftesbury, *Soliloquy*, 1.1, *Characteristicks of Men, Manners, Opinions, Times*, ed. Philip Ayres, 2 vols. (New York: Oxford University Press, 1999), 1:90. Elsewhere Shaftesbury writes of 'the way of Miscellany, or *common* Essay; in which the most confus'd head, if fraught with a little Invention, and provided with *Common-place-Book*-learning, might exert it-self to as much advantage, as the most orderly and well-settled Judgment' (*Miscellaneous Reflections*, 1.1, *Characteristicks*, 2:129–31). See also 2:141 on the seesaw of essay-writers.

34. Jonson and Shaftesbury are wishing essayists did what they said. Cornwallis should keep his writing, done for his own purposes, to himself: 'I write this in an Alehouse, into which I am driuen by night, which would not giue me leaue to finde out an honester harbour. I am without any company but Inke & Paper, & them I vse in stead of talking to my selfe' (67). 'That I am a man, I am bound to doe something; that a Christian, something not ill. So I thinke of this in respect of my purpose, not in my purpose's performance. It is called madnesse to talk to one's selfe, and meditation goeth with so faint a presse in my braine that it is soone wiped out. I write, therefore, to my selfe, and my selfe profits by my writing. If a strange eye carryes it to a stranger's iudgement and hee profits not by it, I am not sorry nor displeased, for I meant it onely to my selfe' (162).

35. For Jonsonian authorship as absolutist see Jonathan Goldberg, *James I and the Politics of Literature* (Baltimore: Johns Hopkins University Press, 1983), esp. 219–20, and Sara van den Berg, 'Ben Jonson and the Ideology of Authorship,' in *Ben Jonson's 1616 Folio*, ed. Jennifer Brady and W. H. Herendeen (Newark: University of Delaware Press, 1991), 111–37. I discuss Shaftesbury in relation to Addison and Steele in Chapter 4.

36. For Shaftesbury's commonplace book, 'Exercises,' see Robert Voitle, *The Third Earl of Shaftesbury* (Baton Rouge: Louisiana State University Press, 1984), 135–7.

37. Ben Jonson, *Timber: or, Discoveries, Made upon Men and Matter: as they have flowed out of his daily Reading; or had their refluxe to his peculiar Notions of the Times*. See Donaldson's Introduction for an account of Castelain's travails (xiv–xv).

38. T. C., *Morall Discourses and Essayes, Upon Severall Select Subjects* (1655), 'Prooemium,' A3–A4v.

39. Edward Blount, publisher of John Earle's *Microcosmographie; or, A Piece of the World Discovered in Essays & Characters* (1628), says he's acting like a midwife to bring forth the infants that the father would have smothered, 'who having left them lapt up in loose sheets, as soon as his fancy was delivered of them, written especially for his private recreation, to pass away time in the country, and by the forcible request of friends drawn from him' ('To the Reader,' 3). Henry Harflete calls his *A Banquet of Essayes* (1653), 'this weak Infant of my Braine' (Epistle Dedicatory, A3v).
40. Tuvill, 'Epistle Dedicatory,' 5.
41. Similarly, John Hall describes his essays as 'Faint breathings of a minde burthened with other literary employments, neither brought forth with Care, nor ripened with Age, yet such as if they bee not now blasted may be the first Fruits of larger Harvest' (*Horae Vacivae, Or, Essays. Some Occassional Considerations* [1646], A3v). *An Essay in Defence of the Female Sex* (1696) emphasizes the scale of essays, describing itself as 'this Essay' (A2v, A4), 'this little Piece' (A2), and 'this little Book' (A9).
42. Vincent Casaregola discusses this aspect of essays. He describes them 'not as finished products but processes, as discourse itself, with the implicit invitation to the reader to respond, just as the essay itself ... is in response to discourse that has preceded it' ('The Literature of the Essay and the Discourse of Values,' in *Values and Public Life: an Interdisciplinary Study*, ed. Gerard Magill and Marie D. Hoff [Lanham, MD: University Press of America, 1995], 57–88, 75). And he says elsewhere, 'the "event" of the essay may not be limited to the expressions of the essayist but may include an invitation to the reader to add his or her own distinctive, and perhaps digressive, patterns of amplification ... the essay implicitly encourages the reader to continue the process initiated by the essayist' ('Orality, Literacy, and Dialogue: Looking for the Origins of the Essay,' in *Time, Memory, and the Verbal Arts*, ed. Dennis L. Weeks and Jane Hoogestraat [Selinsgrove: Susquehanna University Press, 1998], 69–91, 80, 81).
43. Richard Whitlock, *Zootomia, or, Observations on the Present Manners of the English: Briefly Anatomizing the Living by the Dead* (1654), [A8v]. The Montaigne passage is from the beginning 'Of Books' (296). 'Observations' was a synonym for 'essays'; the title on the book's engraved frontispiece is *Zootomia, or a Morall Anatomy of the Liuing by the Dead in Observations Essays, &c*. Edward Blount, the publisher of *Horae subsecivae: Observations and Discourses* (1620), makes clear in his 'To the Reader': 'The Booke, you see, is of mixt matter, by way of obseruations, or Essayes, and Discourses' (A2v). Likewise, Richard Brathwait[e], *Essaies upon the fiue senses* (1620): 'here be certain *Essaies* or *Observations*, or what you will' (A2v–A3). See also Jonson's *Epicoene* (1610):

> Sir John Daw: The dor on Plutarch and Seneca! I hate it! They are mine own imaginations, by that light. I wonder these fellows have such credit with gentlemen.
> Clerimont: They are very grave authors.
> Daw: Grave asses! mere essayists: a few loose sentences, and that's all. A man would talk so his whole age; I do utter as good things every hour, if they were collected and observed, as either of 'em.

(2.3.42–9; ed. Edward Partridge [New Haven: Yale University Press, 1971], 57.)
44. Whitlock, a.
45. See my 'Addison's Aesthetics of Novelty,' *Studies in Eighteenth-Century Culture* 30 (2001), 269–88.
46. Whitlock, as Montaigne and Bacon do, locates the sources of this in the usual suspects, Plutarch and Seneca, and he makes an equally standard claim that 'essay' is what you call what you don't have a name for: 'Among many kindes of writings I finde Plutarchs most inviting Imitation for the form, (call them Discourses, Essayes, or what you will) nor behinde any for matter; if mixt sometimes with those Mucrones Sermonum, Enlivening Touches of Seneca full of smart Fancy, solid sense and accurate reason: such like Peeces compiled by able Pen-men out of Plutarchs fullness and Seneca's quickness, would undoubtedly fill the mouth of the most gaping Expectaltee among Readers' (a). Expectaltee: 'look-out' (OED), critic. Thomas Tuke calls his *New Essayes: Meditations and Vowes* (1614), 'these lines, (for I know not what to call them)' (A3).
47. Whitlock, a7.
48. Osborn writes: 'It being the Custom of some Heads, to afford the greater Reason, the less they are pumped. Such as is Clearest, running commonly quickest, and most Fluent; whereas, the Deeper requires straining, and so becomes Heavyer, and of a lesse sprightfull Tast' (*A Miscellany of Sundry Essayes, Paradoxes, and Problematicall Discourse, Letters and Characters*, in *The Works of Francis Osborn*, 7th edn. [1673], Preface, B4–B4v).
49. See Montaigne's 'Of the Education of Children' for his account of this. Whitlock gives an interesting rationale for citing quotations. Instead of taking a position for or against scholarship, and striking a gentlemanly pose, he offers a principle of justice – doing as I would be done by – as his rationale for citing his sources: 'As for my Quotations (which in the Judgments of some are dasht (like Pedigrees) with a vix ea nostra voco – scarce worth being called our own) I have on purpose confirmed some of my Descants (as well as at first I had them thence hinted) from such able Pens as are unquestionable. All Writings are but Hints, Descant, or Confirmation; if any be our own, it may well enough satisfie Expectation from any Single (unlesse singular) Author. He is a usefull Servant to Truth that serveth her by either, though not by all. Besides such is the peevish-nesse of present times, Contemporaries speaking even the words of the Ancients, have no Authority, unlesse they disown them by Citation: my Citations are from that Principle of doing as I would be done by, doing my Reader Service by a Reference to some usefull Book (or part of it) that may recompense his perusall of mine. I have my selfe sometimes been more beholding to some Books for anothers Sense, then their own. The like may befall this' (18–19). His book may point others to useful books, as he has sometimes found what books cite more helpful than what they say.
50. Whitlock, 21. The Cornwallis quotation is from 'Of Essaies and Bookes,' 202.
51. Felltham, 321–2.
52. 'To the Peruser' is retained as a preface to the 'short century' once the 'long century' is added in the third edition (1628). The long century was printed

first in all subsequent editions, so 'To the Readers' serves as an introduction to the volume, while 'To the Peruser' becomes an introduction to the second part.
53. Felltham, A4.
54. Tuvill, 'Of Poverty,' 142.
55. *Remedies against Discontentment drawen into several Discourses from the writings of auncient Philosophers* (1596) repeats this classical cliché, saying that discourses are the over-rulers of our passions (B1v); its title is a compact description of the humanist practice of moral philosophy appropriate to a world of writings, a practice of reading.
56. Felltham, 322. This final line picks up, to summarize and stress, a couple of key points made earlier in 'To the Pervsers,' the focus on the author's uses and the reader's freedom: 'I writ it without incouragement from another; and as I writ it, I send it abroade. Rare, I know it is not: Honest, I am sure it is: Though thou findest not to admire, thou maist to like. What I aime at in it, I confesse hath most respect to my selfe; That I might out of my owne Schoole take a lesson, and should serue mee for my whole Pilgrimage: and if I should wander from these rests, that my owne Items might set mee in heauens direct way againe. We doe not so readily run into crimes, that from our owne mouth haue had sentence of condemnation' (321–2). 'Request from others, may sway our words, or actions; but our minds will haue their owne free thoughts, as they apprehend the thing. Internall iudgement is not easily peruerted. In what thou shalt heere meete with, vse the freedome of thy natiue opinion: *Et Lectorem, et Correctorem liberum volui*' (321).
57. Osborn, *A Miscellany of Sundry Essayes, Paradoxes, and Problematicall Discourse, Letters and Characters* [1659], in *The Works of Francis Osborn, Esq*, 7th edn. (1673), 'The Preface. The Proem,' B5v–B6v.
58. Osborn takes this remark of Augustine's from Richard Hooker: 'The brethren in Egypt (saith S. Augustine) are reported to have many prayers, but every of them very short, as if they were darts thrown out with a kind of sudden quickness, lest that vigilant and erect attention of mind which in prayer is very necessary should be wasted or dulled through continuance, if their prayers were few and long' (*Of the Lawes of Ecclesiaticall Politie* [1594; rpt. New York: Da Capo Press, 1971], 69).
59. Cornwallis, 190.
60. Ibid.
61. Ibid.
62. Ibid., 190–1.
63. It's interesting that poetry figures art – method – more generally here. Both are machines of language that take you where they want to go, tying you up so you can't walk universally. This is a recurrent feature of the essay. For Boyle too the essay is an alternative to method; method requires you to complete its requirements even if they exceed your needs (see Chapter 3). This also raises a question: how much of essays' opposition to method is a contrast with poetry? Is this prose telling us what it can do, what it enables, and how to think through its exigencies?
64. Cornwallis writes: 'Socrates was the wisest man of his time, and his ground for that was his turning all his acquired knowledge into morality; of whom one saide, he fetched Philosophy from heauen and placed her in Cities'

(191). William Scott, in his *Essay on Drapery* (1635), uses this *topos*, one he almost certainly took from Cornwallis, along with the latter's remarks on what essays promise: 'It was the chiefest commendation of *Socrates*, that he turned all his acquir'd knowledge into morality; of whom one said, hee fetcht Philosophie from Heaven, and plac't her in Cities. Him I try to imitate, wherein if I write nothing but words I write what the Title of my Book promiseth, a tri-all an Essay' (*An Essay on Drapery, or The Compleate Citizen*, ed. and intro. Sylvia L. Thrupp [Boston: Harvard School of Business, 1953], 'To the Reader'). Addison uses this line at a key moment of articulating his practice in *Spectator* #10 (which I discuss in Chapter 4). Cornwallis's remarks on Montaigne (probably the passage to which Osborn refers) echo this shift of focus from knowledge to morality. Montaigne offers 'profitable Recreation' and 'speakes nobly, honestly, and wisely, with little method but with much iudgement. Learned he was and often showes it, but with such a happinesse as his owne following is not disgraced by his owne reading. He speaks freely and yet wisely, censures and determines many things Iudically, and yet forceth you not to attention with a "hem" and a spitting Exordium. In a word – hee hath made Morrall Philosophie speake couragiously, and in steede of her gowne, giuen her an Armour. He hath put Pedanticall Schollerisme out of countenance, and made manifest that learning mingled with Nobilitie shines most clearly' (42).

65. Osborn offers a nice image of this kind of trial: 'There appearing, no way readier, to demonstrate to a man his particular weakness, then by admitting him full leave to try his strength. Wherefore, so long as no body saw me, I was not capable of blame, If wanting the Engines of Learning, I endeavoured, to shake the Pillars of the Schooles. For though the Attempt, is not very likely, to afford any Benefit to others; yet, I cannot but remain, the stronger for it, and the more agile My Selfe: As such do, that swing; though the Beame stirs not, at which they tugge, It being natural to honest labour, still to be followed, by Wisdom or Reward' (B6). Exercise is not about moving the bar but buffing up. This leads to Shaftesbury's question about the point of writing essays if they're only for one's own benefit, or rather the point of publishing them if they are only journals, so to speak, of one's exercise program, records of one's practice of moral self-building, registers of reading that have benefits off the page.
66. Cornwallis, 'Of Fame,' 74.
67. Allen, Introduction, in Cornwallis, xiii.
68. For the evolution of Montaigne's *Essais*, see Donald Frame's 'Pierre Villey (1879–1933): an Assessment,' *Oeuvres & Critiques* 8 (1983), 29–43, a discussion of Villey's foundational account of the three stages of the *Essays*, as well as Frame, 'Considerations on the Genesis of Montaigne's *Essais*', 1–11, and David Maskell, 'The Evolution of the *Essais*,' 23–34, both in *Montaigne*, ed I. D. McFarlane and Ian Maclean (Oxford: Clarendon Press, 1982). Frame says that 'Writing (almost no matter what) probably offered relief from the frustrating futility of giving free rein to his flighty mind,' but eventually 'he must have needed tougher meat to chew on' and so ate, in effect (and in my words), his responses as well as his texts (10). Dudley M. Marchi notes that Montaigne was 'read as an author of the *exemplum*, as a

compiler of the commonplaces of ancient wisdom. The first edition of the *Essais* does in fact give the sense of an accumulation of anecdotes from which the author draws moral lessons, without the independent affirmation of the self-portrait and lacking the complicated attempt to portray the human condition in all its variety and complications, aspects that characterize the later editions' (*Montaigne among the Moderns: Receptions of the Essais* [Providence, RI: Berghahn, 1994], 23). See also Rosalie Colie: 'we might not have had these *Essais* at all without the *Adagia* and the adage-habit' (*The Resources of Kind: Genre-Theory in the Renaisance*, ed. Barbara Lewalski [Berkeley: University of California Press, 1973], 36). For the evolution of Bacon's *Essays*, see Kiernan's 'General Introduction' to his edition; 'Many aphorisms have been culled from Bacon's reading, and it is a feature of the essays, especially in their final form in 1625, that Bacon is engaged in dialogue, if not debate, with such sentences from his reading' (xlii).

69. Ted-Larry Pebworth, *Owen Felltham* (Boston: Twayne, 1976), 64, 65, 69. Laurence Stapleton also discusses the evolution of the *Resolves* in her chapter on Felltham in *The Elected Circle: Studies in the Art of Prose* (Princeton: Princeton University Press, 1973), 81–2. She notes, 'What lends life to his writing is accuracy of language. He observes with words given by words, rather than with words given by eyes or ears' (83). Stanley Stewart, in contrast to both Pebworth and Stapleton, sees in Felltham's final edition 'a crustier, more skeptical, pessimistic' tone ('Authorial Representation in Owen Felltham's *Resolves*,' *Cithera* 28 [1989], 7–33, 25).

70. [Thomas Culpeper,] 'Of Essayes,' *Essayes or Moral Discourses on Several Subjects. Written by a Person of Honor* (1671). Culpeper says of the essay, 'it hath so little to do with the matter it handles; rather expressing a generality of knowledge, then obliged to any particular Science: as we see in building, there are many Artists, that may own the compleating of some parts of the Fabrick, yet not claim the perfecting, of the whole structure' (1). In 'Of Discourse,' Cornwallis says it's good for mercenaries and mechanics to show themselves by talk, but a gentleman should talk like a gentleman, exhibiting general knowledge; 'it becomes him not to talke of one thing too much or to be wayed downe with any particular profession'; and he compares such wise guys to Socrates 'who although a Souldier and a Scholler, yet he discoursed stil like wisedome, which commaunds ouer all. One knowledge is but one part of the house, a baywindowe or a gable-ende. Who builds his house so maimed, much lesse himselfe? No, be complete. If thy Ghests be weary of thy Parlour, carry them into thy Gallery' (36–7). This echo of Cornwallis should be read alongside Culpeper's statement in 'Of Writing' that 'he is not a prudent manager of his knowledge, who doth not commit it to some memorial (it is what I reprehend in my self, that I have so little to shew of what I have observed or read, not having a line in a Note-book taken out of any Author) our Age had otherwise been not so much beholding to the former, and why should not succeeding times look to be as much obliged unto us' (115–16). If his essays seem more free of references than others, that's not because they're less registers of his reading but because he was less careful in the notes he took.

2. By way of essays

1. Thomas Palmer, *An Essay of the Meanes how to make our Trauviles, into forraine Countries, the more profitable and honourable* (1606), 'To the Reader.'
2. Here, for example, is the opening: 'Trauailing is equiuocable, Regular or Irregular. Of Irregular trauelling, most men finde by experience what it is. The Regular is an honorable or honest action of men (and in speciall cases of women) into forreine Countries and States, chiefly for a publike good to that Countrie of which such are, and also for a priuate benefit, and necessitie in cases necessarie and of commendableness. In like sort there are deriued, from this action of trauelling, two order of Trauellers, Regular and Irregular. The Regular are threefould; Non voluntarie, Inuoluntarie, or Voluntarie. Of whome foure things may be considered. First what ought to be the moouing causes of mens trauell. Secondly, what courses such as are iustly mooued must vndertake before trauell, if they will benefit their Countrie, or themselues. Thirdly, how they ought to spend their times in the interim of trauell. Lastly, what commendable carriages and behauiour such are to express at their returnes, to the farther honour of themselues, good of the State, and glorie of God. / The first of these according to the ancient diuision of Causes hath fowre head mouers; but it may be impertinent to intreat of aboue two, at this present, namely of the efficient and finall. For, the formall esteemed causes (which are pedestriall, equestrial, or nauticall) stand either at the diposition of the efficient; or pretend perfection and vse from the finall' (1–2).
3. Cornwallis, 73.
4. Felltham, 'Of Trauaile,' 271. Osborn's Preface opens: 'If, contrary to the Mode of such as lose their Thoughts in the open Aire where they were conceived; I have, with more Diligence, registred Mine; it was out of no Opinion they deserve a longer life, but to prevent Idleness, with a Concourse of some more Tedious, if not Sinful: which in the Vacancy of Imployment, are apt to intrude themselves, under the pretence of a more ancient and Familiar Acquaintance' (Br).
5. Henry Peacham, *The Complete Gentleman and The Truth of Our Times, Reveled out of One's Man's Experience, by Way of Essay*, ed. Virgil B. Heltzel (Ithaca: Cornell University Press, 1962).
6. 'There are more, but mine is but an Essay, not a Catalogue. I thinke well of these Bookes named, and the better because they teach me how to manage my selfe. Where any of them grow subtile or intend high matters, I giue my memory leaue to loose them' (Cornwallis, 202). Essays are the name for the practice of registering thoughts, but here such thoughts are put on the page in order to forget them, husks of a process of use.
7. Peacham, 160.
8. Ibid., 165.
9. Ibid., 217.
10. Ibid., 219.
11. Ibid., 221.
12. Ibid., 179.
13. Montaigne's reading and writing are organized by attention to the ways one moves through books: 'Let attention be paid not to the matter, but to the

shape I give it' ('Of Books,' 296); 'And everyday I amuse myself reading authors without any care for their learning, looking for their style, not their subject' ('Of the Art of Discussion,' 708). For discussions of Montaigne's practice of reading, see Victoria Kahn, 'The Sense of Taste in Montaigne's *Essais,*' *Modern Language Notes* 95 (1980), 129–91; Terence Cave, 'Problems of Reading in the *Essais,*' in *Montaigne*, ed. McFarlane and Maclean, 133–66; Cathleen M. Bauschatz, 'Montaigne's Conception of Reading in the Context of Renaissance Poetics and Modern Criticism,' in *The Reader in the Text*, ed. Susan R. Suleiman and Inge Crosman (Princeton: Princeton University Press, 1980), 264–91.

14. Culpeper, 'Of Knowledge and Reading,' 105.
15. 'Why do we take so much pleasure out of being different not only from others but from our own past?' (Bruno Latour, *We Have Never Been Modern* [Cambridge: Harvard University Press, 1993], 114). I discuss Barthes's notion of the 'readerly' classic text below.
16. Culpeper, 108.
17. Cornwallis, 200.
18. See Chapter 1, note 9 for the passage from Seneca's second moral epistle.
19. Cornwallis, 202.
20. Peacham, 217–18.
21. Ibid., 162.
22. Adorno, 161. 'In the essay discreetly separated elements enter into a readable context; it erects no scaffolding, no edifice. Through their own movement the elements crystallize into a configuration. It is a force field, just as under the essay's glance every intellectual artifact must transform itself into a force field' (161).
23. Certeau, 174.
24. Walking, like reading, has no place: 'walking manipulates spatial organizations, no matter how panoptic they may be: it is neither foreign to them (it can only take place within them) nor in conformity with them (it does not receive its identity from them). It creates shadows and ambiguities within them. It inserts its multitudinous references and citations into them' (Certeau, 103); 'to read is to wander through an imposed system (that of the text, analogous to the constructed order of the city or of a supermarket) ... The reader takes neither the position of the author nor the author's position. He invents in texts something different from what they "intended." He detaches them from their (lost or accessory) origin. He combines their fragments and creates something un-known in the space organized by their capacity for allowing an indefinite plurality of meanings' (169). This jibes with Kittay and Godzich's account of prose literacy; see esp. 124, 130.
25. 'A different world (the reader's) slips into the author's place. The mutation makes the text habitable, like a rented apartment. It transforms another person's property into a space borrowed for a moment ... as pedestrians do, in the streets they fill with the forest of their desires and goals' (Certeau, xxi). This conception of reading contrasts with Paul Heilker's account of the essay: 'what the essay highlights is that thought and language resist domestication' (*The Essay: Theory and Pedagogy for an Active Form* [Urbana, IL: National Council of Teachers of English, 1996], 181). Heilker assumes that

you can only live in a house that's yours, but, I think, with Wilde, that much of one's thinking is with other people's thoughts: you make a home in the language you use.
26. This is Erich Auerbach's description of the task of Montaigne's *Essais* (*Mimesis*, trans. Willard Trask [New York: Doubleday Anchor, 1957], 273).
27. Richard Hurd, who edited Cowley's *Select Works* in 1772, said 'the Sieur de Montaigne and Mr Cowley are our two great models of essay-writing' (qtd. Arthur Tilley, 'Introduction,' *Cowley's Essays* [Cambridge: Cambridge University Press, 1938], xxvi; all citations to Cowley's *Essays* are to this edition). In 1969 James Sutherland introduces his discussion of Cowley by calling him 'a celebrated writer,' and concludes with Lamb's delight in him (*English Literature of the Late Seventeenth Century* [Oxford: Clarendon Press, 1969], 222–3). But the new *Encyclopedia of the Essay* (ed. Tracy Chevalier [Chicago: Fitzroy Dearborn, 1997]) doesn't have an entry for him, and he gets only one bland line in the entry, 'British Essay.'
28. Alan de Gooyer, 'Sensibility and Solitude in Cowley's Familiar Essay,' *Restoration* 25 (2001), 1–18, 6. The source of this anecdote is a letter to Sprat (21 May 1665), cited in Johnson's *Life of Cowley*; it does not make the connection between disappointment in the country and writing that Gooyer suggests: 'The first night that I came hither I caught so great a cold, with a defuxion of rheum, as made me keep my chamber ten days. And, two after, had such a bruise on my ribs with a fall, that I am yet unable to move or turn myself in my bed. This is my personal fortune here to begin with. And, besides, I can get no money from my tenants, and have my meadows eaten up every night by cattle put in by my neighbours. What this signifies, or may come to in time, God knows if it be ominous, it can end in nothing less than hanging. Another misfortune has been, and stranger than all the rest, that you have broke your word with me, and failed to come, even though you told Mr. Bois that you would. This is what they call *Monstri simile*. I do hope to recover my late hurt so farre that within five or six days (though it be uncertain yet whether I shall ever recover it) as to walk about again. And then, methinks, you and I and *the Dean* might be very merry upon St. Anne's Hill. You might very conveniently come hither the way of Hampton Town, lying there one night. I write this in pain, and can say no more: *Verbum sapienti*' (Johnson, *Lives of the Poets*, intro. Arthur Waugh, 2 vols. [New York: Oxford University Press, 1977], 1:11–12). Sutherland also locates a motive for the essays in this kind of story: 'although he complained to his friend Sprat that his tenants would not pay their rent, and that his meadows were 'eaten up every night by cattle put in by neighbours,' he tried to make a virtue out of necessity and wrote his charming essays' (*English Literature*, 222).
29. Cowley, 'Of Solitude,' 24. 'But this you'l say is work only for the Learned, others are not capable either of the employments or the divertisements that arise from Letters. I know they are not, and therefore cannot much recommend Solitude to a man totally illiterate' (25). It bears repeating that reading is a practice of literacy; this doesn't mean that the things that reading does can only be done with books, but to practice them on books is to read.
30. Cowley, 'Of Myself,' 107–8.

31. Gooyer, 6; 'his defense of retirement is traditional; he attacks political ambition and wealth and praises the virtuous simplicities of solitude. Yet for all his bitter – and perhaps warranted – recriminations of the political world, he ultimately ends up appealing to personal sentiment as sufficient justification for his withdrawal' (1).
32. Ibid., 7. Gooyer focuses on 'authenticity' throughout (1, 5, 6, 9, 10), 'an accumulated fullness of inner experience prior to critical understanding and outside the custody of moral logic' (8). His analysis shifts Cowley's 'liberty' into an anachronistic 'liberation': 'Withdrawal bestows liberation' (14).
33. Cowley, 'Of Myself,' 109–10.
34. Gooyer, 9.
35. Ibid., 15.
36. David Hill Radcliffe, *Forms of Reflection: Genre and Culture in Meditational Writing* (Baltimore: Johns Hopkins University Press, 1993), 73.
37. This 'sneer' goes back to Addison, Tilley says, 'In spite of *The Spectator's* sneer that "he praised solitude when he despaired of shining in a court," there is no reason to doubt his earnest affection for obscurity and retirement' ('The Essay and the Beginning of Modern English Prose,' in *The Cambridge History of English Literature*, vol. 8, ed. A. W. Ward and A. R. Waller [Cambridge: Cambridge University Press, 1920], 368–90, 378).
38. The quoted phrase is Gooyer's; see his brief account of this debate (3–4).
39. 'Opting out' is Gooyer's term, 15.
40. Radcliffe, 78. See especially Radcliffe's excellent account of the Pindaric structure of the whole (77). In 'Ode. Upon Liberty,' Cowley contrasts his choice of Pindaric form to heroic ones (20–1).
41. This is the second recommendation Cowley makes for retirees. The first is the 'very eradication of all lusts.' Is this some kind of joke? I wonder if Gooyer's argument takes its shape from this very traditional, stoic notion of *ataraxia*. If this is so, it's worth remembering Cowley's second point as well: 'The first work, therefore, that a man must do to make himself capable of the good of solitude is the very eradication of all lusts, for how is it possible for a man to enjoy himself while his affections are tied to things without himself? In the second place, he must learn the art and get the habit of thinking' (24).
42. Cowley, 'Of Obscurity,' 29–30; quoting *Aeneid* 1.412.
43. 'It is an unpleasant constraint to be always under the sight and observation and censure of others; as there may be vanity in it, so, methinks, there should be vexation too of spirit' ('Of Liberty,' 10). 'Now, as for being known much by sight, and pointed at, I cannot comprehend the honour that lies in that' ('Of Obscurity,' 31).
44. *Aeneid* 1.405. The line is Certeau's epigraph for the section, 'The chorus of idle footsteps' (97).
45. Certeau, 97.
46. Ibid., 131, 174.
47. 'They march, obscure, for *Venus* kindly shrouds / With Mists, their Persons, and involves in Clouds, / That, thus unseen, their Passage none might stay, / Or force to tell the Causes of their Way' (*Aeneid* 1.570–3, trans. Dryden, *The Works of Dryden*, vol. 5, ed. William Frost and Vinton A. Dearing [Berkeley: University of California Press, 1987], 362).

48. See Certeau, 100. Deleuze remarks: 'As a general rule, fantasies simply treat the indefinite as a mask for a personal or a possessive: "a child is being beaten" is quickly transformed into "my father beat me." But literature takes the opposite path and exists only when it discovers beneath apparent persons the power of an impersonal – which is not a generality but a singularity at the highest point: a man, a woman, a beast, a stomach, a child … It is not the first two persons that function as the condition for literary enunciation; literature begins only when a third person is born in us that strips us of the power to say "I" (Blanchot's "neuter")' ('Literature and Life,' *Critical Inquiry* 23 [1997], 225–30, 227). The reference is to Blanchot's *The Infinite Conversation*, trans. Susan Hanson (Minneapolis: University of Minnesota Press, 1993), 384–5. This far from uncanny moment, this most familiar of recognitions, is also mentioned by Hadot and Santner, cited below.
49. Manuel de Landa: 'if instead of taking a planetary perspective we adopted a cosmic viewpoint, our entire planet would itself be a mere provisional hardening in the vast flows of plasma which permeate the universe' (*A Thousand Years of Nonlinear History* [New York: Zone, 1997], 261).
50. Barthes, *S/Z*, 4.
51. Ibid., 16.
52. Ibid., 5.
53. Qtd. ibid., 267. Barthes's reference to it, 16.
54. Adorno's account of the essay seems closer to Bataille than Barthes's is: 'The essay refuses to glorify concern for the primal as something more primal than concern for the mediated … thought may only hold true to the idea of immediacy by way of the mediated, but it becomes the prey of the mediated the instant it grasps directly for the unmediated' (167).
55. Obaldia, 80. For *doxa* as repressive, see 78, 118.
56. Ibid., 67; see also 66, 80. For a similar account of essay as play, evasion, and release, see Snyder, 200.
57. R. Lane Kaufmann, 'Essaying as Unmethodical Method,' in *Essays on the Essay: Redefining the Genre*, ed. Alexander J. Butrym (Athens: University of Georgia Press, 1989), 221–41, 236; qtd. Obaldia, 63. For Obaldia's reading of the essay as a romantic genre, see 39–41. Many critics take the essay as a genre defined by a tension between an individual and the system, the place where one gets to use one's own voice, express oneself lyrically in terms that are not mediated by the system. This is the thesis of Good's *The Observing Self*; he discusses the essay in terms of personal voice (1) and personal reflection (7), as starting from the Cartesian problem of a self facing an unknown world (4), and as an act of personal witness (23). For other accounts of the essay that focus on voice and expression in similar terms, see: Carl H. Klaus, Chris Anderson, and Rebecca Blevins Faery, eds., 'Introduction,' *In Depth: Essayists for Our Time*, 2nd edn. (Philadelphia: Harcourt Brace Jovanovich College Publishers, 1993), 5; Wendell Harris, 'Reflections on the Peculiar Status of the Personal Essay,' *College English* 58 (1996), 934–53, 934; Ruth-Ellen Boetcher Joeres and Elizabeth Mittman, eds., 'An Introductory Essay,' *The Politics of the Essay: Feminist Perspectives* (Bloomington: Indiana University Press, 1993), 19; and Edward Hoagland,

'What I Think, What I Am,' *The Tugman's Passage* (New York: Random House, 1982), 25.
58. Obaldia, 124–5.
59. Bensmaïa, 58; for complication, see 13, 99; for forgoing mastery and system, 31, 56. In contrast to Bensmaïa's Barthesian version of tactics (see *Roland Barthes by Roland Barthes*, trans. Richard Howard [New York: Hill and Wang, 1977], 172), I've adopted Certeau's conception of tactics to describe a way of reading. 'A tactic insinuates itself into the other's place, fragmentarily, without taking it over entirely' (Certeau, xix); for reading in these terms, see 'Reading as Poaching': 'The reader takes neither the position of the author nor the author's position' (169; see also 101).
60. Bensmaïa, 5, 92; for excess, see 12; for the power of procedure as a new system of production, 33, 99; for generative alterity, 92. The 'essential supplement' is Obaldia's notion, 92; she says that essays are all equally secondary and so equally primary (56, 93, 123, 124). This is not the same thing, as Adorno notes in the passage cited above, note 54 above.
61. 'And this is what constitutes the writing of essays (we speak here of Bataille): the amorous rhythm of science and of value: heterology, bliss' (Barthes, *Roland Barthes*, 159; qtd. Bensmaïa, 24). Bensmaïa's account of reading Barthes and reading essays is in such terms, as seduction, as cruising (69). Similarly, John O'Neill reads Montaigne in terms of a 'pleasure [that] lies outside of any literary organization,' 'topics and titles in the Essays serve only as strategies of pleasure' (*Essaying Montaigne: a Study of the Renaissance Institution of Writing and Reading* [Boston: Routledge and Kegan Paul, 1982], 7).
62. '"Friendship" becomes the motif of a reflection that, paradoxically, focuses less on what friendship is supposed to bring to shared experience, than on how it alienates me, distances me from myself and makes me defer, as it were, the moment of taking care of myself' (Bensmaïa, 63). See also the discussion of '*acolouthia*' (going beyond) and friendship (64–5): 'it still represents a "snare" since I have *to yield myself* (to them [friends]), which, in Barthesian terms, means that I have to renounce that which is most authentic in me, most irreducible' (65).
63. 'Each time he is obliged to enter the public arena, Barthes must abandon his "creation of self," be "frozen," become an Image ... If, being "cultivated," the Image loosens its hold a bit and becomes more ethereal, it nevertheless remains an Image. Friendship will thus remain in the final instance on the side of the species, on the side of gregarious values and the Imaginary. Even with "friends," one must still speak the common, general, incorporeal language' (Bensmaïa, 88). This is written in Barthes's own language; for a glossary see Bensmaïa, 76. See also Michèle Richman's 'Foreword' to Bensmaïa on Barthes's 'écriture' as 'the nemesis of writing-as-instrument, the unreflective transcription of the *doxa* or "that which goes without saying"' (xvii).
64. See Obaldia, 144.
65. Stanley Fish, *Self-Consuming Artifacts* (Berkeley: University of California Press, 1972), 98. 'At that moment the reader is transformed from a passive recipient of popular truth into a searcher after objective truth, and this transformation follows upon the transformation of the essay from a vehicle

whose form is designed to secure belief into an instrument of inquiry and examination' (98).
66. Ibid., 119–20.
67. Ibid., 151, 154–5.
68. Ibid., 154. For Fish's discussion of Bacon's 'seeds' see 88; these are different from Socrates' seeds discussed on 8.
69. Ibid., 154, 151; 'they are unfinished with a purposefulness that makes the bestowing of the adjective less a criticism than a compliment' (151).
70. 'The result is a change in the quality of the reader's attention' (Fish, 98). 'This is still another of the essays whose conclusion sends us back with new eyes to its opening' (133). 'Bacon deplores the tendency of the mind to equate its immediate horizons with the horizons of reality, and, again like Plato, he devises a mode of proceeding that prevents the mind from resting too easily in the satisfaction of closed and artificial systems' (152). Plato's answer was to train a mind to grasp that reality in an unmediated fashion; Bacon's answer doubts the possibility of that. The essay offers a tool for this latter kind of practice, a rereading not a dreaming by the book.
71. Georg Lukács, 'On the Nature and Form of the Essay,' *Soul and Form*, trans. Anna Bostock (Cambridge: MIT Press, 1974),1–18, 16–17.
72. Here are some early modern definitions of the word:

John Baret, *An Aluearie or triple dictionarie* (1574): to *Assay* or rather *Essay* of the French worde; To assay: to prooue: to assaile: to sette upon by deceite; To espie or essay priuity; To attempt again, & assay to dooe something; A proofe: a trying: an assaying; Tasted, essayed, sacrificed, taken out of; To thinke deeply: to studie: to muse on a thing: to recorde in ones mind, to practise and assaye how well he can doe: to purpose: to singe or playe sweetly ... To assaye with money, to corrupt a judgement; An assay or flourish, that one maketh to prooue what he can dooe, before he fight in deede; An assaying or proouing before, a grouping or feeling of the way with ones hande or other thing / It is no hard matter to assaye or prooue.

Robert Cawdry, *A Table Alphabeticall* (1604): essay, tryall what one can say, or doe in any matter.

J. B. [John Bulloker], *An English Expositor, or Compleat Dictionary* (1616): Essayes Tryals / Trials.

Henry Cockeram, *The English Dictionarie* (1623, 1658): Essayes Tryals.

John Minsheu, *Guide into Tongues* (1627): essay proue.

Edward Phillips, *The New World of English Words* (1658, 1678): Essay, (French) a tryal, also a preamble. The Essay of a Deer, in Hunting, is the Breast, or Brisket of a Deer, in French *la hampe*; assay: to prove, to try; an Assayer of the King is an Officer of the Mint, for the true trial of Silver.

Edward Phillips, *The New World of Words*, new edition (1696): *Essay*, a Preamble, a Taste, a Tryal; also the Touching and Proof of Gold and Silver, when it comes to the Mint: said figuratively of the Works of the Brain. A Poeticall Essay, Montaign's *Essays*. / The *Essay* of a Deer, in Hunting, is the Breast, or Brisket of a Deer.

Thomas Blount, *Glossographia* (2nd edn., 1661): Essay (Fr.) a proof, a trial, a flourish or preamble; Among Comedians the trial or proof of the action, which they make before they come forth publickly upon the stage, is their *Essay*.

Elisha Coles, *An English Dictionary* (1676, 1692): Essay, f. to try; also a tryal or preamble / Essay, [of a deer] the breast or brisket; Assaier, a Mint-officer for the trial of Silver.

73. Lukács, 17.
74. 'Form is [the essayist's] great experience, form – as immediate reality – is the image-element, the really living content of his writings ... that moment at which things become forms – the moment when all feelings and experiences on the near and the far side of form receive form, are melted down and condensed into form' (Lukács, 8).
75. Lukács, 17.
76. Jean-François Lyotard, *The Postmodern Condition: a Report on Knowledge*, trans. Geoff Bennington and Brian Massumi (Minneapolis: University of Minnesota Press, 1984), 81.
77. Ibid., 80.
78. Ibid., 81, 17, 66; see too the quotation from Medwar on *'having ideas'* as the [new] science (60).
79. 'Modern aesthetics is an aesthetic of the sublime, though a nostalgic one. It allows the unpresentable to be put forward only as the missing contents; but the form, because of its recognizable consistency, continues to offer to the reader or viewer matter for solace and pleasure' (Lyotard, 81). Postmodern aesthetics, in contrast, 'searches for new presentations, not in order to enjoy them but in order to impart a stronger sense of the unpresentable ... Those rules and categories are what the work of art itself is looking for'; 'our business is not to supply reality but to invent allusion to the inconceivable which cannot be presented' (81). In other words, we must grasp for the unmediated, and as we fail (as we must, by definition), think we're the first ones who've so dared.
80. For the two 'modes' of modernity, 'the nostalgia for presence' and 'the increase of being and the jubilation which result from the invention of new rules of the game,' see Lyotard, 80–1.
81. Lukács, 10. 'Essays do not create – neither new worlds nor new philosophies. They are always written about; they are always either Of or On ... Out of old and often ancient texts the essayist makes another to throw like a shawl across the knees of a third. This is an activity for men?' (Gass, 30). 'The essay, always directed to artifacts, does not present itself as a creation; nor does it long for something all-embracing, the totality of which would resemble creation' (Adorno, 165).
82. Thomas Harrison, *Essayism: Conrad, Musil, and Pirandello* (Baltimore: Johns Hopkins University Press, 1992), 217.
83. Ibid., 223. 'Essayism does not extol a new liberalism subtended by subjective self-certainty. Nor does it propose new instruments for the old project of self-determination. Rather, it questions the subject still imagined by this liberal project, a subject that appears not only to be an ideological epiphenomenon but also an all too static, even reflex, reaction to complex operations of being-in-the-world. The invitation by Conrad, Musil, and Pirandello to reconsider the operations of being-in-the-world did not hope to be answered by improved programs for self-realization. If anything, they expected that the subject might begin to outgrow its own self-conception, desisting, as it were, from its projects of practical and ideal desire' (213).

84. Harrison, 224–5.
85. Harrison, 219–20.
86. It's possible I'm mistaking Harrison's point. He could be signaling just this different kind of truth, this reorientation of expectations (*truth* will always be a process not a product), and by *will* he could mean seriousness of purpose in looking (not just a Lyotardesque relativistic happy play with possibilities). He may be arguing against precisely the position I'm saying he holds. I'm saying his *truth* is a condition of asking questions of the sort that yield true/false answers, and that such a true/false grid is organized by categories that skeptical reason recognizes as habitual but not universal (Hume's point and Nietzsche's); so he needs to ask different questions organized by different expectations (our conventions, by definition, give us our truths – which are necessarily local). But if he's already saying that, and truth for him is not just a project of what we know, a way to make sense, but instead a way of resituating the substance of that answer in the undertaking of those questions – truth is not what you get but how you look, and what he calls the 'will to truth' may be his way of articulating just that transfer – then I'm agreeing with him, up to this point. (And if so, if I am mistaking his point by reading his language too rigidly, instead of taking my movement through it as his point, then yes: I get you. These mazes you move through, who's to say that the way you move through them isn't their point? In disagreeing with Harrison, I get – enact – his point.)
87. This is Stanley Cavell's distinction, one used by Eric L. Santner in *On the Psychotheology of Everyday Life* (Chicago: University of Chicago Press, 2001), 23–4. Santner also quotes Hilary Putnam: 'It is true that we do not "know" that there is a world and that there are other people ... but not because (this is the skeptic's misunderstanding) we "don't know" these things. In ordinary circumstances, circumstances in which neither doubt nor justification is called for, our relation to the familiar things in our environment, the pen in our hand or the person in pain whom we are consoling, is not one of either "knowing" or "not knowing." Rather, Cavell suggests, it is one of *acknowledging* (or, sadly, failing to acknowledge). Our task is not to acquire a "proof" that "there is an external world" or that our friend is in pain, but to *acknowledge* the world and our friend' (qtd. Santner, 24).
88. Santner, 5–6.
89. 'Escaping the imaginary totalizations produced by the eye, the everyday has a certain strangeness that doesn't surface, or whose surface is only its upper limit, outlining itself against the visible. Within this ensemble, I shall try to locate practices that are foreign to the "geometrical" or "geographical" space of visual, panoptic, or theoretical constructions. These practices of space refer to a specific form of *operations* ... and to an *opaque and blind* mobility characteristic of the bustling city. A *migrational*, or metaphorical, city, thus slips into the clear text of the planned and readable city' (Certeau, 93).
90. Pierre Hadot, 'Learning How to Read,' *Philosophy as a Way of Life* (New York: Blackwell, 1995), 108, 109. The opening quotation is Luc de Clapiers, Marquis de Vauvenargues, *Réflections et maxims* (no. 400, qtd. Hadot, 108).

'Every thought is new when another expresses it in his own way'; 'There are many things we don't know well enough, and that it is good to have repeated' (nos. 398–9, qtd. Hadot, 124).
91. Montaigne, 'Of Friendship,' 139. 'Our friendship has no other model than itself, and can be compared only with itself' (139).
92. Peacham, 204–5.
93. Not wrong because the essay enables just that kind of work; one updates one's texts in the shape of one's own concerns.
94. Landa, 261.
95. Schlegel: 'The essay is like a mutual galvanism of the author and reader; it is also an inner arousal for each independently. It is a systematic alteration between rest and motion. Its purpose is to cause motion, to combat intellectual arthritis, to promote agility' (qtd. John McCarthy, *Crossing Boundaries: a Theory and History of Essay Writing in German, 1680–1815* [Philadelphia: University of Pennsylvania Press, 1989], 59). Adorno: 'In the essay, discreetly separated elements enter into a readable context; it erects no scaffolding, no edifice. Through their own movement the elements crystallize into a configuration. It is a force field, just as under the essay's glance every intellectual artifact must transform itself into a force field' (161). Terence Cave describes Montaigne's *Essais* as a 'catalyst in a chain reaction which displayed some of the characteristics of reading and rereading as a perennial activity' (153).

3. Boyle's Essay

1. Steven Shapin and Simon Schaffer, *Leviathan and the Air-Pump: Hobbes, Boyle and the Experimental Life* (Princeton: Princeton University Press, 1985), 63; Rose-Mary Sargent, *The Diffident Naturalist: Robert Boyle and the Philosophy of Experiment* (Chicago: University of Chicago Press, 1995), 39.
2. *Sceptical Chymist*, in *The Works of Robert Boyle*, ed. Michael Hunter and Edward B. Davis, 14 vols. (London: Pickering & Chatto, 1999–2000), 2:214; all citations to Boyle's works are to this edition.
3. See Sargent, 14, and Lawrence M. Principe, *The Aspiring Adept: Robert Boyle and His Alchemical Quest* (Princeton: Princeton University Press, 1998), 12, 23, 220.
4. See Latour, esp. 69, 47.
5. Qtd. Steven Shapin, *A Social History of Truth: Civility and Science in Seventeenth-Century England* (Chicago: Chicago University Press, 1994), 140.
6. [Francis Boyle,] 'The Preface to the Reader,' *Moral Essays and Discourses Upon Several Subjects Chiefly Relating to the Present Times* (1690), A2.
7. Felltham, A4.
8. Hall, A3v, 111–12.
9. Gethin, a.
10. Robert Boyle, 'A Proemial Essay, wherein, With some considerations touching *Experimental Essays* in General Is interwoven such an Introduction to all those written by the Author, as is necessary to be perus'd for the better understanding of them,' *Works*, 2:10–12.
11. Ibid., 2:14–15.

12. Ibid., 2:15. Boyle famously declares himself content to be such an 'Underbuilder' (2:20).
13. For Shapin and Schaffer's account of Boyle's three embedded technologies, material, literary, and social, see 25–6; each of the technologies 'contributes to a common strategy for the constitution of the matter of fact,' functioning 'as an objectifying resource' (77).
14. For their account of Boyle's writing in terms of pictures, see Shapin and Schaffer, 62, 64; for the portrayal of a trustworthy author, 65, 69.
15. Shapin, 'Pump and Circumstance: Robert Boyle's Literary Technology,' *Social Studies of Science* 14 (1984), 481–520, 484. 'The literary technology of virtual witnessing extended the public space of the laboratory in offering a valid witnessing experience to all readers of the text' (Shapin and Schaffer, 77; see also 69).
16. 'A greater degree of assurance was required to produce assent in virtual witnesses. Boyle's literary technology was crafted to secure this assent' (Shapin and Schaffer, 61).
17. Michael Hunter, *Robert Boyle, 1627–91: Scrupulosity and Science* (Rochester, NY: Boydell, 2000), 9; Principe, *Aspiring*, 107, 109, 111.
18. For romance, Principe, 'Virtuous Romance and Romance Virtuoso: the Shaping of Robert Boyle's Literary Style,' *Journal of the History of Ideas* 56 (1995), 377–97; for his critique of Shapin, see 396–7. For transmutation histories, Principe, *Aspiring*, 93, 111, and William R. Newman, *Gehennical Fire* (Cambridge: Harvard University Press, 1994), 3–11.
19. Sargent, 211, 127–8. 'The dynamic, open-ended structure of his experimental essays reflected well the nature of experimental practice in general' (185); for her discussion of the 'Proemial Essay' see 183–9.
20. James Paradis, 'Montaigne, Boyle, and the Essay of Experience,' in *One Culture: Essays in Science and Literature*, ed. George Levine (Madison: University of Wisconsin Press, 1987), 59–91, 60, 77, 86.
21. Florio says of Montaigne's *Essais*: 'Why but Essayes are but mens schoolthemes pieced together; you may as well say, several texts. Al is in the choise & handling' (John Florio, 'To the Reader,' *The Essayes of Montaigne*, trans. Florio [1603], A5v). Dudley M. Marchi notes that in the seventeenth century Montaigne was 'read as an author of the *exemplum*, as a compiler of the commonplaces of ancient wisdom' (23). For accounts of the *Essais* as exercises in reading, see Victoria Kahn, 'The Sense of Taste in Montaigne's *Essais*,' and Terence Cave, 'Problems of Reading in the *Essais*.'
22. Boyle, 'Proemial Essay,' 2:14. Sargent notes this too, 300 n. 8.
23. Culpeper, 1.
24. Richard M. Chadbourne, 'French Essay,' *Encyclopedia of the Essay*, ed. Tracy Chevalier (Chicago: Fitzroy Dearborn, 1997), 295; in France the essay 'was categorized – and often dismissed as an English literary type' (306).
25. Pierre Nicole, *Moral Essays* (1677), translation of *Essai de morale* (1671), 'Advertisement,' A2–A2v.
26. John Willis, 'An Essay of Dr. John Willis, exhibiting his Hypothesis about the Flux and Reflux of the Sea,' in The Royal Society of London, *Philosophical Transactions*, vols. *1–2* (New York: Johnson Reprint Corporation, 1963), #16 (6 August 1666), 266–7, 281.

27. Oldenburg writes in his preface to Willis: 'it was thought fit to offer it by Press to the Publick, that other Intelligent Persons also might the more conveniently and at their leisure examine the *Conjecture* (the Author, such is his Modesty, presenting it no otherwise) and thereupon give in their sense, and what Difficulties may occur to them about it, that so it maybe either confirm'd or laid aside accordingly' (2:264).
28. 'And though it be manifest enough, that *Galileo*, as to some particulars, was mistaken in the account which there he gives of it; yet that may be very well allowed, without any blemish to so deserving a person, or prejudice to the *main Hypothesis*: For that Discourse is to be looked upon onely as an *Essay* of the *general Hypothesis*; which as to *particulars* was to be afterwards adjusted, from a good *General History of the Tides*' (Willis, 2:265).
29. Willis, 2:266.
30. Shapin, *Social History*, 309; see 240 for epistemology grounded in decorum.
31. Ibid., 179. 'If, in the context of mathematical practice, absolute certainty and precision were the goals of inquiry, in experimental practice they presented themselves as potential troubles for the development and continuance of an investigative *conversation*' (351); for the contrast in these terms of Boyle and Pascal, see 339; for conversation, see 117–21, 351–3.
32. Michael Hunter sees Shapin's *Social History* as 'dominated by the concept of self-fashioning' (*Scrupulosity*, 11).
33. 'conventions and codes of gentlemanly conversation were mobilized as practically effective solutions to problems of scientific evidence, testimony, and assent' (Shapin, *Social History*, 121; for identity, 131, for authority, 191).
34. Sargent, 44. She argues that contextualist studies 'tend to dismiss the epistemic factors embedded within cultural practices' (43); 'Actors' reasons for what they do are often drawn from the internal dynamics of an activity itself, distinct from any ulterior goals or purposes' (212). In his Introduction to *Robert Boyle Reconsidered*, ed. Michael Hunter (New York: Cambridge University Press, 1994), Hunter argues for combining contextualism with sensitivity to 'the power and complexity of intellectual traditions in their own right' (5).
35. Culpeper, 108. Cornwallis writes that 'it becomes [a gentleman] not to talke of one thing too much or to be wayed downe with any particular profession' (36), and describes his essays in this way: 'I would earne none of these [arts] so dearly as to ty vp the minde to thinke onely of one thing; her best power by this meanes is taken from her, for so her circuit is limited to a distance, which should walke vniuersally' (191).
36. For Sargent on social dimensions, 18; for Shapin on epistemic ones, *Social History*, 118, 123. Both Harwood and Altgoer note that Boyle doesn't reject rhetoric; John T. Harwood, 'Science Writing and Writing Science: Boyle and Rhetorical Theory,' in *Boyle Reconsidered*, 37–56, 48, and Diane B. Altgoer, *Reckoning Words: Baconian Science and the Construction of Truth in English Renaissance Culture* (Madison: Fairleigh Dickinson University Press, 2000), 132. Harwood says Boyle's main purpose is to persuade (41), and Altgoer's account has room for little else (133). Both also emphasize the self-fashioning that is integral to the classical practice of rhetoric (Harwood, 39; Altgoer, 134, 136). For a brief overview of rhetoric in early modern English natural philosophy, see Brian Vickers's 'Introduction,' *English Science,*

Bacon to Newton (New York: Cambridge University Press, 1987); for Boyle, 10, 15.
37. For Shapin and Schaffer, 'The objectivity of the experimental matter of fact was an artifact of certain forms of discourse and certain modes of social solidarity' (77–8). Sargent takes issue with this: '"matters of fact" do not compose a rigid category delineated by linguistic structure. Facts are highly confirmed items of knowledge that may refer to singular effects, regular occurrences, or causal processes. The category of the factual, while foundational, is also dynamic. The material included within the informational basis remains open to revision in the light of further discoveries' (136).
38. Shapin and Schaffer, 66; for Sargent's emphasis on the philosophical, see 183, 186.
39. 'Proemial Essay,' 2:16.
40. In the Preface to *Christian Virtuoso*, Boyle explains his use of figures: 'I make frequent use of Similitudes, or Comparisons: And therefore I think myself here obliged to acknowledge, once for all, that I did it purposely. And my Reasons for this Practise, were, *not only* because fit Comparisons are wont to delight most Readers, and to make the Notions they convey better kept in Memory ... *but* I was induced to employ them chiefly for two other Reasons: 1. ... Comparisons fitly chosen, and well applied, may, on many occasions, usefully serve to illustrate the Notions for whose sake they are brought, and, by placing them in a true Light, help Men to conceive them far better, than otherwise they would do. And, 2. Apposite Comparisons do not only give Light, but Strength, to the Passages they belong to, since they are not always bare Pictures and Resemblances, but a kind of Arguments: being oftentimes, if I may so call them, Analogous Instances, which do declare the Nature, or Way of Operating, of the Thing they relate to, and by that means so in a sort prove, that, as 'tis possible, so it is not improbable, that the Thing may be such as 'tis represented' (11:287); 'proper Comparisons do the Imagination almost as much Service, as Microscopes do the Eye; for, *as* this Instrument gives us a distinct view of divers minute Things, which our naked Eyes cannot well discern ... *so* a skillfully chosen, and well-applied, Comparison much helps the Imagination, by illustrating Things scarce discernible, so as to represent them by Things much more familiar and easy to be apprehended' (11:287–8). See Harwood, 51.
41. Boyle, *New Experiments and Observations Touching Cold* (1665), *Works* 4:222; qtd. Sargent, 202. Sargent characterizes Boyle's experimental philosophy as 'a gradual and dynamic process of inquiry' that is open-ended and depends on the feedback of facts and reflections onto each other (182): 'The experimentalist must remain open to the possibility that new theories or improved technologies may radically alter the way in which inquiry proceeds' (216; see also 127, 208).
42. *The Christian Virtuoso, First Part* (1690), *Works*, vol. 11. 'I am now and then busied in devising, and putting in practice, Tryals of several sorts, and making Reflections upon them' (11:291).
43. Ibid., 11:292.

44. Ibid., 11:306. See Principe's discussion of the *Sceptical Chymist*, vulgar chymists, and systematizers (*Aspiring*, 52, 33, 46–7), and Sargent's discussion of Boyle's critique of speculative theorists (27, 71–5).
45. 'The Person I mean here, is such a one, as by attentively looking about him, gathers Experience, not from his own Tryals alone, but from divers other *matters of fact*, which he heedfully observes, though he had no share in the effecting them; and on which he is dispos'd to make such Reflections, as may (unforcedly) be apply'd to confirm and encrease in him the Sentiments of *Natural Religion*, and facilitate his Submission and Adherence to the *Christian Religion*' (*Christian Virtuoso*, 11:306).
46. *Christian Virtuoso*, 11:295; *Usefulness of Experimental Natural Philosophy* (1663), *Works*, 3:222; see also 11:299, 3:200–1, 3:235.
47. Harwood says that reading is Boyle's most important metaphor, and discusses his reading the world in both his moral and natural philosophy (50–1); for a discussion of the 'two books' in relation to Boyle, see Sargent, 112–15. David R. Olson offers an account of the massive cultural shift entailed by new ways of reading and discusses the links between Protestant theology and scientific methodology in *The World on Paper: the Conceptual and Cognitive Implications of Writing and Reading* (New York: Cambridge University Press, 1994), esp. 168–71, 177.
48. Boyle, *Occasional Reflections Upon Several Subjects, Whereto is premis'd A Discourse About such kinds of Thoughts* (1665), *Works*, 5:16–17, 32.
49. Ibid., 5:52, 26.
50. Reading books 'requires rather that a man be docile than ingenious,' while collecting 'Moral and Spiritual Documents out of a Book of Hieroglyphics, or from a Landscape or a Map, is more than every attentive considerer can do, and is that which argues something of Dexterous and Sagacity that is not very ordinary' (Ibid., 5:27). Boyle construes the difference between taking instructions from books of morality and devotion and taking them from the 'Book of Nature and the Accidents he chances to take notice of' as the difference between an ant who only carries away and a bee who 'does not onely gather, but improve and transform, her food, and live on that which otherwise would be useless, and besides, not onely has the pleasure to gather its food from Flowers, and from a variety of them, but lives upon Honey, an Aliment that is as sweet and delicious as nutritive' (5:28). The classical bee figure is repeated later, again an image of transformative gathering (5:52).
51. Ibid., 5:52.
52. Ibid., 5:30.
53. Ibid., 5:30; see also 5:32.
54. See Principe, 'Virtuous Romance,' 393.
55. *Occasional Reflections*, 5:18, 8, 9. Boyle invites his readers 'to exercise their Pens in some such way of Writing: Divers of whom will probably be incouraged to venture upon making some such composures, when they find Excuses for divers of those things that are most likely to be thought to Blemish such Essays' (5:18). For an account of the relationship between Occasional Meditations and a different genre, diaries, see J. Paul Hunter, *Before Novels: the Cultural Contexts of Eighteenth-Century English Fiction* (New York: Norton, 1990), 199–206. Hunter's account is organized by a sharp

distinction between 'traditional humanists' and modern Protestant diarists (and occasional mediators) (199, 201). He explains the practice as a modern challenge to 'traditional authority' and 'received opinion' (204), an emphasis on personal experience and subjective authority (204, 208) that goes with turning reading into writing: 'every reader becomes, in effect, his or her own writer' (201).

56. Boyle, *Works*, 5:5, 5:49–50.
57. Ibid., 5:10–11. Michael Hunter dates the composition of *Occasional Reflections* c. 1647–48 (5:xi), and 'Proemial Essay' 1657 (2:xi).
58. Uffley, A3–A3v.
59. [William Master,] *Logoi eukoiroi, Essayes and Observations Theologicall and Morall* (London, 1653), A4–A5, 9.
60. Chudleigh, 'To the Reader,' 246. For a similar claim, see William Anstruther, 'The Preface to the Reader,' *Essays, Moral and Divine* (Edinburgh, 1701).
61. Chudleigh defines moral philosophy as 'That [which] will in some measure teach us what we owe to God and our selves, will inform us how we may reduce our Knowledge into Practice, and live those Truths we have been learning' (257–8).
62. Boyle, 'A Physio-Chymical Essay, Containing An Experiment with some Considerations touching the differing Parts and Redintegration of Salt-Petre' ['Essay on Nitre'], section 39, *Certain Physiological Essays* [1661], *Works*, 2:112.
63. For one of Boyle's many accounts of his work being unpolished and unfinished, see *Some Considerations About the Reconcileableness of Reason and Religion* (1675), *Works*, 8:239–40. Harwood writes: 'Indefatigable at identifying topics to discuss, he was far less successful at finding principles of order or organization for the materials he collected. The hope of an "orderly discourse" was all too often only a hope. The "finishing stroke" often eluded him' (47). In contrast, Sargent says Boyle's work is unfinished because he makes no claim to first principles or final conclusions (204–6).
64. *Occasional Reflections*, 5:20.
65. 'Proemial Essay,' 2:34.
66. Principe, *Aspiring*, 111, 220.
67. Anthony Grafton discusses the 'long-term continuities and complex genealogies' between humanism and the new sciences in *Defenders of the Text* (Cambridge: Harvard University Press, 1991): 'the two cultures, in short, were not locked in the battle the pamphleteers of the New Philosophy called for; they co-existed and often collaborated' (4, 5).
68. Grafton, 'The New Science and the Traditions of Humanism,' in *The Cambridge Companion to Renaissance Humanism*, ed. Jill Kraye (New York: Cambridge University Press, 1996), 203–23, 212. 'The late humanist and his pupil – like the humanist of the fifteenth and sixteenth centuries – trained themselves to read with their pens ever ready in their hands' (211).
69. Oldenburg, 'A Preface to the Third Year of these Tracts,' *Philosophical Transactions, vols. 1–2*, 2:410.

4. Social and literary form in the *Spectator*

1. Boyle, *Occasional Reflections*, 5:51.
2. Boyle *Occasional Reflections*, 5:52. 'A Man of Polite Imagination ... looks upon the World, as it were, in another Light, and discovers in it a Multitude of Charms, that conceal themselves from the generality of Mankind' (Addison and Steele, *The Spectator*, ed. Donald F. Bond, 5 vols. [Oxford: Oxford University Press, 1965], #411, 3:538).
3. *Spectator* #101, 1:424.
4. Since the English translation of Jürgen Habermas's *The Structural Transformation of the Public Sphere*, trans. Thomas Burger and Frederick Lawrence (1962; Cambridge: MIT Press, 1989), the mutually-defining developments of the press and the public sphere have (again) become a topos of eighteenth-century studies. For Habermas's remarks on the press, see 15–16, 21–2, and for his remarks on periodical essays, see 42–3. In *The Pleasures of the Imagination* (New York: Farrar Straus Giroux, 1997), John Brewer writes: 'The city had become not only the center of culture but one of its key subjects' (3), and that the periodical essay 'was the literary form of the busy, modern age' (104). I address how the city provided not just a new topic, but also a new structure with which to understand modern life, a structure that, as Brewer notes, was epitomized by the *Spectator*: 'Letters, memoirs, essays and works of fiction throughout the century frequently cite the *Spectator* as the key to understanding modern city life' (39).
5. *Spectator* #124, 1:507. The modernity of print was a standard eighteenth-century topic. In *Spectator* #166, print is called 'this great Invention of these latter Ages' (2:154). And George Colman, in the *Connoisseur* (1754), echoes this: 'We writers of essays, or (as they are termed) periodical papers, justly claim to ourselves a place among the modern improvers of literature' (qtd. in Jeremy Black, *The English Press in the Eighteenth Century* [London: Croom Helm, 1987], 1). For background on the press see also James Sutherland, *The Restoration Newspaper and Its Development* (New York: Cambridge University Press, 1986).
6. Edward and Lillian Bloom's *Joseph Addison's Sociable Animal* (Providence: Brown University Press, 1971) is the classic Whiggish account in both senses. For Addison's identity as a Whig, see 27–8, and for their Whiggish appraisal, see 209–10.
7. The first quotation is Terry Eagleton, *The Function of Criticism from the Spectator to Post-Structuralism* (London: Verso, 1984), 10. The second is Scott Paul Gordon, 'Voyeuristic Dreams: Mr. Spectator and the Power of Spectacle,' *The Eighteenth Century: Theory and Interpretation* 36 (1995), 3–23, 4.
8. The first quotations are Michael Warner, 'The Mass Public and the Mass Subject,' in *Habermas and the Public Sphere*, ed. Craig Calhoun (Cambridge: MIT Press, 1992), 377–401, 381. The last is Stuart Sherman, *Telling Time: Clocks, Diaries, and English Diurnal Form, 1660–1785* (Chicago: University of Chicago Press, 1996), 115.
9. Thomas Woodman writes: 'The *Tatler* and the *Spectator* played a major role in the creation of the "public sphere" of relatively free discourse, secular, non-hierarchical and unimpinged upon by the State. Yet this whole development depends on and results from the weakening of other final

authorities. Because of this Addison and Steele, in a brilliant mystification, use public opinion – consensus – as their source of authority in the very act of helping to create such a consensus. The mode of free, apparently random discourse is used to disguise an ideological program, or rather is its entirely appropriate medium ... This like the social life it mimics, is a genuine, perhaps an enviable cultural achievement. But the whole process is a deeply political and ideological one' (*Politeness and Poetry in the Age of Pope* [Rutherford: Fairleigh Dickinson University Press, 1989], 27).

10. Raymond Williams, 'Ideology,' *Marxism and Literature* (New York: Oxford University Press, 1977), 55.
11. Adam Potkay writes: 'the supreme fiction of polite society is the conversational voice' (*The Fate of Eloquence in the Age of Hume* [Ithaca: Cornell University Press, 1994], 103).
12. See 'The Gazetteer,' ch. 4 of Calhoun Winton, *Captain Steele: the Early Career of Richard Steele* (Baltimore: Johns Hopkins University Press, 1964).
13. Sherman discusses Steele's segue between the *Gazette* and *Tatler* (124), as does Richmond P. Bond, *The Tatler: the Making of a Literary Journal* (Cambridge: Harvard University Press, 1971), 3–4.
14. Addison and Steele, *The Tatler*, ed. Donald F. Bond, 3 vols. (Oxford: Oxford University Press, 1987), 1:16. For details about Steele's appropriation of Swift's Bickerstaff, a satiric character of the astrologer almanac-maker, Partridge, see R. P. Bond, 7–8, and D. Bond's note, *Tatler*, 1:22.
15. *Tatler*, 1:16.
16. Ibid., 1:22.
17. Ibid., 1:16. Shaftesbury calls miscellaneous writing 'satiric' (*Miscellaneous Reflections* 1.3, *Characteristicks*, 2:139).
18. *Tatler*, 1:15.
19. *Tatler* #5, 'Apartment,' 1:51.
20. For this structure of satire, see Ronald Paulson, *The Fictions of Satire* (Baltimore: Johns Hopkins University Press, 1967), 24.
21. Brian McCrea notes that Addison and Steele 'redefine and domesticate satire' (*Addison and Steele Are Dead* [Newark: University of Delaware Press, 1989], 30), and R. P. Bond mentions 'Bickerstaff's general satiric methods' and 'satiric procedures' (164).
22. *Tatler*, 1:23.
23. *Tatler* #164, 2:411.
24. Both R. P. Bond and Sherman comment on this development. Bond notes that Steele 'practically discarded the use of multiple departments' (133); for the details of this 'experimentation' see 179–80. Sherman also discusses the 'shift in form' to a 'single essay on a single topic,' making 'all shunted through a single switching house: Bickerstaff's "Apartment," which is to say his experience, his judgment, his mind' (129).
25. *Tatler* #132, 2:265
26. *Tatler*, 3:364.
27. Steele stresses variety in this final number, saying he 'spoke in the Character of an old Man, a Philosopher, an Humorist, an Astrologer, and a Censor, to allure my Readers with the Variety of my Subjects' (*Tatler* #271, 3:363).
28. *Spectator* #34, 1:141–2.

164 *Notes, pp. 92–4*

29. In *Structural Transformation*, Habermas writes of the public turning 'the principle of publicity against the established authorities' (56), a 'transformation' of 'public authority' (60): 'With the rise of a sphere of the social, over whose regulation public opinion battled with public power, the theme of the modern (in contrast to the ancient) public sphere shifted from the properly political tasks of a citizenry acting in common ... to the more civic tasks of a society engaged in critical debate ... The political task of the bourgeois public sphere was the regulating of civil society (in contradistinction to the *res publica*)' (52).
30. *Spectator*, 1:12–13.
31. William Empson remarks that all politeness had an element of irony in it (*Some Versions of Pastoral* [New York: New Directions, 1968], 230), and these idealized models perhaps sounded sarcastic at the time, perfect icons to criticize the present. Empson's comment recognizes the structural condition of politeness: it can't be compulsory – or it'd be law – and the space between the choice and the exercise of politeness can be the space of irony as well as piety or wit.
32. *Spectator*, 1:144.
33. *Spectator*, 1:449.
34. *Spectator* #81, 1:348. Commenting on his account of 'Party-Patches,' Addison notes that it may 'appear improbable to those who live at a distance from the fashionable World; but as it is a Distinction of a very singular Nature, and what perhaps may never meet with a Parallel, I think I should not have discharged the Office of a faithful Spectator had I not recorded it' (*Spectator* #81, 1:348).
35. *Spectator* #219, 2:351; *Spectator* #249, 2:465.
36. Halifax, in *Essays of Michael, Seigneur de Montaigne*, 3rd edn., trans. Charles Cotton, 3 vols. (London, 1700), 1:1.
37. 'No doubt but he thought that one might take the same Liberty in his Meditations, as is assumed in common Conversations, in which, tho' there be but two or three Interlocutors, 'tis observed that there is such variety in their discourses, that if they were set down in writing, it would appear that by digressions they are run away from their first subject, and that the last part of the conversation is very little answerable to the first. This I verily believe was his true intention, that he might present the World with a free and original Work' (Halifax, 1:5–6).
38. See the methodological statement that opens 'Of Friendship': 'Having considered the Fancy of a Painter, I have that serves me, I had a mind to imitate his way; For he chooses the fairest Place and middle of any wall, or pannel of Wainscote, wherein to draw a Picture which he finishes with his utmost Care and Art, and the vacuity about it he fills with Grotesque; which are odd Fantastick Figures, without any Grace, but what they derive from their variety, and the extravagancy of their Shapes [variété et étrangeté]. And, in truth, what are these things I scribble, other than Grotesques, and monstrous Bodies, made of dissenting parts, without any certain Figure, or any other than accidental Order, Coherence, or Proportion' (Cotton trans., 1:283–4).
39. In his *Dictionary*, Johnson defines 'association' as 'union; conjunction; society'; 'sociable' as 'fit to be conjoined' and 'friendly; familiar;

conversible'; 'conversation' as 'familiar discourse; chat; easy talk' and 'commerce; intercourse; familiarity'; and 'commerce' as 'common or familiar intercourse' (an Addison quotation is the example here).
40. Addison names Montaigne as the model for the essay (*Spectator* #476, 4:185). Hazlitt drew a direct line from 'Montaigne and his imitators, to our Periodical Essayists' ('Of the Periodical Essayists,' *Lectures on the English Comic Writers* [1819; New York: Dutton, 1910], 95).
41. *Spectator* #101, 1:424.
42. Ibid., 1:425.
43. Ibid., 1:425.
44. *Spectator*, 4:27.
45. Ibid., 4:27.
46. Ibid., 4:27.
47. Warner, *Letters of the Republic* (Cambridge: Harvard University Press, 1990), 65–6.
48. Warner writes that print is 'a discourse in which publicity will be impersonal by definition ... the validity of [one's] utterance will be a negative relation to [one's] person' (38), and that, in republicanism, 'virtue comes to be defined by the negation of other traits of personhood, in particular as rational and disinterested concern for the public good' (42). For the relevant part of J. G. A. Pocock's magisterial account of early modernity, see *The Machiavellian Moment* (Princeton: Princeton University Press, 1975), chs. 13 and 14.
49. 'These artifacts represented the material reality of an abstract public: a *res publica* of letters ... an abstraction *never localizable in any relation between persons* ... the mutual recognition promised in print discourse was not an interaction between particularized persons, but among persons constituted by the negating abstractions of themselves. The impersonality ascribed to printed objects was the condition of the promise of a discourse of political interaction' (Warner, 61–2; emphasis in original; see also 72). I take the Latin phrase to indicate that Warner's political imagination, like his subjects', is structured by an ancient conception of politics based on the *polis*, not the modern public sphere. Not all 'republics' were imagined as *res publicae*; Hume, for instance, uses the phrase, 'Republic of Letters,' to describe a condition of dependency and exchange – a commercial republic ('Of Essay-Writing' [1742], in *Essays*, ed. Eugene F. Miller [Indianapolis: Liberty Press, 1987], 536).
50. Warner, 3.
51. Sherman, 114–16. At this point, diaries were a Protestant literary form, a point Sherman makes when he describes the innovation of the periodical essays as 'secular diaries' (22). J. Paul Hunter writes that the 'purposes of [the] diary' were 'to clarify for the autobiographer the patterns and meanings that could presumably be discovered by the close observation of the details of a life' (45). He discusses the 'Puritan diary,' and 'the Protestant culture' in which this 'need to record the self' was rooted, in *Before Novels*, ch. 12; quoted phrases, 307, 304.
52. Sherman, 113, 115.
53. Ibid., 158.
54. Ibid., 113.

55. David S. Shields, *Civil Tongues and Polite Letters in British America* (Chapel Hill: University of North Carolina Press, 1997), 33; the first quoted phrase is the title of his second chapter. Shields writes: 'Belles lettres enabled the transmission of a secularized, cosmopolitan, genteel culture' (12), and Addison and Steele 'infused the politeness of belles lettres into the print world' (267). Based on pleasure and company, not the austere and solitary virtue of either republicanism or Protestantism, sociability defined both community and individual in terms of association (31–3; see also 313–14).
56. Shields starts off his study by discussing Shaftesbury's notion of 'private society' (xiii), and grounds his notion of belles lettres in 'Shaftesbury's social aesthetics' (36).
57. Shields, 44. The movement from Shaftesbury to Addison can be considered the literary or formal dimension of the development of modern Whiggery from old Whig, exemplified by the retired Shaftesbury, to commercial Whig, exemplified by Addison the minister. Shaftesbury wrote: 'thinking I could best serve Him [the king] & my Country in a disinterested Station, I resolv'd absolutely against taking any Employment at Court' (qtd. Voitle, 212). When he started writing for the *Tatler*, Addison was Lord Lieutenant of Ireland (1708–10); his highest office was Secretary of State of the Southern Department (1717–18). See Peter Smithers, *The Life of Joseph Addison*, 2nd edn. (Oxford: Clarendon Press, 1968), chs. 5 and 10.
58. Klein, *Shaftesbury and the Culture of Politeness: Moral Discourse and Cultural Politics in Early Eighteenth-Century England* (New York: Cambridge University Press, 1994), 9.
59. The quoted phrases are Klein's (9, 193); he discusses country Whigs and the politics of the 'landed elite' on 143–4. I refer to Isaac Kramnick's subtitle in order to suggest that a dialectic between Shaftesbury and Addison and Steele can be understood as an earlier version of the mid-century debates Kramnick discusses; see *Bolingbroke and His Circle: the Politics of Nostalgia in the Age of Walpole* (Ithaca: Cornell University Press, 1968), 80. I borrow the term, 'ancienneté,' from Joseph M. Levine, *The Battle of the Books: History and Literature in the Augustan Age* (Ithaca: Cornell University Press, 1991), 6.
60. Klein, 8, 7. He writes: 'In this respect [trying to envision the shape of discourse and culture in new ways], Shaftesbury's project was like that of Joseph Addison and Richard Steele. Indeed, these renowned Whig cultural ideologists were all participants in a significant larger development: politeness was becoming a dominant paradigm, offering the scene of gentlemen in polite conversation as a model for discursive and cultural activity and authority' (9). Earlier Klein suggests a distinction, but one he seems to consider incidental, not defining: 'Whereas Addison and Steele ... used the resources of print culture to disseminate polite moralism to a broad audience, Shaftesbury was, much more, the philosopher of politeness, aiming at an intellectual and social elite' (2). He does recognize that Addison and Steele used a different technology to address a different audience, but still considers their project to be the same as Shaftesbury's (37). Klein outlines very well Shaftesbury's concern with 'the fully autonomous being' (210), and it is precisely this concern, which has both political (republican) and philosophical (stoic) implications, that distinguishes his project from the *Spectator's*.

61. Shaftesbury's books were as elite and exclusionary as the *Spectator* was popular and inclusionary; for details on the production of his books, see Klein, 123–4, and Voitle, 338–9. For Shaftesbury's disembodied – Platonic – disinterest, see Ronald Paulson, *The Beautiful, Novel, and Strange* (Baltimore: Johns Hopkins University Press, 1997), 24, and Voitle, 319–21.
62. Klein, 116. Klein discusses him 'assigning the highest prestige to dialogue' (115). See Shaftesbury's comments on dialogue in *Miscellaneous Reflections* 5.2, *Characteristicks*, 2:265, and 'Soliloquy' 1.3, *Characteristicks*, 1:104; for complaints about essays, see 'Soliloquy' 1.1, *Characteristicks*, 1:90.
63. Shields, 37. In his catalogue of examples of 'conversational' literary forms, Shields doesn't mention the essay (33).
64. This is not to say that urbanity is only possible or proper in the city, or that one can't or shouldn't live in urban areas without urbanity; but rather that in the modern social imaginary, the two were articulated as mutually-defining: the model of behavior associated with urban areas is urbanity.
65. *Spectator* #124, 1:507.
66. Ibid.
67. Ibid.
68. *Spectator* #10, 1:44.
69. *Spectator* #124, 1:506.
70. Addison, 'Essay on Virgil's Georgics' (1697), in *Miscellaneous Works*, ed. A. C. Guthkelch, 2 vols. (London: G. Bell and Sons, 1914), 2:1–11, 6. I discuss this passage in relation to the 'Pleasures of the Imagination' and Addison's category of novelty in my 'Addison's Aesthetics of Novelty.'
71. I take the description of Puritanism as a 'Religion of the Closet' from Warner (33), who quotes it from Cotton Mather's 1718 Diary.
72. Gay (3 May 1711), quoted in *Addison and Steele: the Critical Heritage*, ed. Edward Bloom and Lillian Bloom (Boston: Routledge and Kegan Paul, 1980), 226.
73. *Spectator* #10, 1:44.
74. For an excellent background discussion, see Erika Rummel, *The Humanist-Scholastic Debate in the Renaissance and Reformation* (Cambridge: Harvard University Press, 1995), esp. 11–12.
75. Cicero, *Tusculan Disputations*, trans. J. E. King (Cambridge: Harvard University Press, 1945), 10.
76. Julian wrote that Socrates 'rejected the speculative life and embraced a life of action' ('Letter to Themistes,' 264b–c, in *Works*, trans. W. C. Wright, 3 vols. [Cambridge: Harvard University Press, 1913], 2:229). Xenophon's *Memorabilia*, trans. E. C. Marchant (Cambridge: Harvard University Press, 1923), is one locus for Cicero's statement, 11–13.
77. Xenophon, 16.
78. Plutarch, *Moralia* 796d–e, trans. H. N. Fowler, 15 vols. (Cambridge: Harvard University Press, 1936), 10:147.
79. Cicero, 10.
80. In his famous appraisal of Addison, Johnson praises the 'genuine Anglicism' of his 'idiomatical' style ('Addison,' *The Major Works*, ed. Donald Greene [New York: Oxford University Press, 2000], 676). Johnson's praise, though, had its limit in his claim that 'the graces of writing and conversation are

of different kinds,' and he offers this mild, but I think central, critique: Addison 'sometimes descends too much to the language of conversation' (*Rambler*, ed. Albrecht Strauss and Walter Jackson Bate [New Haven: Yale University Press, 1986], #14, 3:149).

81. Collet quoted in *Spectator*, 1:xcv. In an earlier letter Collet says the Bible 'teach[es] me the whole Compass of my Duty to God and man' (qtd. *Spectator*, 1:lxxxvi). The addition of the *Spectator* to this duty marks its lessons as a complement to divine duty; the *Spectator* addresses the duty of person to person, which has become distinct from divine duty.

82. See Pocock on the early eighteenth-century problem of articulating 'a defense of urban life and politics as neither an ancient *polis* nor a *faeces Romuli*,' 'an understanding of commercial modernity' based on 'social, cultural, and commercial values, ones we associate especially with the name of Addison' ('Varieties of Whiggism,' *Virtue, Commerce, and History* [New York: Cambridge University Press, 1985], 235). Gordon Wood calls the *Spectator* a key text in the shift from 'classical public virtue' to 'modern social virtue,' from the 'social adhesives' of monarchy – 'force, kinship, patronage' – to 'a new, modern virtue' associated with 'sociability' and a 'new emphasis on politeness' that he too calls 'Addisonian' (*The Radicalism of the American Revolution* [New York: Vintage, 1991], 230, 215–16).

83. Shaftesbury complains about 'Party-Pamphlets' and 'new-fashion'd theological Essays' (*Miscellaneous Reflections* 5.2, *Characteristicks*, 2:267). For examples, see *Contemporaries of the Tatler and the Spectator* (Los Angeles: Clark Library, 1954).

84. Fowler, 167. Fowler suggests that the distinction between kind (or genre) and mode contains a historical dimension: form precedes mode, and mode is an effect, 'a selection or abstraction from kind' (106). See also Paul Alpers, *What Is Pastoral?* (Chicago: University of Chicago Press, 1996), ch. 2.

85. Habermas offers a critique of the Weberian 'cognitive-instrumental abridgements of reason' that lie – via Horkheimer and Adorno's *Dialectic of Enlightenment* (1944; trans. John Cumming [New York: Continuum, 1993]) – behind many of the current literary critical approaches to the eighteenth century: 'Instrumental reason is set out in concepts of subject–object relations. The interpersonal relation between subject and subject, which is decisive for the model of exchange, has no constitutive significance for instrumental reason' (*Theory of Communicative Action*, trans. Thomas McCarthy, 2 vols. [Boston: Beacon, 1984, 1987], 1:xlii, 1:379). This methodological distinction lies behind my comments here: 'society is perceived from the perspective of the acting subjects as the lifeworld of a social group. In contrast, from the observer's perspective of someone not involved, society can be conceived only as a system of actions, such that each action has a functional significance according to the maintenance of the system' (2:117).

86. This is not, of course, to say that paradigms derived from Pocock, Marx, or Weber are mistaken about the eighteenth century, just that they're not exhaustive.

5. Fleeting habitations in *Tom Jones*

1. Ford, quoted in *Henry Fielding: a Critical Anthology*, ed. Claude Rawson (Baltimore: Penguin, 1973), 360. Elsewhere Ford remarks, 'there are few books that I more cordially dislike than *Tom Jones* ... as regards *Tom Jones* my personal dislike goes along with a certain cold-blooded, critical condemnation. I dislike Tom Jones, the character, because he is a lewd, stupid, and treacherous phenomenon; I dislike Fielding, his chronicler, because he is a bad sort of hypocrite. Had Fielding been the least genuine in his moral aspirations it is Blifil that he would have painted attractively and Jones who would have come to the electric chair, as would have been the case had Jones lived today' (*The English Novel from the Earliest Days to the Death of Joseph Conrad* [1930; Manchester, UK: Carcanet, 1983], 91–2). After more in this vein, Ford declares: 'For myself, I am no moralist' (93).
2. Martin Battestin's is the standard Christian reading; see Martin C. Battestin and Ruth R. Battestin, *Henry Fielding: a Life* (New York: Routledge, 1989), 452–3, and his 'Introduction,' Henry Fielding, *The History of Tom Jones* (Wesleyan: Wesleyan University Press, 1975); all references to the novel are to this edition. For accounts of *Tom Jones* as neo-classical, see Ian Watt, *The Rise of the Novel* (Berkeley: University of California Press, 1957), ch. 9, Martin Price, *To the Palace of Wisdom: Studies in Order and Energy from Dryden to Blake* (Garden City, NJ: Doubleday, 1964), ch. 10, and Claude Rawson, *Henry Fielding and the Augustan Ideal under Stress* (Boston: Routledge & Kegan Paul, 1972), ch. 2. For accounts of various aspects of Fielding's conservatism, see Michael McKeon, *The Origins of the English Novel 1600–1740* (Baltimore: Johns Hopkins University Press, 1987), ch. 12, James Thompson, *Models of Value: Eighteenth-Century Political Economy and the Novel* (Durham, NC: Duke University Press, 1996), ch. 4, and John Richetti, *The English Novel in History 1700–1780* (New York: Routledge, 1999), ch. 5.
3. R. S. Crane critiques Fielding's insistence on 'stating' instead of 'rendering' ('The Plot of *Tom Jones*,' in *Twentieth-Century Interpretations of Tom Jones*, ed. Martin C. Battestin [Englewood Cliffs, NJ: Prentice-Hall, 1968], 68–93, 89). Watt has a hard time fitting Fielding into a history of a novel defined by formal realism, an illusion of 'a full and authentic report of human experience' (32). And Richetti reads him as a stumbling block in the novel's long march towards properly representing 'a deliberately unassimilated contemporaneity' (150).
4. Wayne C. Booth reads the witty voice as a character and finds a second 'plot' or 'subplot' concerning the 'growing intimacy between the narrator and the reader, an account with a kind of plot of its own and its own separate denouement' (*The Rhetoric of Fiction*, 2nd edn. [Chicago: University of Chicago Press, 1983], 216–17). Robert L. Chibka modifies and extends Booth's argument, noting there is not 'a consistent conceit' in the images of the narrator or a plot in the reader's relationship to him, while taking up Booth's key insight about a 'harmony' between the two aspects of the novel ('Taking "The Serious" Seriously: the Introductory Chapters of *Tom Jones*,' *The Eighteenth Century: Theory and Interpretation* 30 [1990], 23–45, 30). Chibka stresses the 'interwoven' nature of the whole (26) and reads thematic continuities between the plot and the essays without privileging one

over the other; the essays are 'a coexisting level of discourse that plays against the others without necessitating hierarchical distinctions' (24). Robert Alter also remarks this kind of interweaving (*Fielding and the Nature of the Novel* [Cambridge: Harvard University Press, 1969], 34, 70), and so does Martin Price: 'Fielding is neither essayist nor realistic novelist, nor both in turn. He is rather both at once and therefore something different from either' (298).

5. Thomas Lockwood, 'Matter and Reflection in *Tom Jones*,' *English Literary History* 45 (1978), 226–35, 227. Lockwood argues that, rather than a 'unified fictional whole,' Fielding's approach to the novel is rooted in the periodical essay and works like an essay, 'a revitalization of the essayist's role in what amounts to a new kind of essay' – a long story 'communicated through the presence of an author who retains the essayist's privilege of talking freely in his own person. In this sense *Tom Jones* is an essay in which the "matter" or illustrative material has been vastly extended and elaborated' (226–7). Lockwood's account is excellent, especially his readings of 'the book's capacity to transform matter into reflection' (228) and his remarks on its occupying a middle ground where concrete images become general and vice versa (233). His account of the essay, though, as an expressive genre, one voice talking freely, may be anachronistic. I understand the early modern genre to be as interactive as expressive, an occasion to read as well as write, and it's this digestive quality of the genre that informs *Tom Jones*. Leopold Damrosch also focuses on the essayistic element of *Tom Jones*: 'He [the narrator] is no mere device for getting the story told, but the essential medium through which it makes sense, so the essayistic element in this kind of novel is its absolute *sine qua non*' (*God's Plot and Man's Stories: Studies in the Fictional Imagination from Milton to Fielding* [Chicago: University of Chicago Press, 1985], 275). An extreme version of this way of reading *Tom Jones* is Robert Withington's stripping away of the narrative altogether; he includes the introductory chapters from *Tom Jones* in his collection, *Essays and Characters: Montaigne to Goldsmith* (New York: Macmillan, 1933), saying they 'partake of the nature of essays' (459).

6. *Tom Jones*, 209.
7. Ibid., 488.
8. Ibid., 32, 487.
9. In an extremely valuable study, *Henry Fielding's Novels and the Classical Tradition* (Newark: University of Delaware Press, 1996), Nancy Mace has situated Fielding's novels within the classical tradition and shown how integral this kind of learning is to them. Fielding 'regards his work as a continuation of the classical tradition' (127) and 'believed his novels to be an outgrowth of ancient, rather than modern, traditions' (135). This is not a simple, uncritical transmission but one that recognizes the need to self-consciously adapt these traditions. So when Fielding adapts the epic, for instance, he also critiques it and draws attention to its artifice (70–3). Such self-conscious uses of traditional forms allow readers to become as self-conscious as the narrator about the novel's construction and to examine their own assumptions about literature (104, 136). In both his periodical essays and novels, Fielding's 'use of classical references encourages his readers to become "learned"; as they read his essays, they begin to adopt his attitudes

towards classical learning, and discover indirectly the moral and critical truth of the ancients' (60). I take this kind of learning to include both an appreciation of classical materials and a stimulus to reflection, another aspect of learning that Mace points to (47, 133). Fielding stresses both the materials of 'learning' and the skill of reflection they enable.
10. *Tom Jones*, Book 9, Chapter 1. The order is slightly different when Fielding returns to this in Book 13, Chapter 1: genius, humanity, learning, experience (685–7).
11. A classical source of this point is Horace: 'Natura fieret laudabile carmen an arte, / quaesitum est; ego nec studium sine diuite uena / nec rude quid prosit uideo ingenium; alterius sic / altera poscit opem res et coniurat amice' [It has been long a question, whether a poet was formed by art or nature: I neither see what art can do without a rich vein, or a fine genius without the help of art; for each requires the other's aid, and conspires with it in a friendly manner] (*Ars poetica*, lines 408–11; *The Works of Horace*, trans. David Watson, ed. W. Crakelt, 2 vols. [1792; New York: AMS, 1976], 2:398).
12. *Tom Jones*, 491–2.
13. Ibid., 492.
14. Ibid., 178–83, 331.
15. Alter uses the phrase, 'fleeting juxtaposition,' to describe Fielding's use of a Horatian line about Cybele's priests to figure a knock at the door by Lady Bellaston's servant (104, about *Tom Jones*, 697). I'm combining this with Gass's *Habitations of the Word*. Tom both is and isn't like Milton's Adam. The space between Tom's 'fall' and the Fall makes his look domestic, modern, and petty, but these are precisely the effects of a different, and one hopes less mistaken, expulsion by an all-worthy Father. Recognizing in Tom's slight echo of Adam a disappointingly reduced human world offers a greater horizon against which to view that world – and so in these terms we can recognize Tom, indeed, as another Adam, a continuation of that story and a realization of its effects. As we gloss the space between the texts, we engage the layers of mediation (Fielding's, Milton's, the Bible's, and indeed the several Bibles') that seek to grasp an exile at once banally mundane and cosmically significant – or significant *as* mundane. The significance of being exiled from God is that we only grasp our experience within human limits; Fielding's Tom realizes Milton's Adam, or God's Adam, or vice versa, or all of these at once.
16. *Tom Jones*, 150–1.
17. Ibid., 151–2.
18. Ibid., 152–3.
19. Ibid., 153.
20. A moment similar to this, perhaps not a direct source but in the same spirit, is in *Don Quixote* when Quixote and Sancho are hunting boar with the Duke and Duchess and are surprised by attacking 'Moors': 'trumpets and clarions blared, drums boomed, fifes shrilled, all at the same time, and so fast and continuously that only a person with no sense at all could have failed to lose it in the pandemonium created by all those instruments. The Duke was amazed, the Duchess was astonished, Don Quixote was dumbfounded, Sancho Panza was trembling and, in short, even those in on the

secret were alarmed' (Miguel de Cervantes, *Don Quixote*, trans. John Rutherford [New York: Penguin, 2000], 723–4).
21. *Tom Jones*, 153–4.
22. Ibid., 398.
23. Jill Campbell has a different account of the effect of this 'layered' passage: 'As Fielding describes it, this layered consciousness is created by the process of historical change; we inherit the heathens' reverence for or awe of Flora, because they believed in her, though we do not' (*Natural Masques: Gender and Identity in Fielding's Plays and Novels* [Stanford: Stanford University Press, 1995], 169). Ancient belief doesn't exactly cause our reverence for Flora but offers a different version of what we do. We *do* believe in Flora, or at least in what we understand Flora to signify (politics, literature, or perhaps even just 'reverence' as such), and one of the ways we gain access to that understanding is by replaying the form the ancients used to signify what Flora means. History offers a reservoir of possibilities as much as a residue of differences; the shifting between those two ways of approaching history is the content of the passage, and of our layered consciousness.
24. Fielding declares his love for Sophia just before this chapter (149). He critiques the modern philosophical reduction of love to appetite in Book 6, Chapter 1.
25. 'Hushed be every ruder Breath. May the Heathen Ruler of the Winds confine in iron Chains the boisterous Limbs of noisy *Boreas*, and the sharp-pointed Nose of bitter-biting *Eurus*. Do thou, sweet *Zephyrus*, rising from thy fragrant Bed, mount the western Sky, and lead on those delicious gales, the Charms of which call forth the lovely Flora from her Chamber, perfumed with pearly Dews, when on the first of *June*, her Birth-day, the blooming Maid, in loose Attire, gently trips it over the verdant Mead, where every Flower rises to do her Homage, till the whole Field becomes enamelled, and Colours contend with Sweets which shall ravish her most' (154).
26. *Tom Jones*, 154–5. The chapter is titled, 'A short Hint of what we can do in the Sublime, and a Description of Miss Sophia Western' (154).
27. Ibid., 154.
28. Ibid., 155–7.
29. Eric Rothstein, 'Virtues of Authority in *Tom Jones*,' in *Critical Essays on Henry Fielding*, ed. Albert J. Rivero (New York: G. K. Hall, 1998), 141–63, 160. Rothstein's account nicely tracks how stock characters are self-consciously appropriated and how genres are revised, but it's framed in terms of a realism that I think he, not Fielding, brings to the table: 'As visible, discrete modes, [generic patterns] have something of the independent solidity of his characters, but their autonomous logic, like the characters', leads them to their being inadequate to the "real life" with which Fielding tests them, and so he corrects and revises them' (156–7). Rothstein querulously asks, 'What is one to say, too, about the freedom of the reader in a book that trains us to employ certain modes of reading – irony and analogy – which are designed to lead us into error as well as knowledge?' (150). Well, isn't that precisely *freedom*?
30. *Tom Jones*, 156.
31. Ibid., 157. Sophia's introduction ends by bringing us back to the introduction to her introduction: Fielding announcing of his announcement of

Sophia by calling her 'a Lady with whom we ourselves are greatly in Love, and with whom many of our Readers will probably be in Love too before we part' (149). We see as much of Sophia as we love; she takes her final shape in our response, in the shape of our love (and our own beloveds).

32. Ronald Paulson, *Satire and the Novel in Eighteenth-Century England* (New Haven: Yale University Press, 1967), 139; referring to George's feeling 'gratitude towards him' (*Tom Jones*, 314). For 'double irony,' see William Empson, 'Tom Jones,' in *Fielding: a Collection of Critical Essays*, ed. Ronald Paulson (Englewood Cliffs, NJ: Prentice Hall, 1962), 123–45, 124.
33. Paulson, *Satire and the Novel*, 140.
34. Price writes, 'All these forms of self-justification Fielding renders with ironic courtesy; he is detached enough to make us see through them with ease, but he is attentive enough to their logic to make us respect its formal rigor' (288). Lockwood too notes a moment of this dynamic (Square's exposure): 'Fielding ironically sympathizes here with a certain sort of rationalization' (232).
35. *Tom Jones*, 264.
36. Ibid., 265.
37. For examples of invitations to apply our sagacity, see 116 and 614. We're offered occasions to do so in completing the satire and revealing 'other reasons' in passages like this one: 'Mr *Western* was become so fond of *Jones* that he was unwilling to part with him, tho' his Arm had been long since cured; and *Jones*, either from the Love of Sport, or from some other Reason, was easily persuaded to continue at his House' (240). For another example, see 352.
38. Ibid., 255–6. In Battestin's note, he points out that the 'June' in this scene is a vestige of the original time-scheme of the novel, but it's also worth noting that June could be a condition of romance, as it's a condition of Flora in Sophia's introduction, where there's another vestigial mention of June (154).
39. *Tom Jones*, 256.
40. Ibid., 256.
41. '*Sophia, Sophia* alone shall be mine. What Raptures are in that Name! I will engrave it on every Tree' (256). Tom's carving could sublimate his desire into writing or figure his masturbation as writing; likewise Fielding's writing either hints at the desublimation of his instrument as a penis or records its sublimation as a pen-knife.
42. Ibid., 256.
43. Alter discusses two other suggestions of masturbation in the novel: Blifil's self-satisfaction (44) and Square figured as a dildo in Molly's closet (32).
44. Dorothy Van Ghent, *The English Novel: Form and Function* (1953; New York: Harper, 1961), 80; Alexander Welsh, *Strong Representations: Narrative and Circumstantial Evidence in England* (Baltimore: Johns Hopkins University Press, 1992), 54.
45. Alter reads the scene in this way (50).
46. *Tom Jones*, 298, 731.
47. Ibid., 730.
48. Ibid., 318, 360.

49. Ibid., 268–70.
50. Ibid., 739.
51. Ibid., Book 6, Chapter 1. Swift writes: 'if the materials be nothing but dirt, spun out of your own entrails (the guts of modern brains), the edifice will conclude at last in a cobweb' (*The Battle of The Books*, in *A Tale of a Tub and Other Works*, ed. Angus Ross and David Woolley [New York: Oxford University Press, 1999], 113).
52. *Tom Jones*, 159.
53. Sophia sees the real object of Blifil's love: 'To say the truth, Sophia, when very young, discerned that Tom, though an idle, thoughtless, rattling rascal, was nobody's enemy but his own; and that Master Blifil, though a prudent, discreet, sober young gentleman, was at the same time strongly attached to the interest only of one single person; and who that single person was the reader will be able to divine without any assistance of ours' (165). Blifil's love is the exemplification of love as hunger, and the suggestion is that, with only the self as the object of affection, love is finally cruel as well as hungry, compounded of jealousy, revenge, and sadism (346).
54. Watt, 264–5, 272–4; Paulson, 141; Alter, 67.
55. Campbell writes: 'Fielding neither conceals the conflicts created for his main characters by the coexistence, within them, of competing, "residual" and newly dominant models of gendered identity, nor consistently works to "naturalize" the terms of their individual identities as man and woman. At times in fact Fielding underlines the specifically "adoptive" or constructed nature of both Tom's and Sophia's gendered identities, though he does not thereby renounce the ideological potential of his fictional creations' (135). Tom is located 'in a network of specifically adoptive relations' that indicate 'that features of identity (including one's gender), historical in nature, are as much characterized by confusion, multiple reference, and fluidity as the features of this novel's political world' (166).
56. Watt, 278; Alter, 50, 195.
57. *Tom Jones*, 485, 720.
58. Ibid., 486, 328, 526, 570. The statement about perfect characters that Fielding argues against in Book 11, Chapter 1 is exemplified by the puppet-master who brags that his 'rational Entertainment' corrects 'a great deal of low Stuff that did very well to make Folks laugh; but was never calculated to improve the Morals of young People' (639; for another dig against the correction of the 'low' stage, see 210). His explanation is interrupted by the discovery of the Merry Andrew improperly coupled with Grace (640) – laughter never goes with grace in this kind of moralizing discourse. As Battestin's note points out, this satirizes the puppet-master's play, Cibber's *Provok'd Husband*, by naming the naughty maid after its lady of 'Exemplary Virtue' and so mocks the effects such plays are claimed to have (640, n. 1).
59. *Tom Jones*, 719–21, 768–9.
60. Ibid., 628. For a fascinating reading of the Man of the Hill as an allegory of history, see John Allen Stevenson, *The Real History of Tom Jones* (New York: Palgrave Macmillan, 2005), ch. 1, esp. 32–3.

61. Ibid., 601, 607–8.
62. Ibid., 75, 151.
63. Ibid., 591, 585.
64. Ibid., 271.
65. Ibid., 593. On Sophia's combining political opposites, see Peter J. Carlton, 'Tom Jones and the '45 Once Again,' Studies in the Novel 20 (1988), 361–73, 369. We might apply to Fielding Western's comment to his sister: 'You have made a Whig of the Girl' (336).
66. Bakhtin, 'Discourse in the Novel,' *The Dialogic Imagination*, ed. Michael Holquist, trans. Caryl Emerson and Michael Holquist (Austin: University of Texas Press, 1981), 409; see also 416.
67. Lockwood, 227.
68. *Tom Jones*, 833.
69. Watt, 288; Richetti, 150. Richetti argues: 'Fielding's fiction seems to resist the liberating principle that Bakhtin proposes as the secret of the novel's achievement, that "it is precisely the diversity of speech, and not the unity of a normative shared language, that is the ground of style." ... The narrator separates himself and his audience from these linguistic strata and implicitly appeals ... to a cognitively meaningful and stable discourse' (133). The principle of 'unassimilated contemporaneity' (150) invoked by Richetti is discussed by Bakhtin in 'Epic and Novel,' where he characterizes novelization as 'an indeterminacy, a certain semantic openness, a living contact with the unfinished, still-evolving contemporary reality (the openended present)' (7). But the line quoted by Richetti comes from the later 'Discourse in the Novel,' where it is part of a discussion of 'Comic style (of the English sort)' that describes, among others, Fielding and his parodying of Richardson (308–9). As Bakhtin develops his account of heteroglossia in the novel, he discusses two kinds of novels. The 'second stylistic line' is characterized by a 'radical skepticism toward any unmediated discourse and any straightforward seriousness' (401); it is distinguished from the 'first stylistic line,' which includes 'the sentimental novel,' 'characterized by psychology and pathos' and inhabiting 'the zone of the letter, the diary' (396–7). Richardson is part of the first line, and Fielding the second (414). It is precisely Fielding's refusal to claim an unmediated access to 'unassimilated contemporaneity' that makes his novels heteroglossic in Bakhtin's terms. The constant reminders of a mediating presence by the narrative voice and the essays don't keep *Tom Jones* from realizing the potential of the novel; according to Bakhtin they are the very conditions of that realization: 'Thus the category of literariness characteristic of the First Line, with its dogmatic pretensions to lead a real life, is replaced, in novels of the Second Line, by a trial and self-critique of novelistic discourse ... The Second Line opened up once and for all the possibilities embedded in the novel as a genre' (414).
70. Influential accounts that have modified Watt's 'rise of the novel' include McKeon, J. Paul Hunter, *Before Novels*, and William Warner, *Licensing Entertainments: the Elevation of Novel Reading in Britain, 1684–1750* (Berkeley: University of California Press, 1998).
71. Patrick Reilly remarks: 'Fielding's supporters insist that its alleged faults are so only on the supposition that *Tom Jones* should have been another

kind of novel' (*Tom Jones: Adventure and Providence* [Boston: Twayne, 1991], 21). See also Lockwood, 226.
72. Bakhtin, 366–415; Alter, 11, 102–3 (Alter pursues this thought in the preface to his *Partial Magic: the Novel as a Self-Conscious Genre* [Berkeley: University of California Press, 1975]); Mace, 134–5.
73. Important studies along these lines include Paulson, *Satire and the Novel*, ch. 4, John Preston, *The Created Self: the Reader's Role in Eighteenth-Century Fiction* (London: Heinemann, 1970), ch. 6, and Welsh, ch. 2.
74. Watt, 288.
75. The latter is Wolfgang Iser's argument about a virtual aesthetic object that isn't represented on the page but rather realized off the page by the reader through a process of judgment; see *The Implied Reader* (Baltimore: Johns Hopkins University Press, 1974), ch. 2, and *The Act of Reading* (Baltimore: Johns Hopkins University Press, 1978), 198–203.
76. Alter notes the novel 'generally proceeds by pointing up a contrast not between life and its representation in literature but between one kind of representation of reality and another' (102).
77. Henry James famously comments on Tom's having enough 'life' (or 'health and spirits') to count 'almost' as 'having a mind,' that is, 'reactions and full consciousness.' Happily this is supplemented by his author, '*he* handsomely possessed of a mind,' 'an amplitude of reflexion for him and round him' (qtd. in Rawson, *Critical Anthology*, 328).
78. Price, 289.
79. See Paulson, *Satire and the Novel*, 137–8, Price, 286, Alter, 88, Iser, *Implied Reader*, 52–5, and Battestin, *Life*, 453.
80. *Tom Jones*, 211, 743.
81. Richard A. Rosengarten, *Henry Fielding and the Narration of Providence: Divine Design and the Incursions of Evil* (New York: Palgrave Macmillan, 2000), 17. The 'retrospective viewpoint as practiced by the narrator results in cautious, ambivalent attribution, while those in the midst of the fray readily, even eagerly invoke the triumph of the divine design against their apprehensions of ominous, foreboding tragedy ... *Tom Jones* actually presents the sagacious reader with two perspectives on providence: that of the actors of the moment, and that of the narrator in retrospect. They are not perfectly symmetrical. Those whose circumstances are immediate can do no other than attribute their happy conclusion to the designs of providence. The one who considers events retrospectively wavers' (85).
82. McKeon: 'Fielding's subsumption of questions of virtue by questions of truth transfers the major challenge of utopian projection from the substantive to the formal realm. And a central reason for this, we may speculate, is the relative uncertainty of his commitment to the utopian institutions and communities envisioned by conservative ideology ... Accordingly, what "happens" at the end of *Joseph Andrews* (and *Tom Jones*) is less a social than an epistemological event' (408). See also Eve Tavor, *Scepticism, Society and the Eighteenth-Century Novel* (New York: St. Martin's Press, 1987).
83. McKeon, 403. Rawson finds in Fielding 'a sense of beleaguered harmony, of forms preserved under stress, of feelings of doom and human defeat ceremoniously rendered' (*Augustan Ideal*, ix). Hunter echoes this: 'Implicit in the use of ancient structural models is a sense of lost order and the hope

of attaining standard analogues to the attainments of the past' (*Occasional Form: Henry Fielding and the Chains of Circumstance* [Baltimore: Johns Hopkins University Press, 1975], 137). Mace, in contrast, argues that Fielding's project is rooted in, but significantly distinct from, the Scriblerians' works (118–27, 133).

84. Preston, 96; Alter, 101.

Bibliography

Addison, Joseph, 'Essay on Virgil's Georgics,' *Miscellaneous Works*, ed. A. C. Guthkelch, 2 vols. (London: G. Bell and Sons, 1914), 2:1–11.
Addison, Joseph, and Richard Steele, *The Spectator*, ed. Donald F. Bond, 5 vols. (Oxford: Oxford University Press, 1965).
——, *The Tatler*, ed. Donald F. Bond, 3 vols. (Oxford: Oxford University Press, 1987).
Adorno, Theodor, 'The Essay as Form,' trans. Bob Hullot-Kentor and Frederic Will, *New German Critique* 32 (1984), 151–71.
Aesop Naturaliz'd and expos'd to the Publick view in his own shape and dress by way of Essay on a hundred fables (London, 1697).
Alpers, Paul, *What Is Pastoral?* (Chicago: University of Chicago Press, 1996).
Alter, Robert, *Fielding and the Nature of the Novel* (Cambridge: Harvard University Press, 1969).
——, *Partial Magic: the Novel as a Self-Conscious Genre* (Berkeley: University of California Press, 1975).
Altgoer, Diane B., *Reckoning Words: Baconian Science and the Construction of Truth in English Renaissance Culture* (Madison: Fairleigh Dickinson University Press, 2000).
An enquiry (by way of essay) into the origin of feudal tenures, and the rights of eventual succession to lands in primogeniture only, as the laws of England now stand. By a member of the Middle Temple Society (London, 1764).
An Essay in Defence of the Female Sex (London, 1696).
Andersen, Jennifer, and Elizabeth Sauer, eds., *Books and Readers in Early Modern England* (Philadelphia: University of Pennsylvania Press, 2002).
Anstruther, William, *Essays, Moral and Divine* (Edinburgh, 1701).
Ashwick, Samuel, *The eighth book of the Iliad of Homer; attempted by way of essay* (London, 1750).
Atkins, G. Douglas, *Estranging the Familiar: Towards a Revitalized Critical Writing* (Athens: University of Georgia Press, 1992).
Auerbach, Erich, *Mimesis*, trans. Willard Trask (New York: Doubleday Anchor, 1957).
Austin, William, *Haec Homo, Wherein the Excellency of the Creation of Woman is described; By Way of an Essay* (London, 1637).
Bacon, Francis, *The Essayes or Counsels, Civill and Morall*, ed. Michael Kiernan (Cambridge: Harvard University Press, 1985).
Bakhtin, M. M., *The Dialogic Imagination*, ed. Michael Holquist, trans. Caryl Emerson and Michael Holquist (Austin: University of Texas Press, 1981).
Barthes, Roland, *Roland Barthes by Roland Barthes*, trans. Richard Howard. (New York: Hill and Wang, 1977).
——, *S/Z: an Essay*, trans. Richard Miller (New York: Hill and Wang, 1974).
Battestin, Martin C., ed., *Twentieth-Century Interpretations of Tom Jones* (Englewood Cliffs, NJ: Prentice-Hall, 1968).

Battestin, Martin C., and Ruth R. Battestin, *Henry Fielding: a Life* (New York: Routledge, 1989).
Bauschatz, Cathleen M., 'Montaigne's Conception of Reading in the Context of Renaissance Poetics and Modern Criticism,' in *The Reader in the Text*, ed. Susan R. Suleiman and Inge Crosman (Princeton: Princeton University Press, 1980), 264–91.
Bensmaïa, Réda, *The Barthes Effect: the Essay as Reflective Text* (Minneapolis: University of Minnesota Press, 1987).
Benson, John, *England in its condition, briefly and most lively characterized, by way of essay* (London, 1648).
Black, Jeremy, *The English Press in the Eighteenth Century* (London: Croom Helm, 1987).
Black, Scott, 'Addison's Aesthetics of Novelty,' *Studies in Eighteenth-Century Culture* 30 (2001), 269–88.
Blair, Ann, 'Humanist Methods in Natural Philosophy: the Commonplace Books,' *Journal of the History of Ideas* 53 (1992), 541–51.
Blanchot, Maurice, *The Infinite Conversation*, trans. Susan Hanson (Minneapolis: University of Minnesota Press, 1993).
———, *The Station Hill Blanchot Reader*, ed. George Quasha (Barrytown, NY: Station Hill, 1999).
Bloom, Edward Alan, and Lillian D. Bloom, *Joseph Addison's Sociable Animal* (Providence: Brown University Press, 1971).
Bloom, Edward Alan, and Lillian D. Bloom, eds., *Addison and Steele: the Critical Heritage* (Boston: Routledge and Kegan Paul, 1980).
Bond, Richmond P., *The Tatler: the Making of a Literary Journal* (Cambridge: Harvard University Press, 1971).
Booth, Wayne C., *The Rhetoric of Fiction*, 2nd edn. (Chicago: University of Chicago Press, 1983).
Boyle, Francis, *Moral Essays and Discourses Upon Several Subjects Chiefly Relating to the Present Times* (London, 1690).
Boyle, Robert, *Certain Physiological Essays* (London, 1661).
———, *The Works of Robert Boyle*, ed. Michael Hunter and Edward B. Davis, 14 vols. (London: Pickering & Chatto, 1999–2000).
Brathwait[e], Richard, *Essaies upon the fiue senses* (London, 1620).
Bretz, Mary Lee, *Voices, Silences and Echoes: a Theory of the Essay and the Critical Reception of Naturalism in Spain* (London: Tamesis, 1992).
Brewer, John, *The Pleasures of the Imagination* (New York: Farrar Straus Giroux, 1997).
Burgand, Peter, *Idioms of Uncertainty: Goethe and the Essay* (University Park: Pennsylvania State University Press, 1992).
Butrym, Alexander J., ed., *Essays on the Essay: Redefining the Genre* (Athens: University of Georgia Press, 1989).
Calhoun, Craig, ed., *Habermas and the Public Sphere* (Cambridge: MIT Press, 1992).
Campbell, Jill, *Natural Masques: Gender and Identity in Fielding's Plays and Novels* (Stanford: Stanford University Press, 1995).
Carlton, Peter J., '*Tom Jones* and the '45 Once Again,' *Studies in the Novel* 20 (1988), 361–73.

Casaregola, Vincent, 'The Literature of the Essay and the Discourse of Values,' in *Values in Public Life: an Interdisciplinary Study*, ed. Gerard Magill and Marie D. Hoff (Lanham, MD: University Press of America, 1995), 57–88.

——, 'Orality, Literacy, and Dialogue: Looking for the Origins of the Essay,' in *Time, Memory, and the Verbal Arts*, ed. Dennis L. Weeks and Jane Hoogestraat (Selinsgrove: Susquehanna University Press, 1998), 69–91.

Cavallo, Guglielmo, and Roger Chartier, eds., *A History of Reading in the West* (Amherst: University of Massachusetts, 1999).

Cave, Terence, 'Problems of Reading in the *Essais*,' in *Montaigne*, ed. I. D. McFarlane and MacLean (Oxford: Clarendon Press, 1982), 133–66.

Certeau, Michel de, *The Practice of Everyday Life*, trans. Steven Rendell (Berkeley: University of California Press, 1984).

Cervantes, Miguel de, *Don Quixote*, trans. John Rutherford (New York: Penguin, 2000).

Chadbourne, Richard M., 'French Essay,' in *Encyclopedia of the Essay*, ed. Chevalier.

Chartier, Roger, 'Reading Matter and "Popular" Reading: From the Renaissance to the Seventeenth Century', in *A History of Reading in the West*, ed. Guglielmo Cavallo and Roger Chartier (Amherst: University of Massachusetts, 1999), 269–83.

Cheare, Abraham, *Sighs for Sion: or, Faith and Love ... In way of Essay* (1656).

Chevalier, Tracy, ed., *Encyclopedia of the Essay* (Chicago: Fitzroy Dearborn, 1997).

Chibka, Robert L., 'Taking "The Serious" Seriously: the Introductory Chapters of *Tom Jones*,' *The Eighteenth Century: Theory and Interpretation* 30 (1990), 23–45.

Chudleigh, Mary, *The Poems and Prose of Mary, Lady Chudleigh*, ed. Margaret J. M. Ezell (New York: Oxford University Press, 1993).

Cicero, *Tusculan Disputations*, trans. J. E. King (Cambridge: Harvard University Press, 1945).

Clarendon, Edward Hyde, Earl of, *Reflections upon Several Christian Duties – Divine and Moral, by Way of Essays* (London, 1668).

Clerk, James, *The practice of discipline, or some directions for the right managing of ecclesiastick discipline. In way of essay* (Edinburgh, 1705).

Cochrane, Robert, ed., *The English Essayists: Lord Bacon to John Ruskin* (London: William P. Nimmo, 1877).

Colie, Rosalie, *The Resources of the Kind: Genre-Theory in the Renaissance*, ed. Barbara Lewalski (Berkeley: University of California Press, 1973).

Contemporaries of the Tatler and the Spectator (Los Angeles: Clark Library, 1954).

Cornwallis, William, *Essayes*, ed. Don Cameron Allen (Baltimore: Johns Hopkins University Press, 1946).

Cowley, Abraham, *Essays*, ed. Arthur Tilley (Cambridge: Cambridge University Press, 1938).

Craig, Alexander, *The Poeticall Essaies of Alexander Craig* (London, 1605).

Crane, R. S., 'The Plot of *Tom Jones*,' in *Twentieth-Century Interpretations of Tom Jones*, ed. Martin C. Battestin (Englewood Cliffs, NJ: Prentice-Hall, 1968), 68–93.

Culpeper, Thomas, *Essayes or Moral Discourses on Several Subjects. Written by a Person of Honor* (London, 1671).

Damrosch, Leopold, *God's Plot and Man's Stories: Studies in the Fictional Imagination from Milton to Fielding* (Chicago: University of Chicago Press, 1985).
Deleuze, Gilles, 'Literature and Life,' *Critical Inquiry* 23 (1997), 225–30.
Dryden, John, *An Essay of Dramatick Poesie'* (London, 1668).
Du Plessis, Rachel Blau, 'F-words: an Essay on the Essay,' *American Literature* 68 (1996), 15–45.
Eagleton, Terry, *The Function of Criticism from the Spectator to Post-Structuralism* (London: Verso, 1984).
Earle, John, *Microcosmographie; or, A Piece of the World Discovered in Essays & Characters* (London, 1628).
Empson, William, *Some Versions of Pastoral* (New York: New Directions, 1968).
——, 'Tom Jones,' in *Fielding: a Collection of Critical Essays*, ed. Ronald Paulson (Englewood Cliffs, NJ: Prentice Hall, 1962), 123–45.
Felltham, Owen, *Resolves: A Duple Century*, 4th edn. (London, 1631).
Fielding, Henry, *The History of Tom Jones*, ed. Martin C. Battestin (Wesleyan: Wesleyan University Press, 1975).
Fischer, Steven Roger, *A History of Reading* (London: Reaktion, 2003).
Fish, Stanley, *Self-Consuming Artifacts* (Berkeley: University of California Press, 1972).
[Fontenelle, M. de,] *A Discovery of New Worlds. From the French. Made English By Mrs. A. Behn. To which is prefixed a Preface, by way of Essay on Translated Prose* (London, 1688).
Ford, Ford Maddox, *The English Novel from the Earliest Days to the Death of Joseph Conrad* (1930; Manchester, UK: Carcanet, 1983).
Fowler, Alastair, *Kinds of Literature* (Cambridge: Harvard University Press, 1982).
Frame, Donald, 'Considerations on the Genesis of Montaigne's *Essais*,' in *Montaigne*, ed. I. D. McFarlane and Ian Maclean (Oxford: Clarendon Press, 1982), 1–11.
——, 'Pierre Villey (1879–1933): an Assessment,' *Oeuvres & Critiques* 8 (1983), 29–43.
Fuller, Thomas, *The Holy State and The Profane State*, ed. Maximilian Graff Walton, 2 vols. (New York: Columbia University Press, 1938).
Gass, William H., *Habitations of the World* (New York: Simon and Schuster, 1985).
Gethin, Grace, *Misery's Virtues Whetstone. Relique Gethinianae. Or, Some Remains of the Most Ingenious and Excellent Lady, the Lady Grace Gethin, Lately Deceased: Being a Collection of Choice Discourses, Pleasant Apothegmes, and Witty Sentences. Written by Her for the most part, by way of Essay, and at spare Hours* (London, 1699).
Ginzburg, Carlo, *The Cheese and the Worms* (Baltimore: Johns Hopkins University Press, 1980).
Glanvill, John, *Scepsis Scientifica: or, Confest Ignorance, the way to Science; In an Essay of The Vanity of Dogmatizing, and Confident Opinion* (London, 1665).
Goddard, Thomas, *Miscellanea; Or, Serious, Useful Considerations, Moral, Historical, Theological. Together with the Characters of A True Believer In Paradoxes and Seeming Contradictions. An Essay* (London, 1661).
Goldberg, Jonathan, *James I and the Politics of Literature* (Baltimore: Johns Hopkins University Press, 1983).

Good, Graham, *The Observing Self: Rediscovering the Essay* (New York: Routledge, 1988).
Gooyer, Alan de, 'Sensibility and Solitude in Cowley's Familiar Essay,' *Restoration* 25 (2001), 1–18.
Gordon, Scott Paul, 'Voyeuristic Dreams: Mr. Spectator and the Power of Spectacle,' *The Eighteenth Century: Theory and Interpretation* 36 (1995), 3–23.
Gould, S. J., and E. S. Vrba, 'Exaption: a Missing Term in the Science of Form', *Paleobiology* 8 (1982), 4–15.
Grafton, Anthony, *Commerce with the Classics: Ancient Books and Renaissance Readers* (Ann Arbor: University of Michigan Press, 1997).
——, *Defenders of the Text* (Cambridge: Harvard University Press, 1991).
——, 'The Humanist as Reader,' in *A History of Reading in the West*, ed. Guglielmo Cavallo and Roger Chartier (Amherst: University of Massachusetts, 1999), 179–212.
——, 'Is the History of Reading a Marginal Enterprise? Guillaume Budé and His Books,' *PBSA* 91 (1997), 139–57.
——, 'The New Science and the Traditions of Humanism,' in *The Cambridge Companion to Renaissance Humanism*, ed. Jill Kraye (New York: Cambridge University Press, 1996), 203–23.
Grafton, Anthony, and Lisa Jardine, '"Studied for Action": How Gabriel Harvey Read His Livy,' *Past and Present* 129 (1990), 30–70.
Greene, Thomas M., *The Light in Troy: Imitation and Discovery in Renaissance Poetics* (New Haven: Yale University Press, 1982).
Habermas, Jürgen, *The Structual Transformation of the Public Sphere*, trans. Thomas Burger and Frederick Lawrence (1962; Cambridge: MIT Press, 1989).
——, *Theory of Communicative Action*, trans. Thomas McCarthy, 2 vols. (Boston: Beacon, 1984, 1987).
Hadot, Pierre, *Philosophy as a Way of Life* (New York: Blackwell, 1995).
Halifax, George Savile, Marquis of, 'Vindication,' *Essays of Michael, Seigneur de Montaigne*, 3rd edn., trans. Charles Cotton, 3 vols. (London, 1700).
Hall, John, *Horae Vacivae, Or, Essays. Some Occasional Considerations* (London, 1646).
Hall, Michael L., 'The Emergence of the Essay and the Idea of Discovery,' *Essays on the Essay: Redefining the Genre*, ed. Alexander J. Butrym (Athens: University of Georgia Press, 1989), 73–92.
Harflete, Henry, *A Banquet of Essayes* (London, 1653).
Harris, Wendell, 'Reflections on the Peculiar Status of the Personal Essay,' *College English* 58 (1996), 934–53.
Harrison, Thomas, *Essayism: Conrad, Musil, and Pirandello* (Baltimore: Johns Hopkins University Press, 1992).
Harwood, John T., 'Science Writing and Writing Science: Boyle and Rhetorical Theory,' in *Robert Boyle Reconsidered*, ed. Michael Hunter (New York: Cambridge University Press, 1994), 37–56.
Hazlitt, William, *Lectures on the English Comic Writers* (1819; New York: Dutton, 1910).
Heilker, Paul, *The Essay: Theory and Pedagogy for an Active Form* (Urbana, IL: National Council of Teachers of English, 1996).

Hesse, Douglas, 'Saving a Place for Essayistic Literacy,' in *Passions, Pedagogies, and 21st-Century Technologies*, ed. Gail E. Hawisher and Cynthia L. Selfe (Logan: Utah State Press, 1999), 34–48.

Hoagland, Edward, *The Tugman's Passage* (New York: Random House, 1982).

Hooker, Richard, *Of the Lawes of Ecclesiastical Politie* (1594; rpr. New York: Da Capo Press, 1971).

Horace, *Works*, trans. David Watson, ed. W. Crakelt, 2 vols. (1792; New York: AMS, 1976).

Horae subsecivae: Observations and Discourses (London, 1620).

Horkheimer, Max, and Theodor Adorno, *The Dialectic of Enlightenment*, trans. John Cumming (1944; New York: Continuum, 1993).

Hume, David, *Essays*, ed. Eugene F. Miller (Indianapolis: Liberty Press, 1987).

Hunter, J. Paul, *Before Novels: the Cultural Contexts of Eighteenth-Century English Fiction* (New York: Norton, 1990).

——, *Occasional Form: Henry Fielding and the Chains of Circumstance* (Baltimore: Johns Hopkins University Press, 1975).

Hunter, Michael, *Robert Boyle, 1627–91: Scrupulosity and Science* (Rochester, NY: Boydell, 2000).

Hunter, Michael, ed., *Robert Boyle Reconsidered* (New York: Cambridge University Press, 1994).

Iser, Wolfgang, *The Act of Reading* (Baltimore: Johns Hopkins University Press, 1978).

——, *The Implied Reader* (Baltimore: Johns Hopkins University Press, 1974).

James VI, *The Essayes of a Prentice in the Divine Art of Poesie* (Edinburgh, 1584).

Joeres, Ruth-Ellen Boetcher, and Elizabeth Mittman, eds., *The Politics of the Essay: Feminist Perspectives* (Bloomington: Indiana University Press, 1993).

Johnson, Ralph, *The Scholars Guide from the Accidence to the University* (1665; Menston, England: The Scholar Press, 1971).

Johnson, Robert, *Essaies, or Rather imperfect offers* (London, 1601).

Johnson, Samuel, *The Major Works*, ed. Donald Greene (New York: Oxford University Press, 2000).

——, *Rambler*, ed. Albrecht Strauss and Walter Jackson Bate (New Haven: Yale University Press, 1986).

Jonson, Ben, *Discoveries*, in *The Oxford Authors: Ben Jonson*, ed. Ian Donaldson (New York: Oxford University Press, 1985).

——, *Epicoene*, ed. Edward Partridge (New Haven: Yale University Press, 1971).

Julian, *Works*, trans. W. C. Wright, 3 vols. (Cambridge: Harvard University Press, 1913).

Kahn, Victoria, 'The Sense of Taste in Montaigne's *Essais*,' *Modern Language Notes* 95 (1980), 1269–91.

Kaufmann, R. Lane, 'Essaying as Unmethodical Method,' in *Essays on the Essay: Redefining the Genre*, ed. Alexander J. Butrym (Athens: University of Georgia Press, 1989), 221–41.

Kittay, Jeffrey, and Wlad Godzich, *The Emergence of Prose* (Minneapolis: University of Minnesota Press, 1987).

Klaus, Carl H., Chris Anderson, and Rebecca Blevins Faery, eds., *In Depth: Essayists for Our Time*, 2nd edn. (Philadelphia: Harcourt Brace Jovanovich, 1993).

Klein, Lawrence E., *Shaftesbury and the Culture of Politeness: Moral Discourse and Cultural Politics in Early Eighteenth-Century England* (New York: Cambridge University Press, 1994).

Kramnick, Isaac, *Bolingbroke and His Circle: the Politics of Nostalgia in the Age of Walpole* (Ithaca: Cornell University Press, 1968).
Landa, Manuel de, *A Thousand Years of Nonlinear History* (New York: Zone, 1997).
Latour, Bruno, *We Have Never Been Modern* (Cambridge: Harvard University Press, 1993).
Lee, Hermione, 'Virginia Woolf's Essays,' in *The Cambridge Companion to Virginia Woolf*, ed. Sue Roe and Susan Sellers (New York: Cambridge University Press, 2000), 91–108.
Levine, George, ed., *One Culture: Essays in Science and Literature* (Madison: University of Wisconsin Press, 1987).
Levine, Joseph M., *The Battle of the Books: History and Literature in the Augustan Age* (Ithaca: Cornell University Press, 1991).
Locke, John, *An Essay concerning Human Understanding*, ed. Peter H. Nidditch (New York: Oxford University Press, 1975).
Lockwood, Thomas, 'Matter and Reflection in *Tom Jones*,' *English Literary History* 45 (1978), 226–35.
Lukács, Georg, 'On the Nature and Form of the Essay,' *Soul and Form*, trans. Anna Bostock (Cambridge: MIT Press, 1974), 1–18.
Lyotard, Jean-François, *The Postmodern Condition: a Report on Knowledge*, trans. Geoff Bennington and Brian Massumi (Minneapolis: University of Minnesota Press, 1984).
Mace, Nancy A., *Henry Fielding's Novels and the Classical Tradition* (Newark: University of Delaware Press, 1996).
Manguel, Alberto, *A History of Reading* (New York: Penguin, 1996).
Marchi, Dudley M., *Montaigne among the Moderns: Receptions of the Essais* (Providence, RI: Berghahn, 1994).
Maskell, David, 'The Evolution of the *Essais*,' in *Montaigne*, ed. I. D. McFarlane and Ian Maclean (Oxford: Clarendon Press, 1982), 23–34.
Mason, William, *A Handfvl of Essaies. Or Imperfect Offers* (London, 1621).
Master, William, *Logoi eukoiroi, Essayes and Observations Theologicall and Morall* (London, 1653).
McCarthy, John A., *Crossing Boundaries: a Theory and History of Essay Writing in German, 1680–1815* (Philadelphia: University of Pennsylvania Press, 1989).
McCrea, Brian, *Addison and Steele Are Dead* (Newark: University of Delaware Press, 1989).
McFarlane, I. D., and Ian Maclean, eds., *Montaigne* (Oxford: Clarendon Press, 1982).
McKeon, Michael, *The Origins of the English Novel 1600–1740* (Baltimore: Johns Hopkins University Press, 1987).
Middleton, Richard, *Monologues* (London: T. Fisher Unwin, 1913).
Montagu, Walter, *Miscellanea Spiritualia: or, Devout Essayes* (London, 1648).
Montaigne, *The Complete Essays*, trans. Donald Frame (Stanford: Stanford University Press, 1957).
——, *The Essayes of Montaigne*, trans. John Florio (London, 1603).
Moss, Ann, 'Commonplace-Rhetoric and Thought-Patterns in Early Modern Culture,' in *The Recovery of Rhetoric*, ed. R. H. Roberts and J. M. M. Good (Charlottesville: University Press of Virginia, 1993), 49–60.

——, 'The *Politica* of Justus Lipsius and the Commonplace-Book,' *Journal of the History of Ideas* 59 (1998), 421–36.
——, *Printed Commonplace Books and the Structuring of Renaissance Thought* (New York: Oxford University Press, 1996).
Newman, William R., *Gehennical Fire* (Cambridge: Harvard University Press, 1994).
Nicole, Pierre, *Moral Essays* (London, 1677).
Nourse, Timothy, *A Discourse of Natural and Reveal'd Religion in Several Essays* (London, 1691).
O'Neill, John, *Essaying Montaigne: a Study of the Renaissance Institution of Writing and Reading* (Boston: Routledge and Kegan Paul, 1982).
Obaldia, Claire de, *The Essayistic Spirit: Literature, Modern Criticism, and the Essay* (New York: Oxford University Press, 1995).
Olson, David R., *The World on Paper: the Conceptual and Cognitive Implications of Writing and Reading* (New York: Cambridge University Press, 1994).
Osborn, Francis, *A Miscellany of Sundry Essayes, Paradoxes, and Problematicall Discourse, Letters and Characters (1659)*, in *The Works of Francis Osborn*, 7th edn. (1673).
Palmer, Thomas, *An Essay of the Meanes how to make our Trauviles, into forraine Countries, the more profitable and honourable* (London, 1606).
Paradis, James, 'Montaigne, Boyle, and the Essay of Experience,' in *One Culture: Essays in Science and Literature*, ed. George Levine (Madison: University of Wisconsin Press, 1987), 59–91.
Paulson, Ronald, *The Beautiful, Novel, and Strange* (Baltimore: Johns Hopkins University Press, 1997).
——, *The Fictions of Satire* (Baltimore: Johns Hopkins University Press, 1967).
——, *Satire and the Novel in Eighteenth-Century England* (New Haven: Yale University Press, 1967).
Paulson, Ronald, ed., *Fielding: a Collection of Critical Essays* (Englewood Cliffs, NJ: Prentice Hall, 1962).
Peacham, Henry, *The Complete Gentleman and The Truth of Our Times, Revealed out of One's Man's Experience, by Way of Essay*, ed. Virgil B. Heltzel (Ithaca: Cornell University Press, 1962).
Pebworth, Ted-Larry, *Owen Felltham* (Boston: Twayne, 1976).
Plutarch, *Moralia*, trans. H. N. Fowler, 15 vols. (Cambridge: Harvard University Press, 1936).
Pocock, J. G. A., *The Machiavellian Moment* (Princeton: Princeton University Press, 1975).
——, *Virtue, Commerce, and History* (New York: Cambridge University Press, 1985).
Pope, Alexander, *An Essay on Man* (London, 1733).
Potkay, Adam, *The Fate of Eloquence in the Age of Hume* (Ithaca: Cornell University Press, 1994).
Preston, John, *The Created Self: the Reader's Role in Eighteenth-Century Fiction* (London: Heinemann, 1970).
Preston, Richard, *An elementary treatise, by way of essay, on the quantity of estates &c.* (London, 1791).
Price, Martin, *To the Palace of Wisdom: Studies in Order and Energy from Dryden to Blake* (Garden City, NJ: Doubleday, 1964).

Price, Michael W., 'Cornwallis,' *DLB 151: British Prose Writers of the Early Seventeenth Century* (Washington, DC: Gale, 1995).

Principe, Lawrence M., *The Aspiring Adept: Robert Boyle and His Alchemical Quest* (Princeton: Princeton University Press, 1998).

——, 'Virtuous Romance and Romance Virtuoso: the Shaping of Robert Boyle's Literary Style,' *Journal of the History of Ideas* 56 (1995), 377–97.

Radcliffe, David Hill, *Forms of Reflection: Genre and Culture in Meditational Writing* (Baltimore: Johns Hopkins University Press, 1993).

Ramesey, William, *The Gentlemans Companion: or, A Character of True Nobility, and Gentility: In the way of Essay* (London, 1672).

Rawson, Claude, *Henry Fielding and the Augustan Ideal under Stress* (Boston: Routledge and Kegan Paul, 1972).

Rawson, Claude, ed., *Henry Fielding: a Critical Anthology* (Baltimore: Penguin, 1973).

Reilly, Patrick, *Tom Jones: Adventure and Providence* (Boston: Twayne, 1991).

Remedies against Discontentment drawen into several Discourses from the writings of auncient Philosophers (London, 1596).

Richetti, John, *The English Novel in History 1700–1780* (New York: Routledge, 1999).

Rivero, Albert J., *Critical Essays on Henry Fielding* (New York: G. K. Hall, 1998).

Robinson, John, *Essayes; or, Observations Divine and Morall. Collected Ovt of holy Scriptures, Antient and Moderne Writers, both divine and humane* (London, 1638).

——, *Observations Divine and Morall for the Furthering of Knowledge, and Vertue* (London, 1625).

Rosengarten, Richard A., *Henry Fielding and the Narration of Providence: Divine Design and the Incursions of Evil* (New York: Palgrave Macmillan, 2000).

Rothstein, Eric, 'Virtues of Authority in *Tom Jones*,' in *Critical Essays on Henry Fielding*, ed. Albert J. Rivero (New York: G. K. Hall, 1998), 141–63.

Rummel, Erika, *The Humanist-Scholastic Debate in the Renaissance and Reformation* (Cambridge: Harvard University Press, 1995).

Sacheverell, William, *An Account of the Isle of Man: Its Inhabitants, Language, Soil, Remarkable Curiosities, The Succession of its Kings and Bishops, Down to the Eighteenth Century: By Way of Essay* (London, 1702).

Santner, Eric L., *On the Psychotheology of Everyday Life* (Chicago: University of Chicago Press, 2001).

Sargent, Rose-Mary, *The Diffident Naturalist: Robert Boyle and the Philosophy of Experiment* (Chicago: University of Chicago Press, 1995).

Savage, John [trans.], *Spanish Letters, Historical, Satyrical and Moral of the famous Don Antonion de Guevara, Bishop of Mondonedo ... written by way of essay on different subjects* (London, 1697).

Scott, William, *An Essay on Drapery, or The Compleate Citizen*, ed. and intro. Sylvia L. Thrupp (Boston: Harvard School of Business, 1953).

Seneca, *Epistulae Morales*, trans. R. M. Gummere, 3 vols. (New York: Putnam's Sons, 1925).

Shaftesbury, Anthony Ashley Cooper, 3rd Earl of, *Characteristicks of Men, Manners, Opinions, Times*, ed. Philip Ayres, 2 vols. (New York: Oxford University Press, 1999).

Shapin, Steven 'Pump and Circumstance: Robert Boyle's Literary Technology,' *Social Studies of Science* 14 (1984), 481–520.

——, *A Social History of Truth: Civility and Science in Seventeenth-Century England* (Chicago: Chicago University Press, 1994).

Shapin, Steven, and Simon Schaffer, *Leviathan and the Air-Pump: Hobbes, Boyle and the Experimental Life* (Princeton: Princeton University Press, 1985).

Sharpe, Kevin, *Reading Revolutions: the Politics of Reading in Early Modern England* (New Haven: Yale University Press, 2000).

Sharpe, Kevin, and Steven Zwicker, eds., *Reading, Society, and Politics in Early Modern England* (New York: Cambridge University Press, 2003).

Sherman, Stuart, *Telling Time: Clocks, Diaries, and English Diurnal Form, 1660–1785* (Chicago: University of Chicago Press, 1996).

Shields, David S., *Civil Tongues and Polite Letters in British America* (Chapel Hill: University of North Carolina Press, 1997).

Skynner, Stephen, *Christian Practice described by way of essay upon the Life of our Savior* (London and Boston, 1693).

Smith, Alexander, *Dreamthorpe: A Book of Essays Written in the Country*, ed. Christopher Morley (1863; New York: Doubleday, Doran & Co., 1934).

——, 'Last Leaves: Sketches and Criticisms,' *The English Essayists: Lord Bacon to John Ruskin*, ed. Robert Cochrane (London: William P. Nimmo, 1877).

Smithers, Peter, *The Life of Joseph Addison*, 2nd edn. (Oxford: Clarendon Press, 1968).

Snyder, John, *Prospects of Power: Tragedy, Satire, the Essay, and the Theory of Genre* (Lexington: University of Kentucky Press, 1991).

Stapleton, Laurence, *The Elected Circle: Studies in the Art of Prose* (Princeton: Princeton University Press, 1973).

Stevenson, John Allen, *The Real History of Tom Jones* (New York: Palgrave Macmillan, 2005).

Stewart, Stanley, 'Authorial Representation in Owen Felltham's *Resolves*,' *Cithara* 28 (1989), 7–33.

Stillingfleet, Benjamin, *An Essay on Conversation* (London, 1738).

Suleiman, Susan R., and Inge Crosman, eds., *The Reader in the Text* (Princeton: Princeton University Press, 1980).

Sutherland, James, *English Literature of the Late Seventeenth Century* (Oxford: Clarendon Press, 1969).

——, *The Restoration Newspaper and Its Development* (New York: Cambridge University Press, 1986).

Swift, Jonathan, *A Tale of a Tub and Other Works*, ed. Angus Ross and David Woolley (New York: Oxford University Press, 1999).

T. C., *Morall Discourses and Essayes, Upon Severall Select Subjects* (London, 1655).

Tavor, Eve, *Scepticism, Society and the Eighteenth-Century Novel* (New York: St. Martin's Press, 1987).

Temple, William, *Essay Upon Ancient and Modern Learning* (London, 1690).

Thompson, Elbert N. S., *The Seventeenth-Century English Essay* (Iowa City: University of Iowa Press, 1928).

Thompson, James, *Models of Value: Eighteenth-Century Political Economy and the Novel* (Durham, NC: Duke University Press, 1996).

Thoughts on friendship. By way of essay; for the use and improvement of the ladies. By a well-wisher to her sex (London, 1725).

Tilley, Arthur, 'The Essay and the Beginning of Modern English Prose,' in *The Cambridge History of English Literature*, vol. 8, ed. A. W. Ward and A. R. Waller (Cambridge: Cambridge University Press, 1920), 368–90.
Tuke, Thomas, *New Essayes: Meditations and Vowes* (London, 1614).
Tuvill, Daniel, *Essays Politic and Moral and Essays Moral and Theological*, ed. John L. Lievsay (Charlottesville: University of Virginia Press, 1971).
Uffley, John, Gent., *Wits Fancies: or, Choice Observations and Essayes, Collected out of Divine, Political, Philosophical, Military, and Historical Authors* (London, 1659).
Van den Berg, Sara, 'Ben Jonson and the Ideology of Authorship,' in *Ben Jonson's 1616 Folio*, ed. Jennifer Brady and W. H. Herendeen (Newark: University of Delaware Press, 1991), 111–37.
Van der Laan, J. M., 'Essayistic Orders of Chaos,' in *Disrupted Patterns: On Chaos and Disorder in the Enlightenment*, ed. John McCarthy and Theodore E. D. Braun (Amsterdam: Rodopi, 2000), 191–202.
Van Ghent, Dorothy, *The English Novel: Form and Function* (New York: Harper, 1961).
Vickers, Brian, *English Science, Bacon to Newton* (New York: Cambridge University Press, 1987).
Virgil, *Aeneid*, trans. John Dryden, *The Works of Dryden*, vol. 5, ed. William Frost and Vinton A. Dearing (Berkeley: University of California Press, 1987).
Voitle, Robert, *The Third Earl of Shaftesbury* (Baton Rouge: Louisiana State University Press, 1984).
W. C., *A discourse (By way of Essay) Humbly offer'd to the Consideration of the Honourable House of Commons Toward the raising Moneys by an Excise* (London, 1695).
Ward, Seth, *A philosophicall essay toward an eviction of the being and attributes of God* (London, 1652).
Warner, Michael, *Letters of the Republic* (Cambridge: Harvard University Press, 1990).
——, 'The Mass Public and the Mass Subject,' in *Habermas and the Public Sphere*, ed. Craig Calhoun (Cambridge: MIT Press, 1992), 377–401.
Warner, William, *Licensing Entertainments: the Elevation of Novel Reading in Britain, 1684–1750* (Berkeley: University of California Press, 1998).
Watt, Ian, *The Rise of the Novel* (Berkeley: University of California Press, 1957).
Welsh, Alexander, *Strong Representations: Narrative and Circumstantial Evidence in England* (Baltimore: Johns Hopkins University Press, 1992).
Whitlock, Richard, *Zootomia, or, Observations on the Present Manners of the English: Briefly Anatomizing the Living by the Dead* (London, 1654).
Wilkins, John, *An Essay Towards a Real Character and a Philosophical Language* (London, 1668).
Williams, Raymond, *Marxism and Literature* (New York: Oxford University Press, 1977).
Willis, John, 'An Essay of Dr. John Willis, exhibiting his Hypothesis about the Flux and Reflux of the Sea,' in *The Royal Society of London, Philosophical Transactions*, vols. 1–2 (New York: Johnson Reprint Corporation, 1963).
Winton, Calhoun, *Captain Steele: the Early Career of Richard Steele* (Baltimore: Johns Hopkins University Press, 1964).

Withington, Robert, ed., *Essays and Characters: Montaigne to Goldsmith* (New York: Macmillan, 1933).
Wood, Gordon, *The Radicalism of the American Revolution* (New York: Vintage Press, 1991).
Woodman, Thomas, *Politeness and Poetry in the Age of Pope* (Rutherford: Farleigh Dickinson University Press, 1989).
Woolf, Virginia, 'Montaigne,' *The Common Reader: First Series,* ed. Andrew McNeillie (New York: Harcourt Brace, 1984), 58–68.
Xenophon, *Memorabilia*, trans. E. C. Marchant (Cambridge: Harvard University Press, 1923).

Index

Addison, Joseph   10, 26, ch. 4 passim, 108
Adorno, Theodor   42, 138n30, 149n22, 152n54, 157n95, 169n85
Allen, Don Cameron   33, 134n2
Alter, Robert   109, 123, 171n4, 172n15
Altgoer, Diane B.   159n36
anachronism   7, 20
Andersen, Jennifer   140n21
Anderson, Chris   152n57
Ashwick, Samuel   134n1
Atkins, G. Douglas   138n32
Auerbach, Erich   150n26
Augustine of Hippo   29, 145n58
Austin, William   134n1

Bacon, Francis   15, 18, 24, 30, 33–4, 54–5, 132
Bakhtin, Mikhail   121, 123, 176n69
Baret, John   154n72
Barthes, Roland   52–4, 153n61
Bataille, Georges   53
Battestin, Martin C.   170n2
Battestin, Ruth R.   170n2
Bauschatz, Catherine M.   149n13
Bensmaïa, Réda   54, 136n13, 153n59, 153n63
Benson, John   135n3
Black, Jeremy   163n5
Blair, Ann   2
Blanchot, Maurice   11, 152n48
Bloom, Edward A.   163n6
Bloom, Lillian D.   163n6
Blount, Edward   143n39, 143n43
Blount, Thomas   154n72
Boetcher Joeres, Ruth-Ellen   152n57
Booth, Wayne C.   170n4
Boyle, Francis   68–9
Boyle, Robert   9, ch. 3 passim, 108, 135n3
  "Christian Virtuoso"   78–9
  "Essay on Nitre"   81
  "Occasional Reflections"   79–80, 82, 86
  "Proemial Essay"   9, 67, 69–70, 73, 76–8, 80, 82
  "Sceptical Chymist"   68
Brady, Jennifer   142n35
Brathwaite, Richard   135n3, 143n43
Braun, Theodore E. D.   136n14
Bretz, Mary Lee   138n31
Brewer, John   163n4
Bulloker, John   154n72
Burgand, Peter   136n14

Campbell, Jill   119, 173n23, 175n55
Carlton, Peter J.   176n65
Casaregola, Vincent   143n42
Cavallo, Guglielmo   18
Cave, Terance   149n13, 157n95, 158n21
Cavell, Stanley   156n87
Cawdry, Robert   154n72
Certeau, Michel de   2, 43, 50, 149n24, 153n59
Cervantes, Miguel de   172n20
Chadbourne, Richard M.   158n24
Chartier, Roger   18, 140n19
Cheare, Abraham   134n1
Chibka, Robert L.   170n4
Chudleigh, Mary   1, 8–9, 81
Cicero   102–3
Clarendon, Henry Hyde, Earl of   134n1
Clerk, James   134n1
Cockeram, Henry   154n72
Coles, Elisha   155n72
Colie, Rosalie   147n68
Collet, Joseph   103–4
commonplaces, commonplace books   2, 6, 16–18, 37–8, 49, 63
conversation   93–4, 97–8, 101, 103, 104

Cornwallis, William   1, 2, 8, 9, 26–7, 29–35, 37, 41, 75, 128–31, 134n2, 142n34
Cotton, Charles   1
Cowley, Abraham   1, 9, 36, 44–51
Cox, Elizabeth   6
Crane, R. S.   170n3
Culpeper, Thomas   9, 11, 34–6, 40, 72, 75, 132–3

Damrosch, Leopold   171n5
Deleuze, Gilles   152n48
diaries   95–6, 161n55
digestion   2, 9, 16, 41, 52, 57, 108, 130
Drake, William   16–18
Dryden, John   135n3
Du Plessis, Rachel Blau   136n13

Eagleton, Terry   163n7
Earle, John   143n39
Empson, William   115, 165n31, 174n32
Erasmus   38–9
exaptation   9

Faery, Rebecca Blevins   152n57
Felltham, Owen   9, 27–9, 32, 33–4, 37, 69, 75
Fielding, Henry   1, 10, ch. 5 passim
Fischer, Steven Roger   135n7
Fish, Stanley   54–5, 58
Florio, John   1, 36, 158n21
Fontenelle, M. de   134n1
Ford, Ford Maddox   107
Fowler, Alistair   104, 136n15
Frame, Donald   146n68
friendship   41–2, 49–50, 61, 94, 98
Fuller, Thomas   15

Galileo   73
Gass, William   138n31, 172n15
Gay, John   101
Gazette (London)   88–9
genre   11, 17–18, 67
gentlemanly reading   28–9, 32, 40, 69, 74–5, 84
Gethin, Grace   7–8, 9, 69
Ginzburg, Carlos   18

Glanvill, Joseph   135n3
Goddard, Thomas   16
Godzich, Wlad   140n22
Goldberg, Jonathan   142n35
Good, Graham   136n13, 152n57
Gooyer, Alan de   44–8
Gordon, Scott Paul   163n7
Gould, Stephen Jay   9
Grafton, Anthony   82–3, 141n31
Greene, Thomas   20–1

Habermas, Jürgen   95, 163n4, 165n29, 169n85
Hadot, Pierre   60–1
Halifax, George Savile, Marquis of   93–4
Hall, John   69, 143n41
Hall, Michael L.   136n14
Harris, Wendell   152n57
Harrison, Thomas   58, 60, 156n86
Harwood, John T.   159n36
Hawisher, Gail E.   136n12
Hazlitt, William   166n40
Heilker, Paul   149n25
Herendeen, W. H.   142n35
Hesse, Douglas   136n12
historicism   6–7, 21, 47, 63
Hoagland, Edward   152n57
Homer   109, 112
Hooker, Richard   29, 145n58
Horace   141n30, 172n11
humanism   2–3, 8–9, 17, 20–1, 33, 68, 83–4
Hume, David   166n49
Hunter, J. Paul   161n55, 166n51, 177n83
Hunter, Michael   159n34
Hurd, Richard   150n27

ideology   87–8
imitation   19–20
Iser, Wolfgang   177n75

James VI (Scotland)   135n3
James, Henry   177n77
Jardine, Lisa   142n31
Johnson, Ralph   16
Johnson, Robert   137n27

Johnson, Samuel 150n28, 165n39, 168n80
joke 41–2, 62
Jonson, Ben 21–3, 143n43
Julian 168n76

Kahn, Victoria 149n13, 158n21
Kauffman, R. Lane 54, 152n57
Kiernan, Michael 147n68
Kittay, Jeffrey 140n22, 149n24
Klaus, Carl H. 152n57
Klein, Lawrence 95, 97, 167n60
Kramnick, Isaac 167n59

Landa, Manuel de 52, 63
Latin 42
Latour, Bruno 149n15
Lee, Hermione 138n29
Levine, Joseph M. 167n59
Lievsay, John L. 19–20, 21, 141n23, 141n24
Lipsius 26–7
Locke, John 7–9, 135n3
Lockwood, Thomas 107, 121, 171n5
Lukács, Georg 55–7, 59
Lyotard, Jean-François 57–8, 60

Mace, Nancy 123, 171n9, 178n83
Manguel, Alberto 135n7
Marchi, Dudley M. 146n68, 158n21
Maskell, David 146n68
Mason, William 137n27
Master, William 80–1
McCarthy, John 157n95
McCrea, Brian 164n21
McKeon, Michael 124–5, 170n2
Milton, John 109
Minsheu, John 154n72
Mittman, Elizabeth 152n57
modernity 12, 40, 57–8, 60, 85, 104–5, 117
Montagu, Walter 135n3
Montaigne, Michel de 1, 12, 18, 21, 25–6, 29, 30, 32, 33–4, 36, 39, 61, 71–2, 93–4, 98, 101, 105, 127, 128, 130–1, 132, 146n68, 148n13, 165n38, 166n40

moral philosophy 15, 24, 28, 33, 45, 68, 81, 84, 129–31
Moss, Ann 2

Newman, William R. 158n18
Nicole, Pierre 72
Nourse, Timothy 135n3
novels 121–3
novelty 26, 100

Obaldia, Claire de 54, 136n13, 152n57
Oldenburg, Henry 73, 83
Olson, David R. 161n47
O'Neill, John 136n14, 153n61
Osborn, Francis 29, 144n48, 146n65, 148n4
Ovid 32, 128

Palmer, Thomas 9, 36–7, 148n2
Paradis, James 71–2
Paulson, Ronald 115, 164n20, 168n61
Peacham, Henry 1, 9, 37–42, 61–2
Pebworth, Ted-Larry 33
Phillips, Edward 154n72
Plato 130
Plutarch 30, 103, 127, 128, 144n46
Pocock, J. G. A. 95, 169n82
Pope, Alexander 135n3
Preston, John 177n73
Preston, Richard 134n1
Price, Martin 124, 170n2
Price, Michael W. 134n2
Principe, Lawrence M. 82
print culture 1–3, 8, 10–11, 35, 64
postmodernity 57–8
Potkay, Adam 164n11
public sphere 86, 89, 96–7, 104, 122
Putnam, Hilary 156n87

Radcliffe, David Hall 47–8
Ramesey, William 134n1
Rawson, Claude 170n2, 177n83
readerly writing 2–3, 9, 55
Reilly, Patrick 176n71
Richetti, John 122, 170n2, 176n69
Robinson, John 135n3, 139n10
Rosengarten, Richard 124

Rothstein, Eric 113, 173n29
Royal Society 72, 83
Rummel, Erika 168n74

Sacheverall, William 134n1
Santner, Eric L. 60
Sargent, Rose-Mary 67, 71, 75, 76, 84
satire 90
Sauer, Elizabeth 140n21
Savage, John 134n1
Schaffer, Simon 67, 71, 73, 76
Schlegel, Friedrich von 157n95
Scott, William 146n64
Scriblerians 125, 178n83
Selfe, Cynthia L. 136n12
Seneca 9, 16, 21, 41, 127, 130, 139n9, 141n30, 144n46
Shaftesbury, Anthony Cooper, Earl of 10, 22–3, 97–8, 142n33
Shapin, Steven 67, 71, 73–6, 84
Sharpe, Kevin 16–18, 135n4
Sherman, Stuart 95–6
Shields, David 97–8, 167n55
Skynner, Stephen 134n1
Smith, Alexander 138n31
Smithers, Peter 167n57
Snyder, John 136n14, 152n56
sociability 96–8
Socrates 33, 102–3, 130, 145n64
Spectator 9, 10, 26, ch. 4 passim, 108, 151n37
Stapleton, Laurence 147n69
Steele, Richard 10, 26, ch. 4 passim, 108
Stevenson, John Allen 175n60
Stewart, Stanley 147n69
Stillingfleet, Benjamin 135n3
Sutherland, James 150n27

T. C. 23–5
Tatler 88–92
Temple, William 135n3
Thompson, Elbert N. S. 134n2
Thompson, James 170n2
Tilley, Arthur 151n37
Tuke, Thomas 144n46
Tuvill, Daniel 9; 19–20, 25, 28

Uffley, John 3–6, 80

Van der Berg, Sara 142n35
Van der Laan, James M. 136n14
Van Ghent, Dorothy 117
Vickers, Brian 159n36
Virgil 49–51, 100
Voitle, Robert 142n36
Vrba, Elizabeth 9

Ward, Seth 135n3
Warner, Michael 95, 98
Warner, William 176n70
Watt, Ian 122–3, 170n2
Welsh, Alexander 117
Whitlock, Richard 25–30, 32, 127
Wilkins, John 135n3
Williams, Raymond 87
Willis, John 73
Winton, Calhoun 164n12
Withington, Robert 171n5
Wood, Gordon 169n82
Woodman, Thomas 163n9
Woolf, Virginia 138n29

Xenophon 168n76

Zwicker, Steven 135n4